ON THE EDGE OF THE
OF THE
SPOTLIGHT

ON THE EDGE
OF THE
SPOTLIGHT:

Celebrities' Children
Speak Out About Their Lives

by

KATHY
CRONKITE

WILLIAM MORROW AND COMPANY, INC.
New York   1981

Library of Congress Cataloging in Publication Data

Cronkite, Kathy.
    On the edge of the spotlight.

    Includes index.
    1. United States—Biography.   2. Children of entertainers—United States—Biography.
3. Parent and child—United States.   4. Cronkite, Kathy.   I. Title.
CT220.C7   920'.073   80-21255
ISBN 0-688-00326-5

Printed in the United States of America

First Edition

1 2 3 4 5 6 7 8 9 10

BOOK DESIGN BY MICHAEL MAUCERI

In memory of
ALAN SCOTT NEWMAN

September 23, 1951–November 20, 1978

DEDICATED WITH LOVE TO:

Mary Elizabeth Maxwell Cronkite, my mother,
and
Walter Leland Cronkite, my father,
who did everything right;
and to
Albert Ing Duvall, who loved me,
and from whom I learned so much.

THANKS TO:

Arthur Pine, who had faith in me;
Marcy Rudo, who put up with and taught me;
and, of course,
Bill, my best friend, and so much more.

Also to:

Toby Axelrod, Hillel Black, Kathy Connell, Chip Cronkite, Byron
and Jana Lee Dare, Patti Davis, Samantha Drake, Barbara Hallie
Foote, Paula Fuller, Susan Haymer, Howard Kaminsky, George
Laye, Bob Linkletter, Betty and Jock Leslie-Melville, Helen
Markell, Gary Marker, Addie O'Davoren, Kathryn Segura, Amy
Shapiro, David Sheehan, Rose Sommer, Elizabeth Tobin, Irving
and Sylvia Wallace, Nancy Cronkite Whitney, Gerrie Williams,
and all who consented to be interviewed, whether they appear
herein or not, and who in the last three years have suggested,
encouraged, advised, discussed, typed, and otherwise given
assistance.

Foreword by Walter Cronkite

Kathy didn't intend it that way, I don't believe. But this book may prove to be one of the best guides ever to parental behavior.

There were moments when reading this book that I wanted to say of it: "shocking," "appalling."

There were others, however, when I found my throat tightening and my eyes welling with the warm tears of overwhelming love.

This roller coaster of emotions was propelled by the same electric drive of discovery. I was upset to learn of some of the youthful peccadilloes of my daughters; I was delighted to learn that the love they hold for their mother and me, occasionally at doubt in past times of stress, runs deeper than I had dared hope.

There are moments here which brought me up short—episodes that seemed unimportant to the adult mind but which apparently had a great impact on the children. How much were their perceptions, their attitudes, their behavior, their very lives—how much of what they have become was affected by these actions or words of ours that were but accidents of the moment? Some of the simplest and most spontaneous parental reactions seem to have provoked the longest-lasting impressions.

There is a lesson here as to the value of each moment of a child's life—each moment brings the opportunity to open new vistas, to create memorable experiences, for good or for bad. This should be so obvious, but for parents wrapped up in their own concerns, how easy to ignore!

The value of this book will not be in celebrity voyeurism, for Kathy has done all an author who assayed this difficult project could do to avoid that, but in underlining that intimacy that exists betwen parent and offspring regardless of life's station or life-style and in exposing the interesting fact that this intimacy some-times is most obvious when it would seem to be absent. There are some particularly touching examples of that seeming contradic-tion in these pages.

This is a provocative book. Since reading it I have spent long periods in contemplation of the past—not normally a pursuit of mine. Moments with Nancy, Kathy, and Chip portrayed here ex-posed a tapestry of bright memories, but through them runs the thread of regret that more was not made of those times together, and, indeed, that there were not more of them.

Other parents of those interesting people who have sat for these interviews, I should think, will have similar reactions. The inter-views were remarkably candid, and I suppose "shocking" and "appalling" will come to mind as others read of the experiences of their children and their memories of the interaction with the old folks. But I hope they find, too, that silver lining of genuine affection that it seems to me is almost invariably there. Readers will pity the poor child and parents where it is not.

Contents

11

Every child has his Pooh, but one would think it odd if every man still kept his Pooh to remind him of his childhood. But my Pooh is different, you say: he is *the* Pooh. No, this only makes him different to you, not to me. My toys were and are to me no more than yours were and are to you. I do not love them more because they are known to children in Australia or Japan. Fame has nothing to do with love.

I wouldn't like [my toys in] a glass case that said: "Here is fame"; and I don't need [them in] a glass case to remind me: "Here was love."

—CHRISTOPHER (ROBIN) MILNE,
The Enchanted Places

ON THE EDGE
OF THE
SPOTLIGHT

Introduction

Are You
Any Relation To...?

"What is it like to be Walter Cronkite's daughter?" Of all the questions I've had to deal with since childhood, I've found that question the most common and annoying.

My standard answer, which I thought was original before conducting the interviews for this book, has been, "I really can't tell you. Since I've never been anything else, I have no basis for comparison." When I'm in a more communicative mood, I may offer that it has its advantages and disadvantages, but rarely will I take the time to elaborate.

I've heard all the related questions and can answer them, in order, before they're asked. They fall into two categories: curiosity about how foreign and special my life must be, such as, "What is it like . . . ?" and an attempt to get to know the idol better through me, such as, "What does he *really* think about Carter?" I find both types of questions to be personally disparaging. The former makes me feel like a caterpillar in a jar, and the latter attempts to make me a spokesperson for my father, without concern for my own thoughts or identity. It is particularly unfair when I am asked to state his opinion about something on which he must remain impartial, like political candidates. There are even people who go so far as to accuse me of lying when I explain that he doesn't discuss his choices with his family.

It is the insensitivity of well-meaning fans that is most destructive to the children of the famous and that helps create and perpetuate the lack of discrete identity that we must live with. I was fortunate that my parents were aware of some of the difficulties their children might face. They took pains to protect us from too public a life by keeping us out of the press wherever possible and by taking us on isolated family vacations on our boat away from the fans' frequent interruptions.

Only once that I can remember did my father and I discuss the influence of his fame on us. We were dining together in one of Manhattan's small, intimate restaurants when, midway through the meal, a couple of fans came over to the table requesting his autograph. Dad put down his knife and fork, swallowed, and accepted the pieces of paper thrust toward him. He signed them, chatted a bit with the strangers, and dismissed them with a handshake.

"Has all this been very hard on you growing up?" my father asked me quietly as the fans departed. I assured him that it hadn't. Though I had grown up in his shadow, on the edge of his spotlight, I had never known anything else.

Growing up as the child of a celebrity, I experienced both privileges and problems, but I felt justified telling my father that I'd come through it okay. Many others born into similar situations have sought self-destructive methods of coping with that role. Too many become dopers or teenage alcoholics, and there are those who never use their last names to avoid that awful question, "Are you any relation to . . . ?" At one time or another, I have had some of those same problems, but to a lesser degree. I think I'm one of the lucky ones.

It wasn't until I grew up and started trying to come to terms with myself that it became important for me to sort out what it means to be Walter Cronkite's daughter. When I went out into the world to make my own life, I began to learn what effect my father's fame has had on me, and I sought to identify the mechanisms I developed in order to deal with it. Once I had put several thousand miles between myself and my family, and spent several years pursuing my own career, I began to put my father's fame and its impact on me in the proper perspective.

When I moved to Hollywood to start my acting career, I was introduced to Paul Newman's son, Scott. I experienced for the first time the awe and curiosity that others must feel toward the children of celebrities. Ironically, I wanted to ask him all those "what is he really like?" questions about his father, but I knew I could not. There is an unspoken law among celebrities' children, a tacit understanding that precludes all but the most casual questions about one's parents. Only with each other can we relax in the knowledge that no one will ask, "What's it like?"

Scott and I became better friends, and the aura of his father's fame dissolved. I saw Scott himself more clearly. As I did, I discovered how troubled he was and the excesses to which he submitted. Much of his anxiety was directly related to his father's fame.

One evening, I heard Scott drunkenly accuse someone of being interested in him only because of his father, when in fact the "antagonist" did not even know who his father was. Later, at the same party, he said belligerently to someone else, "Don't you know who my father is?"

I couldn't cope with his drinking, his drug taking, and the weird "therapies" he subjected himself to, one after another. He tried yoga, astral projection, nutrition therapy, and even twenty-four-hour-a-day psychologists, but whether he was looking for answers or for escape, I couldn't say. I didn't know how to help him, and I couldn't stand watching his self-destruction.

Scott made me sharply aware of the different reactions children have to the fame that surrounds them. I saw him at one end of the spectrum and myself at the other. What had I learned that he hadn't? What had my parents said or done? What steps had I taken? What strengths did I have? Why didn't Scott make it? I asked myself, what could I have told him, which of my experiences or thoughts could I have shared that would have helped him survive? How could I have reached out to him and perhaps been allowed to know him better?

It was only through writing this book that I could break the silence and ask others, "What is it like to be the child of a celebrity? How does it affect your life?" Maybe I could find some answers, not only for myself, but for some of the victims, the casualties, as well.

Perhaps then the next tragic, premature death of a child of a celebrity will not be dismissed with a remark like, "Oh, those kids of stars are all screwed up," but instead will be viewed as what it truly is: an individual human tragedy. On the other hand, when one of us is successful in a chosen field, it won't be written off as inherited talent or good fortune but will be an accomplishment acknowledged as a personal triumph.

1.

Who's Whose

You only grow by coming to the end of something and by beginning something else.
—JOHN IRVING, *The World According to Garp*

Scott's death prompted only more questions. I needed more than ever to find out how other children of the famous felt: whether we felt isolated or allied by the fame of our parents; whether we held in common feelings of inadequacy or privilege, of anger or embarrassment or pride. I am not an expert on famous people's children, but because I am the child of a well-known man, I am more aware of some of the pressures and influences on our lives. I wanted to offer a forum in which we could share our thoughts with each other and with the public.

In general, the issues that seemed most important related to identity, independence, and career. Consequently, most of the people I talked to were at least in their twenties and had been out on their own. Their parents came from a cross section of professions, since I did not want to rely too heavily on the hothouse products of Hollywood or highly publicized second-generation stars like Jane Fonda or Liza Minnelli.

The children of famous women are sadly under-represented. Except for entertainers, women who have achieved publicly recognized success are often of the generation in which women did not have both a career and children. Those of the new generation, who may indeed have both, have children too young to interview.

One afternoon I took a long walk to downtown Edgartown, Massachusetts, and strolled through some of its narrow tree-shaded side streets. I poked about several white clapboard houses that through the years had been converted to tiny gift shops, clam bars, and art galleries until I came upon a clothing store featuring antique dresses. Once inside, I fell in love with a turn-of-the-century silk suit, but it was definitely outside my clothing budget. I started joking with the salesperson about whether NBC would buy it for me for the TV show on which I was appearing. She was a young woman about my age, and she asked with sudden interest, "Do you work for NBC?"

I told her that I was about to start filming a situation-comedy series for that network, and we chatted about the show for a minute until she mentioned in an offhand way, "My father works for NBC."

"Oh? What does he do?" I asked.

She hesitated, then said, "Well, he . . . uh, writes for them."

"What does he write?"

"Oh, different stuff. For the news department, mostly," she answered, trying to change the subject.

Her reluctance to discuss her father's career was familiar and immediately identifiable. Most people will say outright what their fathers do; the children of the famous often try to avoid it or sneak up on it sideways. I had often identified my father to a stranger as just a journalist, or even, as this girl had, as a network news writer. I might not have pursued it except that I saw something of myself in her, even though I was the curious outsider producing that familiar discomfort. I was less interested in who her father was than in how she felt about being his daughter.

"Does your father ever work on camera?" I asked, following my instinct.

"Oh, well, yes," she answered quietly.

"Anyone I might recognize?" Unintentionally, I was drawing my questions from the catechism I had endured so many times.

She seemed to slump in resignation, sighed, and told me the

name of her father, a man who would be recognized anywhere in the United States.

I responded by telling her about my book, which deals in part with the slow dance we had just performed. I watched the skepticism on her face until, finally, I remembered to introduce myself.

"Oh!" she said with a smile. "You're one of the *CBS* Cronkites! Well, then, you know what it's like."

Realizing I was an ally, her mood lightened considerably, and, after we talked another few minutes, she tentatively agreed to let me interview her. When I reached her the following evening, however, she told me that she had changed her mind. She explained that her family had always fiercely guarded its privacy and that, regardless of the interviewer, they had advised against talking to me. I was disappointed but understood the desire for privacy.

Shortly after I began this book, I ran into Carrie Fisher at a membership-only Beverly Hills nightclub. Thinking that the daughter of Eddie Fisher and Debbie Reynolds might have some interesting observations about what it's like to grow up in Hollywood, I approached her, explained my project, and asked if she would contribute.

She gave me an icy stare and snapped, "Good luck." Then she turned and strode off. It was the first refusal I experienced, and it was formidable to think that in the months ahead I might frequently have to face such rude responses.

Another Hollywood child I approached simply said, "I don't know anything about my childhood. I've blocked it all out."

Many of us have been raked over the coals by the press. I was not looking for sensationalism but for honest insights into what makes our lives different from others. It would be essential to make that clear to the people I approached.

The children of politicians were even more cautious and protective than the Hollywood kids. Some, like the Kennedys, have an almost impenetrable shield of advisers, managers, and secretaries. Others choose less conventional ways of removing themselves from the public eye.

One young woman I met, the daughter of a nationally known politician, had broken all communication with her family years ago when she moved to California and changed her name. When questioned about her family, she claimed to be an orphan. We met, and I liked her instantly. She wore her hair long and loose to her waist, and a flowing skirt swirled around her ankles. She embodied a peculiar blend of strength and vulnerability, of child and woman.

After several weeks of casual conversation, of carefully winning her confidence, I asked her if she would be willing to talk about her family. She replied that if her father had been an actor or a writer, she would gladly discuss him, but since she considered politics to be "disgusting and reprehensible," she wished to disassociate herself from his politics entirely. She tentatively agreed to be interviewed anonymously, but I felt the particulars of her family history made it difficult to guarantee her privacy, so I pursued it no further.

I also approached the son of an infamously hard-nosed mayor of national renown.

"I've spoken with my father," he said when I finally reached him. "He didn't *forbid* me to do it, but he advised me not to, and he's mostly given me good advice in the past. Some of the people close to my father have made me feel bad for *not* doing it. They said, 'Don't you have enough guts to do what you want to do?' I could do it if I wanted to, but, well, this is just an example of what it's like to be the mayor's son."

Among the other rebuffs, the most frustrating was my rejection by Loretta Lynn's children. A friend had spoken directly to Loretta, and she loved the idea and passed along a phone number where I could reach her manager. It was the manager who rejected the interview, refused even to ask the kids about it, and effectively blocked me from any further communication.

Unfortunately, it was not always possible to avoid the parents and their representatives entirely. Famous people can usually be tracked down one place or another, but I had no idea how to reach the kids. Where, for example, would you start looking for Charles Schulz's children, none of whom live at home?

Mr. Schulz replied to my inquiry with a terse, "They wouldn't be interested."

But, summoning up all the courage I could, I persevered. "Excuse me, sir, but don't you think that that should be *their* decision?"

"I know my kids," was his answer, "and that *would* be their decision."

"Well, but would you ask them?"

A week or so later, I received a most gracious note from him. All five of his children had been enthusiastic, and he cheerfully put me in touch with them.

One of the more subtle reminders of our subordinate position to our illustrious parents is that their names are so frequently appended to our own, as in Kathy, Walter's daughter, or Jack, Gerald's son. In order not to perpetuate that practice and so as not to distract from the substance of the interviews, I would like to introduce us all now. In the time that has passed since the first of these interviews took place, I have added three years to my age, moved several times, had both failures and successes in my career, and been married. Undoubtedly the people I interviewed have also grown and changed.

Rick Armstrong, twenty-two at the time we met, is the eldest son of Neil Armstrong, the ex-test pilot, college professor, amateur musician, atheist, and the first human being to set foot on the moon. I interviewed Rick in his sparsely furnished apartment near Marineland, where he had a summer job working with the cetaceans. He is a college student, unsure of his major, but he is interested in marine biology and "would like to learn to fly someday."

A science fiction fan, Rick admitted, "I've always been interested in astronomy and space travel, but I've never really thought seriously about joining the space program. Maybe someday. Who knows?"

John Blyth Barrymore, twenty-four, carries not only the legacy of his parents' fame, but of generations of Barrymores, Drews, and Blyths. His mother is the actress Cara Williams, his father, John Drew Barrymore, and his grandfather, the most famous Barrymore of them all, John, Sir.

"I got busted once in Ojai, California, for walking on wet cement. I called my father and said, 'Oh, man, I'm in jail,' and he said, 'What for?' I said, 'Walking on wet cement.'

"He said, 'Take 'em down to the Grauman's Chinese [Theater] and show 'em where they pushed your grandfather's face in it.'

"My relationship with my father is unlike any other father-son relationship I've ever run into; we're much closer than most.

"He'll walk into my house and say, 'Gimme five bucks.'

"I'll say, 'What for?'

"He'll say, 'Child support,' " John told me, laughing his wheezing laugh. "He's more like my son than my father—I always have to be looking out for him."

John has an astonishingly irreverent attitude toward his father, but it is countered by a deep and sincere respect for his father's talent.

"The most chilling thing I've ever seen an actor do was something he did for me in the living room one night. We were just sitting around, and he stood up and started to recite the ghost's speech from *Hamlet*. My father looks like the ghost; he's got white hair down to here and a long white beard, a sunken face, and intense eyes. He didn't even need any makeup. It's an incredible speech, one of the heaviest speeches in Shakespeare, and he just did it. It had me in tears.

"He's mad, but he's vulnerable, and sensitive, and brilliant."

John's parents were divorced when he was very small, and he was raised in Los Angeles primarily by his mother, stepfather, and grandmother.

"My relationship with my mother is better now than it has ever been," he said, "but it'll never be like my relationship with my father because she'd never come down to my level. With my father, there's no false respect, no 'He's my father and I have to respect him.' He looks up to me in a lot of ways, because I'm doing all this stuff that he can't, and he thinks I'm a fine actor, too. We both feel that we're a part of each other, that we're outgrowths of the same thing, not that I'm his creation."

John, who has inherited his mother's thick red hair and his father's famous profile, has been a carpenter, musician, music copyist, and waiter, but at heart he is an actor. He had appeared in the TV series *Kung Fu* with his friend and patron David Carridine, and in several other small parts in television and movies, including *Baby Blue Marine*, before borrowing a hundred dollars and riding the bus to Broadway.

Jennifer Buchwald is the frenetic youngest child of the columnist and satirist Art Buchwald and literary agent and author Ann Buchwald. According to Jenny, her sister is "a mother in North Carolina" and her brother an assistant producer with ABC. When I met with her in an outdoor café on Martha's Vineyard, she was on her way back to Boston for her summer school graduation from Emerson College with a degree in photography.

"Ever since the day I graduated from high school, my parents have treated me like an adult. We had a hard time when I was younger and doing crazy stuff, getting in trouble, but I've got most of that out of my system. I still love to raise hell, but I'm more careful nowadays, and they trust my judgment.

"I always keep in touch with my parents. I call them every week, religiously, no matter where they are. Now I go to see them all the time. I never used to want to, but now I really enjoy being around them.

"We all went to a masquerade party the other night. I went as a mummy, and by the time they arrived, I was coming unraveled and looked like, well, a very seductive mummy. My father cleared his throat and said, 'Um, Jennifer, that's not very . . . proper.' My mother was enjoying it. What the hell, it was fun."

Christopher Buckley is the twenty-eight-year-old son of William F. Buckley, the author, nationally syndicated columnist, and host of "Firing Line."

Chris was raised as a Catholic in the New York area. Currently, he lives alone in New York's Greenwich Village.

Chris worked for *Esquire* magazine for several years, with great success. He was recently offered a position as European editor of *Esquire* but chose instead to take a leave of absence to write a book about the merchant marine. He sailed with them briefly when he was younger and often considered making a career of it. He is currently on a four-month trip to Antarctica, researching his book.

Chris, an enthusiastic sailor, accompanied his father on the transatlantic sailing adventure that became the basis of William Buckley's highly acclaimed book, *Airborne*. Chris advised, "If you ever get a chance to make that trip, do it."

Nancy Cronkite Whitney, who at the time the interview took place was married to Gifford Whitney, writes consumer articles for a small Manhattan newspaper and longs to live in the country. She is older than I by two years and has lived in such diverse places as Frank Lloyd Wright's architectural community, Taliesin West; a vanilla bean farm in Hawaii; a tepee in Vermont; a dairy farm, also in Vermont; a Zen commune; and a sixty-foot schooner at City Island, New York. She has had poems published in national magazines, including *Mademoiselle*, and has appeared on film in *Feedback*, Bill Doukas's movie which was shown at the New York and Los Angeles film festivals. Her hobbies include bellydancing and needlepoint, and she bakes a hell of a pie.

Chip Cronkite ranges in age from sixteen to forty, though he was born twenty-three years ago. He attended Brown University and is pursuing a career in cinematography. He made his first film in MOS 8mm when he was ten. Chip worked as a production assistant for such filmmakers as Robert Altman and John Cassavetes before being admitted to the film editors' union.

He once made me a standing offer that if I will go see Werner Herzog's movies any time I get a chance, he will refund the price of admission if I don't like them. He is alternately witty, charming, and cheerful, or dour and terse.

Mary Crosby has the same long, silky brown hair and wide, pale eyes as her mother, the former Kathryn Grant. At twenty, she is the oldest of Bing's second batch of children and his only daughter. Her brothers, Harry and Nat, are one and two years younger, and her half brothers, Gary, Philip, Dennis, and Howard, are all in their forties.

Mary received her Actor's Equity union card at age four, when she appeared on the stage with her mother in *Peter Pan*. She has been an entertainer since she was a child, although until recently she had never worked in a production without at least one member of her immediate family.

After two years as a drama major at the University of Texas, she decided that she needed more intensive training and was accepted as the youngest student at the renowned American Conservatory Theater in San Francisco. Once enrolled, she said, "It took me three months to find out that I was accepted on my own merit, not just because of my name. I was really glad to know that."

She has appeared in several television shows and movies, including *With This Ring*, in which she played a "silly ingenue," *Pearl*, and the ill-fated situation comedy *Brothers and Sisters*. Currently, she has a featured role in the hit television series *Dallas*.

"As an actress on my own," Mary noted, "I have an identity of my own. But working with the family, I learned to be a professional."

Although Bing had a reputation as a strict and standoffish parent, as well as a rigid Catholic, it is clear when Mary speaks that she was very much Daddy's girl.

Nora Davis and I met when we were both asked to appear at a promotional event for a hair product. I hadn't spoken to Nora since then and was very happy to have an excuse to renew our acquaintance. Nora is the kind of bright, pretty, amusing, good-natured friend one can't have too many of.

Nora's mother, Ruby Dee, an actress, writer, civil rights and political activist, is married to Ossie Davis, who is also a writer, actor, and activist as well as a producer, director, and Sunday-school teacher. Nora is two years older than her brother, Guy. He is a minstrel and musicologist who plays twelve instruments, some of which he built himself. Nora also has a married sister,

Laverne, who is a writer and photographer.

Nora has worked for *Essence* magazine and is now working for the public relations firm Carl Byoir and Associates, but aspires to be an actress. She has appeared in a television special that her parents wrote and produced, entitled "Today is Ours." She also appeared in the 1974 film, *Countdown at Kusini*, filmed in Lagos, Nigeria, and has narrated children's books for Spoken Arts. She attended Vassar, for two years and then transferred to New York University.

"Then I went through a period where I decided I didn't want to live in this country. It was just too much for me to bear. That's part of the reason I married my Nigerian husband and went off to Africa." The marriage lasted only eight months, ending in divorce in 1974. "God bless the Dominican Republic," says Nora.

"I'm told that in my gestures, in my voice, in my eye and my hand movements, and in my vulnerability, I'm very much like my mother. My mother is very easily touched, and I am, too. We're very close in that way.

"But I'm more like my father in that I'm more outgoing, less private—we talk alike," she laughed. "I'd say I'm closer to being a Southern girl—my father is from the South—rather than a Cleveland girl, like my mother. I think I have my father's diplomatic nature, but I have my mother's straight-ahead approach to a lot of things. It's sometimes like the sun and the moon.

"I've had a problem sometimes being tactful. Once in a while you have to come *right out* with your gut feelings and what your intuition is telling you, and sometimes I just don't want to hurt anybody's feelings. *That* I inherited from my father!"

Jack and Debby Erhard are the two younger children of Werner Erhard's first marriage. Werner, who has been described by *Current Biography* as "America's foremost entrepreneur-guru," is the founder and leader of *est* (Erhard Seminars Training), probable the largest consciousness-raising business in the world.

Jack and Debby were raised by their mother, Pat, in Philadelphia after their father, who was then known by the name John Rosenberg, left them. He returned to claim them after he started est, almost fifteen years later. They live with their mother and two older sisters across the street from est headquarters, where Werner lives with his second family. Pat works fifteen hours a day in the est office.

Jack Ford, a very handsome, glib young man, is the second son of former President Gerald Ford and his First Lady, Betty. His older brother, Michael, is in the ministry; Steven is riding professionally in rodeos and studying animal husbandry; and Susan, who has recently been married, appears on television commercials between photography assignments.

"I pride myself on having made a substantial contribution to the environment," Jack said. He is one of the youngest board members of the World Wildlife Fund, and has a syndicated radio show about the environment and outdoorsmanship. He also runs a small newspaper in San Diego, California.

Jack grew up mostly in Alexandria, Virginia, a suburb of Washington, D.C., while his father was a member of Congress. In August 1974, the Fords moved into the White House.

Betty Ford has been active in charity work, particularly in the areas of mental health and cancer, and has written two books.

Arlo Guthrie, best known for his rambling ballad of 1966, "Alice's Restaurant," is one of two sons of dancer Marjorie Mazia (Greenblatt) and writer, folksinger, balladeer, union supporter, and legend Woody Guthrie. It is interesting to note that Arlo's sister, Nora Lee Guthrie, has followed in their mother's footsteps with her own dance company in New York, while the boys take after their father; Arlo's brother, Joady, is a guitar teacher.

Arlo starred in the 1967 movie based on "Alice's Restaurant" and is planning a new film using the Romeo and Juliet theme. He tours extensively, performing mostly to college audiences, and produces his records at home on his Massachusetts farm. He has been married for ten years to Jackie Hyde. They have four children, Abraham, Cathyalicia, Annie Hays, and Sarah Lee.

Christie Hefner at twenty-seven is the youngest vice-president at Playboy Enterprises. After she had held a variety of jobs, including free-lance writing, working at the Boston Playboy Club as an assistant bunny mother in charge of interviewing prospective bunnies and chaperoning promotions, and a secretarial stint in the Chicago editorial, art, and research departments, her father, Hugh Hefner, asked her to join Playboy on a permanent basis. After spending some time getting acquainted with the operation, her first task was to develop and implement the idea of Playboy Boutiques—including marketing research, setting up accounting systems, buying and design—although she had no experience in any of those areas. The store appeared to be failing, but, with a six-month deadline to show a profit or close down, Christie led the effort that turned it around. Once the store was firmly established, she moved on to other projects. In 1978, she was promoted—not by her father, though she admits, "I suspect there were some discussions about it"—to vice-president of the company and placed in charge of Corporate Communications and Promotion and the Playboy Foundation.

Christie presents herself as very much the young executive—sharply dressed, articulate, and intelligent. It is clear that there is more than nepotism at work and that she is extremely capable.

Although she grew up apart from her father and, in fact, did not even use her father's name until she was grown, she has developed a loving respect for him and strives to correct an erroneous image of him.

"He is extremely down-to-earth and is not in the least bit jaded by his wealth; in fact, he's not particularly money-conscious at all. He's an extremely generous man—not many people know that. He's also very relaxed and easy to talk to, although he's very shy. He's extremely funny, and I don't think that comes through very often. He's very boyish in a positive way—he really loves his life.

"He's very romantic. Perhaps people think his relationships with women tend to be [shallow], that there's this big scorecard up in his bedroom. Instead, I think he's the kind of person who likes to send flowers and hold hands at the movies. He is the kind of romantic who has been able to join sex and love."

Francesca Hilton's parents are the late hotelman Conrad Hilton and noted actress Zsa Zsa Gabor. Francesca received a very strict upbringing, as is considered proper in Ms. Gabor's native Hungary. For example, Francesca remembers her mother standing at the door while Francesca was trying to say good-night to her dates. Francesca's current aspirations seem to combine the two worlds of business and entertainment; among other things, she wants to be a producer.

"I'm trying to produce a cartoon written by Hoyt Axton. It shows kids how to treat their parents when they're grumpy, and it's got all his songs in it. He's an incredible songwriter.

"I worked on the Oscars and the Grammys last year. Production assistant. It's a lot of work—fifteen hours a day—but you learn a lot. And the contacts you make can always help.

"I wanted to be a producer ten years ago, and people laughed at me then. Now there are lots of girls who produce. But it's very hard—because it's still a man's world. I think *that's* the hardest thing of all—much harder than being the kid of a star. I'm just beginning to realize that it's harder just being a woman than it is to be anything."

Michael Keeshan looks exactly like his father, Bob "Captain Kangaroo" Keeshan. He is small and round, with thinning hair and a kindly face. He describes his position of vice-president at an advertising agency as "on the account side—more a business job than a creative job."

He has two younger sisters: Laurie is a law student in Washington and Maeve is a banker in Indiana. They grew up in the suburbs of Manhattan.

Michael, who travels a great deal on business, said that the only time he watches his father's show now is when he's in a strange hotel room. "It's like going home, without going home. I just sit there and feel generally warm.

"My father's Captain Kangaroo whether he's on TV or sitting in the living room. By that I mean, Irish temper aside, he's basically gentle, soft-spoken, and he has the same ideals.

"The show was born out of my imminent birth. As a soon-to-be parent, my father became more conscious of the need to improve children's programming. I think when I was born, and subsequently my sister Laurie, he was thinking about what we were going to be exposed to on television—cartoon fare, *Howdy Doody*, in which he had participated as Clarabelle—and wondering where that was going.

"Our household was strict in the sense that we knew what was expected of us," he said, "but, at the same time, everything was open, was discussed. Everyone knew everyone's point of view. It was a very low-key environment. As I said, if you heard my father scream—which one could prompt him to do, as a child—just the thunderous roar would make you want to back down. He does have somewhat of a temper."

Michael seemed to be one of the most down-to-earth, sensible, and happy people I interviewed.

Lorenzo Lamas, the twenty-one-year-old son of actor-director Fernando Lamas and actress Arlene Dahl, has achieved remarkable success in Hollywood in just a few short years. He landed his first bit part on *Switch* after only four months of acting classes sandwiched between parking cars, cleaning pools, and working in a health club.

Several bit parts followed, including the role of Olivia Newton-John's boyfriend in *Grease*, but it was his second *Switch* episode, directed by his father, that gave Lorenzo a chance to show what he could do.

"Dad wanted me to do the part so that I would have a good piece of film on me," he said. It was that piece of film that led to a costarring role in the feature film *Take Down*, in which he played a steelworker who becomes a champion wrestler.

"Essie cried at the premiere of *Take Down*," Lorenzo said, referring to his stepmother, Esther Williams. "We all got very choked up. He's very proud of me. It was one of the happiest moments of my life, to have them come to *my* premiere of the movie *I* starred in."

Lorenzo's parents were divorced when he was two, and when he was ten, he moved to New York with his mother. Within two years, he had returned to live with his father and stepmother in California, where he could pursue the outdoor activities he loves. As well as skiing, surfing, running, and swimming, Lorenzo holds a brown belt in judo and a green belt in karate. He also wrestled and played football on his high school varsity teams. It is little wonder that the six-foot two-inch actor is so often cast as an athlete, although his strong, dark good looks and soft brown eyes have led to speculation that he may be slipstreaming behind John Travolta's success.

Lorenzo was one of the few people I interviewed who had had the opportunity to work with his father. "We were both very professional when we worked together," he said. "He's Dad, but he's Mr. Lamas on the set. I mean I *call* him Dad, but . . .

"You're paid to do something, so you do it well. There are no altercations on the set—that would be silly. Not to be biased or anything—of course, I do love him, and he is my closest friend —but he's a very good director. It's a pleasure to work for him because he is an actor and can identify with other actors. He knows what's going through my mind and my heart, so he knows what to say to me. He's really a very talented fellow and a strong, strong director."

Chris Lemmon is a tall, curly-haired actor who tends to enter a room doing cartwheels; he bounces off the ceiling and walls as you speak. Like his father, Jack Lemmon, he is an actor and a musician. He has appeared in the TV series *Class of '65* and *Brothers and Sisters.* He has a B.F.A. (Bachelor of Fine Arts) in classical piano and composition, writes and sings pop songs, and wants to be a dancer as well. His parents were divorced when he was a small child.

"I just finished writing a piece for clarinet and piano in four movements, ten pieces for piano solo, a piece for small orchestra, piano and oboe, and three songs which I'm going to record— a couple of funny songs and a couple of serious songs and a waltz or two," he said, with little modesty.

When I asked him if it was hard to live up to his father's reputation, he replied emphatically, "No.

"I have nothing to prove to anyone," he elaborated. "All I want to do is to be as good as I can at what I do, that's it. Why make it hard on myself? I'm already making it hard doing a fucking sit-com and trying to write classical music at the same time as I want to be a dancer. The last thing I need," he laughed, "is a personality conflict."

Bela Lugosi, Jr., is a lawyer in downtown Los Angeles. Although he has no accent, and, in fact, has forgotten virtually all of the Hungarian that was his second language as a child, his father's inflections still creep occasionally into his speech in disconcerting ways. When he turns in the doorway with elegant grace to ask in deep tones, "May I offer you a . . . drink?" one almost hears the swirl of the cape. His walls and shelves are hung with mementos and photographs—a Dracula statuette; a shot of his new black Shelby Mustang with plates reading DRAQLA; a group of childhood photos including one of himself, his parents, and three large, dangerous-looking dogs ("I'm the one with the short ears," he joked). Behind them in the photo is a large painting of Clara Bow, nude.

Bela Lugosi, Sr., best known for his portrayal of Count Dracula in the famous film, was close to sixty when his only son was born. "He and my mother's father were within a couple of years of each other in age," Bela said. "Probably the fact that he was older made a lot of physical activity that fathers and sons do together out of the question. But he also probably had more worldly experience and knowledge to impart."

Bela, Jr., lived with his grandmother during seventh and eighth grades and later boarded at military school.

"Of course, on visiting day I'd see my father," he said, "when he wasn't traveling. But he was traveling a lot, so there were long absences during the formative years.

"He had his ups and downs. I would get used to a very extravagant life-style and then, in other years, a very economically hard life-style. Getting a taste of the latter is what has given me more ambition than anything else. It was the down side of the later years of his life that has driven me.

"He was a perfectionist, and I think I've picked that up. I do work hard, I try to do everything well, and I do strive to improve myself. A lot of people took advantage of Dad, and I won't let that happen if I can prevent it."

One of the ways in which his father is still being taken advantage of, even after his death, is in the exploitation without compensation of his image on Dracula products. Bela, Jr., brought suit against Universal Studios in what could be a landmark case concerning the rights of children of the famous. After fifteen years of litigation, the California Supreme Court decided in favor of Universal, that the rights to exploit a name and likeness are personal to the artist and must be exercised during his or her lifetime.

Bela lives in a fashionable area in the hills outside Los Angeles with his wife and two children.

Linda McMahon looks like a little doll, with long blond hair and big blue eyes. She is a musician and a teacher, and a very nice person to know. Her father, Ed McMahon, is best known for his seventeen years on the *Tonight* show and for his notable role in *Fun with Dick and Jane*.

Linda grew up in the New York area with her sister, Claudia, and two brothers, Michael and Jeffrey. Jeffrey is eighteen, a college student interested in two of his father's loves—drama and architecture. Michael is twenty-seven and is studying broadcasting and psychology. Claudia, thirty-three, is a patient-service coordinator for Muscular Dystrophy who also works in consumer affairs, especially with an antinuclear group.

"Claudia has been one of the most important people in my life," Linda said, "in shaping my ideas. Besides loving them because they're your family, my brothers and sister are my best friends.

"It's just been the last few years that my dad's been like a friend to me. I always loved him and liked him—he's my father and I'm his little girl—but now I see him in a different way. He shares things with me that make me feel like he must really have respect for any advice I would give him.

"He has a real zest for life—the littlest thing is a celebration," Linda said with a laugh. "He has a toast: he just lifts his glass and says, 'To the festival!' and, in essence, it's to the festival of life.

"He creates an atmosphere that's very infectious. Nothing is insignificant. He really likes living, he likes people, and I think he's transmitted that to all of us. When we're together, nothing is taken for granted; everything is special.

"I wish I had his incredible drive. He's fifty-five, and I'm twenty-five, and following him around I get exhausted, and he's still got all kinds of energy. He's never been idle since he was little—but I *love* to relax."

Susan Newman is a bright, cynical, multitalented, exotic-looking woman. She is the oldest of Paul Newman's five daughters, with one sister and three half sisters. Her father and her mother, actress and teacher Jacqueline Witte, were divorced when Susan was five, and Susan has another half sister from her mother's second marriage. Her stepmother is actress Joanne Woodward.

"So there are lots of girls. Being the eldest girl, everybody said, 'Oh, my God, you had to break Dad in for everything, curfews, dating. . . .' But I was very atypical. I was very antisocial during the time that everybody was dating, so he never really had to worry. He said he used to have a fantasy of sitting out on a porch with a shotgun keeping my suitors away.

"I think they expected me to get married and have kids right away. I've really surprised them. Actually, some of my sisters were doing a lot more advanced things long before I was."

Susan has appeared in such films as *A Wedding*, *I Want to Hold Your Hand*, and *Slapshot*—in which her father starred— as well as in stage productions. Her current projects include producing specials for television.

Susan is the only one of Paul Newman's children who is seriously interested in acting, although half sisters Nell and Lissie have had roles in projects with their mother, Joanne Woodward. "Nell is in school in Massachusetts, and she specializes in birds —falcons and hawks. Lissie is a wonderful artist, and how she will eventually focus that, I don't know. She could be a wonderful clothes designer or she may want to be an interior decorator. Clea is thirteen, and all she's into is horses. My real sister, Stephanie, is in Guatemala on a government grant, living with the Mayan Indians and doing a photojournalism thing to be used in school systems in this country. Then Kathleen [her mother's other daughter] is ten years old, and I don't know what she'll do. She's a real bright little kid, though."

"And how old are you?"

"Twenty-six." She paused. "Freshly turned, somewhat trauma- tized, worse for wear and tear."

John Ritter is famous himself as one of the three stars of the popular television comedy, *Three's Company*. His father, country musician, songwriter, and singer Tex Ritter, and his mother, Dorothy Fay Southworth, were popular in early Westerns; Tex appeared in almost eighty films.

John grew up in Nashville, Tennessee, and the San Fernando Valley north of Los Angeles. His brother Tom is pursuing law, which, after show business, was Tex's other love. John lives with his wife, Nancy Morgan, who is an actress and a model. Since the interview took place, Nancy and John have welcomed their first child.

Monte Schulz is the twenty-six-year-old son of Charles Schulz, creator of the beloved comic strip, *Peanuts*. Monte is an aspiring writer, currently studying for his Ph.D. at the University of California, Santa Barbara. As a slow, meticulous worker who spent a full year writing one short story, Monty admires his father's ability to compose his comic strip so quickly and con- sistently every day.

Monte also admires his father for his exemplary patience with the five children. Monte, who is the self-described intellectual of the family, has three sisters: twenty-eight-year-old Meredith; twenty-two-year-old Amy, who is a psychiatric technician; and twenty-one-year-old Jill, who is studying to be a teacher. His brother, Craig, twenty-five, recently became engaged in his home town of Sebastapol, California, and has just received his pilot's license.

Monte said, "My father sees himself as a cartoonist, not as a writer. I see him as an artist. He's the very best in his field. The Strip isn't really a good example of his talent. He can draw any character from any strip; he can do real-life scenes. He took a trip to Yosemite Valley and did some sketches while he was there, and they were very, very good."

Nancy Sherman is the twenty-seven-year-old daughter of Allan Sherman, best known for his song about summer camp, "Hello Mudda, Hello Fadda." In the early sixties, his comedy album, "My Son, the Folksinger," was the fastest-selling album in history, according to Nancy. It was followed by another album the very next month and an engagement at Carnegie Hall the month after that. Previously, Allan Sherman had been on unemployment, after years as a producer and a comedy writer. The sudden change was confusing to Nancy, then ten years old.

At school, she felt that some of her classmates only wanted to be her friend to meet her father, so much so that she concealed her identity at summer camp. At one point she turned to drugs, partially, she feels, because she couldn't cope with her father's fame. "I had no concept of who I was and had a very hard time coping with myself until my father died. Whether that's relevant to his death or not, God knows. I kept saying I'd never be in the biz, and then he died, and here I am in the biz."

Nancy is a scriptwriter for television. Her brother Tommy, thirty, is also involved in the production end of show business, as a producer of television game shows.

"Nobody should be born the child of a celebrity," she once told me with a laugh. "They should be adopted right away."

Polly Styron is the daughter of William Styron, author of *Confessions of Nat Turner, Sophie's Choice*, and other highly acclaimed works of fiction. Polly is twenty-one years old and after several intermittent years at Brown University she is now a dance student in New York City.

Polly's attitude toward education is outspoken. "I have always had a hard time being a full-time student. The concept of aiming your education towards becoming something at age eighteen, foreseeing your life that way, that's pathetic to me. That's why I'm taking semesters off here and years off there, and I don't know if I'll ever finish school. I'm interested in learning, and I'd much rather take courses on the side and dance and live a normal life."

Polly has a twenty-five-year-old sister, Susanna, who is a documentary filmmaker. Her brother Tommy, twenty, is a student of English literature at Columbia University. There is also a thirteen-year-old in the family, Alexandra. Polly's mother, Rose, is a poet, and human-rights activist. The entire family respects each other intellectually; William Styron often reads passages from his works in progress to the family for their honest criticism, and Polly has recognized in print, in *Confessions of Nat Turner*, some dreams which she had told her father. Polly seems to respect her father's opinion almost too much, to the extent that she's wary of showing her own writings to him, explaining, "I have no confidence in it, anyway; I don't need to show it to a good writer."

Mark Vonnegut is an intern outside of Boston, preparing to be a pediatrician. He grew up in Massachusetts with his father, writer Kurt Vonnegut, Jr., his mother, two sisters, and three "cousin-brothers," the orphaned children of his uncle. His father, who has been, among other things, an ad copywriter and a used-car salesman and has worked in public relations for General Electric and taught at Harvard, published his first book, *Player Piano*, in 1951. Mark's first book, a detailed account of his trip into and back from mental illness entitled *The Eden Express*, was published in 1976. His wife, Pat, is an educational consultant.

"I didn't grow up as the son of a famous man" Mark said. "I grew up as the son of a not very good car salesman. I was eighteen or so before he really became well known. My younger sister, Nanny, grew up as the daughter of a famous man."

Nanny, who graduated from Rhode Island School of Design, is an artist, a printmaker. Mark's other sister, Edith, works in ceramics and has her pieces in galleries in New York. One brother is a goat farmer and furniture maker, another a musician and scriptwriter for Donny and Marie Osmond, and the third a pilot for Air New England.

When I asked Mark how he and his father are similar, he seemed stumped. It was Pat who answered: "You both work hard and take pride in your work."

"Are your politics similar?"

"Yes," he said. "We're both sort of eclectic lefties."

"Well, what do you admire most about each other?"

"Being reasonable. Because I think most people aren't reasonable; you can't talk to most people, and we can talk to each other. We can differ on things and not have a helpless feeling of giving up on each other. It's pretty much always been like that.

"I think I'm proud of him mostly because he hasn't become terribly full of himself. He's not a wild, far-out guy. He buys his clothes at Brooks Brothers. He's really quite straight."

"You'd better watch it," Pat laughed.

"Why? Am I going to ruin his image?"

"He'll have a heart attack!"

"People probably think you're really different from what you are, too," I commented.

"You know, you gotta be really straight to make a book," he said. "You can't be too far-out.

"He's not different, particularly," he said, referring to his father. "All parents are weird and drive you crazy from time to time. He wanted me to work hard and all the usual stuff; he didn't tell bedtime stories about flying saucers. We played chess a lot, and he seemed very proud of the fact that I could beat him. Of course, he threw the board occasionally. He can be very childish. I think all parents can sometimes be very childish. He's not very out of touch, except in ways that all people get out of touch.

"What writers do is, they cultivate something everybody has. In essence, writers have an advantage because they're not acting stuff out; they're writing it and making a living on it."

Amy Wallace, twenty-five, is the daughter of authors Irving (*The Fan Club, The Word,* and twenty-two other books) and Sylvia (*The Fountain, Empress,* et al) Wallace. She describes herself as "a part-time psychic healer and full-time writer," who has published six books, five of which were cowritten with various members of her family, including her brother, David Wallechinsky. The most recent is *The Intimate Sex Lives of Famous People.* She and her husband, rock musician Josef Marc, live in

Berkeley when he is not on the road with his band, The Hit-
makers, and she is not in Los Angeles, collaborating.

For me, the most exciting aspect of this project was talking to
people. Month after month, I would say, "Just one more interview—I've *got* to talk to . . ." until finally I realized that there
would always be "just one more" person I wanted to get to know.
Even now, I go to sleep at night thinking, "Damn! I wish I had
time to add . . ." But I take comfort in the words of Garp.
Writing this book has indeed been a learning process, and one
of the valuable lessons I have had to learn is when to stop.

2.

Growing Up

"... I say you can dance to *anything* if you really feel like dancing." To prove it, he got up and danced to the news.
—TOM ROBBINS, *Even Cowgirls Get the Blues*

I've gotten used to my father being omnipresent—not only on television every night, but also on magazine covers when I go to the supermarket, imitated in comedy skits, mentioned in passing in novels—but once in a while it still takes me by surprise.

For example, one evening I was at my boyfriend's house. We were draped across the couch, drinking wine and nuzzling each other, lit only by the flickering blue haze from the TV set, when suddenly I heard the rumbling tones of my father's voice!

The son of another newsman told me a similar story from his more ignominious days. The Mexican police had caught him messing with drugs; confiscated his car, cash, and belongings; and escorted him out of the country. Embarrassed and afraid to contact his parents, he found himself in a Salvation Army flophouse in a Texas border town. He was eating with the rest of the down-and-outers when his father appeared on TV, and the drunks and derelicts provided a running commentary on the news. "It was," he told me, "an education."

On the other hand, there have been times when it has provided me with a sense of security to know that almost any evening I can turn on the television and see my dad. As a homesick teenager away at boarding school, or a runaway in a strange part of town, I've always had the knowledge that by simply turning a knob I can see a friendly face, hear his deep, reassuring voice, feel that I have some kind of contact with those I love.

When I was a child, every evening at six or seven o'clock, Mom would line us up in front of the TV to wait for Dad to come on. We tried to stay quiet, but I don't think I listened much.

Just about the time the pretaped newscast was over, we would hear his key in the front door and his special "Hello, I'm home" whistle, and we'd race down the stairs to greet him.

After I left home, I stopped watching the news every night, but when I do, I watch him. Exclusively.

It was reassuring to find that most of the people I interviewed did not watch their parents regularly, or read all their books, or attend all their speeches. Exceptions were Michael Keeshan and his sisters. They were avid Captain Kangaroo fans.

"For the longest time *I* didn't know he was Captain Kangaroo," Michael said. "Oh, I've got a classic story! My sister Maeve, who was about three and a half at the time, went into the studio with my mother where the show was being taped. When my father finished taping, he went back to his dressing room and then came back as himself. He asked my sister how it was, and she said, 'Oh, Daddy, Daddy! You just missed Captain Kangaroo!'

"I don't know when I found out, but I stood in line with my mother for three hours outside of Carnegie Hall to see him in concert; I must have been no more than five at the time. I don't know whether kids at the age of three or four really know what their fathers do anyway."

Bela Lugosi concurred, but he did remember very clearly the first time he saw his father on the screen.

"I think it was *Son of Frankenstein.* I must have been younger than school age—four or five—and my mother took me and some of my playmates to the movies. They kept going down and hiding beneath the seats, afraid to look at the screen. To me, it was just seeing Dad up there; it didn't scare me at all. But, you see, they could fantasize about it. He was mysterious to them.

"Then, from the first grade through the sixth grade, I attended a military boarding school. Every Sunday the students would have a dress parade. The parents would watch, and afterwards was visiting time. But every time my dad would show up, he just created a stir. He was a very imposing man, and the other children were afraid of him. I think that was when I first began to realize that he was recognized by most people."

Nora Davis remembers seeing her parents on TV for the first time: "That was so *strange*," she said, but she had more difficulty than Bela differentiating between fantasy and reality.

"I think the first memory I have is of my father being on something about John Brown. He played some guy who got shot down in the street, and I *freaked out*, even though he was sitting right there watching with me. As I look back on it now, it's hysterically funny, but I made him promise me then and there never to die again. He kept his promise, with one exception, which I never saw because it just gets to me."

I have always appreciated my father's devotion to the family. Even though he is often out of town on business, when he is home, we see more of him than many families of men with less peripatetic jobs. He does not spend all weekend playing golf or go out drinking with the guys after work—he comes home to be with us. In fact, one of the reasons he gave up race-car driving in favor of sailing was that sailing was an activity that we could all enjoy together.

The family always came first, and by my father's example I learned that one can be deeply committed to both family and career without either suffering. On the other hand, I grew up accepting last-minute changes in plans—the possibility of having to postpone my wedding, for example, if a moonshot was scheduled that week, or never being sure whether a long-awaited African safari might be cut short because of a political crisis.

On the date that Debby Erhard was graduated from high school, her father's staff had mistakenly scheduled him to be out of the country.

"At first," Debby said, "there was sadness there. It's a big thing in your life to graduate, and your father should be there. But then I imagined coming down the stairs and having him not there, but having that be exciting, and having that mean something." She had come to understand, she explained, the importance of her father's work.

The lack of time to spend together is one of the hardships of having a successful parent, but, in most cases, the children and parents will agree that there are ways to compensate for that lack. Bela Lugosi disagreed.

"I don't know that it ever can be [compensated for]," he said. "You're talking about the theory parents have who leave their children with someone else while they go pursue careers, the rationalization that it's okay 'because when I *do* spend time with them it is really a *good* time.' I don't buy that. I think there is no substitute for time."

Yet later Bela added, "I'm proud of my father for his loyalty to his family. It was unquestioned. And to my mom while they were married, which was most of my life. He was strictly a family man, and I've always been proud of him for that."

Many of us had absentee fathers, and each found a way to deal with it. Jack Ford said, "My father wasn't there like most fathers, but, in a way, that can be a blessing. Familiarity breeds contempt, right?

"Even though he traveled a lot and was not home a lot, he made a big effort to get there when something was important to one of us. He just had ironclad rules about those kinds of things. Even if the President, the most important person in his sphere of life, said, 'Would you do this?' unless it was absolutely a national disaster, he would say, 'No.' So you never felt like you were playing second fiddle to his career."

"I used to think I couldn't imagine what it would be like to have my father sitting at the dinner table with us," Linda McMahon said. It was a common thought. "You know," she elaborated, "just like a Monday-through-Friday thing, your father comes home from work, and you talk about what happened at school. That was so far away from me, I couldn't even imagine it. But the time he spent with us was spent really well; the *quality* of the time was great. I have really good memories.

"Saturdays were always family days: we either raked the lawn together or cooked a big brunch together or something. But there were times, as much as I love my family, when my friends were going downtown and hanging out at the drugstore, and I was home raking leaves.

"When I look at what those kids are up to now, how they turned out, I'm glad it was different for me. Their parents were always away, and they had parties all the time, could stay out late, and at that time it seemed great. But now I look back, and *I* can remember being *with* my family, having them there. I know now they were strict because they cared about me, though at the time I didn't think so.

"I'm his little girl, and he loves that," Linda told me. "And I love to be treated like that. . . . He still plays the little games with me that he did when I was a girl. The other night I was in bed, and he came in," she started to tell me, very seriously. "And he does this thing, 'walking in his sleep.'" She broke off, laughing, and said, "This is going to sound so ridiculous! But I just wanted to cry, it brought back such memories. He comes in, 'I'm walking in my sleep . . .' and he does this thing where he makes a hotdog out of me, and he smothers me with onions and relish and ketchup. And it was so *cute*, I just wanted to squeeze him. It brought back such good memories.

"As I got to be fifteen, sixteen, seventeen," she said later, "he'd take me on trips that he thought would be interesting for me. He used to do the Junior Miss Pageant every year, and he took me along, thinking it would be great for me to be around a lot of girls my age."

"Was it?" I asked.

"It was all right," she said. "But, you know, it was just being with *him* that was fun."

Sometimes in their efforts to entertain us, I think fathers forget how precious just being in their company is.

Michael Keeshan also accompanied his father on certain trips. "The deal was that my two sisters and I would each get to take one trip on one of his 'Fun with Music' concerts. I liked it very much, and I traveled around most of the states as a child. It was a good chance to spend time with my father, who was gone forty weeks of the year."

Some of my most precious memories of my father were those

rare occasions when I had him all to myself—a midtown meeting for lunch, Christmas shopping for Mom, a shared watch on the boat with the rest of the family asleep below. But the times together as a family were special, too, from my earliest memories of him sitting through our protracted childhood meals in the kitchen, making bird noises to amuse us and to keep our minds off the dreaded vegetables being shoveled into our mouths, to our most recent family evenings, playing cards, talking, and laughing together.

One of Polly Styron's childhood recollections is of her father's bedtime stories. "He's a wonderful storyteller. Even relating a little incident that happened in town would take on fictional qualities. It's just the way his mind works. When we were little, he had certain stories that he would continue, like Irving the Worm. I wish I could remember what some of *his* trials and tribs were!

"My father never played baseball with us, and he never knew what my new dress was, and occasionally he had to ask which birthday this was for us, but he was incredibly supportive. He was not removed, in a neglectful 'I don't care what you do' way, but just as a positive force for giving us responsibility. He definitely treated us like human beings and adults.

"I realize, when talking to other people about their parents, how lucky I am. I think of the things I've missed: When I was thirteen or fourteen, I would love to go to my friends' houses where the father would say, 'Let's go play football,' and they'd all have dinner together, and he'd know all their grades. And I used to think, 'God, my father doesn't do any of that stuff,' but I had other advantages."

Nora, too, prized her parents' storytelling. "We grew up on everything from African folktales to Yiddish folktales and everything else, at bedtime. They've given me an understanding of history and culture that has kept me grounded; that Americans aren't the only people in the world, that black is beautiful, and white is beautiful, and yellow—it's been like a United Nations attitude at home. And a lot of love. A lot of love.

"We mostly get anecdotes from Georgia," she elaborated, "my father's home state, about his father who worked on the railroad, and his time on the chain gang, what my grandmother had to do to survive, and all the family jokes, laughing at some of the good and bad times that my father came out of, how he had to pretend to be a West Indian to eat because there was a lady in Harlem who was feeding West Indians. And we'd have family round-table discussions; we'd ask him about people like Malcolm X and Leon Davis.

"As we got older, there got to be less time for that. But we didn't watch television—we didn't have one for the longest time—and we were encouraged to pursue other kinds of things. And that led us, my brother towards music, my sister towards writing, and me towards—pandemonium!"

One of the most important and sometimes trying lessons we learn growing up is how to get along with our peers. When one's parents are celebrities, other children can make life very difficult. Or sometimes we make it difficult for ourselves. Christopher Lemmon felt that he always had to prove himself to everyone, especially at boarding school.

"I was so obnoxious at fourteen or fifteen that finally one of the guys in my dorm had to sit me down and say, 'Lemmon, Jesus Christ, will you cool it? Come on, man! I mean, what do you think this is?'

"A group of people would be sitting around a table having a wonderful discussion, and I would come bouncing in and do everything but tap-dance in the middle to get their attention. That was the way I coped with it."

But it is in early childhood particularly that our peers can be very cruel.

"There's always some segment of the kids," Michael Keeshan said, "who say, 'Aaaaw, your father's Captain Kangaroo,' or what they think is an absolutely cutting remark about a dancing bear or Mr. Greenjeans. That's obviously supposed to hurt you, that you hang out with people who know dancing bears.

"But none of my *friends* ever made comments. None of my *friends* ever thought it was unusual. It was always the people who you didn't know, who didn't know my father, didn't know us. I tell you, it does tend to make a five-year-old tremendously callous. Anyone can say anything to you, and it doesn't bother you because at a very early age you get to meet that fringe of people who want to make comments or, in theory, make fun of you. You get used to it.

"My annoyance level rose most when I was in high school, but it was a different kind of annoyance. I was starting to identify with values that my father had and to appreciate his work, or at least respect it. I would occasionally get comments like, 'When is your father going to grow up and do something serious?' "

It all seems to indicate the importance of learning to have faith in ourselves, to become comfortable with who we are. I commented to Michael that most of the people I had talked to seemed to be making it, surviving, and, in many cases, succeeding.

"Well," Michael reflected, "being exposed to a lot of grown-up situations at a young age, you have a lot of self-confidence when you go out into the world on your own.

"To me, the biggest handicap to intelligence, to success, is lack of self-confidence. If you have self-confidence, you can literally do whatever you want to do. You just have to persevere."

3.

Advice

Children aren't happy with nothing to ignore
And that's what parents were created for.
                              —OGDEN NASH

The best advice my father ever gave me—that I took—was
when I told him I wanted to move to Los Angeles and become
an actress. He had seen me change my mind over and over about
what I wanted to do with my life, dropping out of and going
back to school every time a new interest struck, so when I proposed this drastic move he said, "Okay"—my first surprise—"but
make a definite time commitment, say a year, during which time
you will diligently pursue this course, whether you get discour-
aged or tired of it or not." For some reason, instead of getting my
back up and hollering that he didn't have any faith in me, I said,
"Okay. That sounds like a good idea."

I wasn't in Los Angeles for very long before I realized that one
year was simply not a realistic amount of time, and I extended it
to five—five years within which to achieve at least total support
from my acting, if not stardom. That was the best bargain I ever
made, because, whether or not I would have actually quit, that
promise to myself carried me through some nasty early days and
discouraging, hopeless weeks. And on my birthday, September 15,

1978, we taped the first episode of my first costarring show, and a series to boot. Three months from my deadline.

Other children were offered the following advice:

Lorenzo Lamas
"Bring all the contracts to me first. Don't sign anything."

Nora Davis
Well, my father's full of it. Advice, that is. I think the best advice was about keeping some personal idea about yourself through success and failure, so that the strong winds don't blow you down. He once said, "You don't have to worry about the struggle; you have to worry about the success."

I think the best advice my mother gave me was that I should always try to function as a woman, as a whole entity, a person in my own right. To share myself with others, but to have some hold on myself.

Nancy Cronkite Whitney
I don't know. I never took any of his advice, so I don't know whether it was good or not.

Jack Ford
"Life is good experiences or bad experiences, and it's up to you to decide which it is."

Rick Armstrong
I know the best advice they gave me and I disregarded was when I wanted to quit piano lessons, and they said, "You'll be sorry when you're older." And I was, of course.

Susan Newman
"Learn how to relax when you're not on. And hope that Grace Kelly-type movies come back and you'll work a lot."

Nancy Sherman
At one point I decided I wanted to transfer to Smith College. I was into urban studies, and they had the best department in

the country. I called my father and said I was thinking of going to Smith, and he said, "Do you want to be known the rest of your life as a Smithy?" That was it, no way I was going.

Debby Erhard
"Tell the truth. Everything comes from that. Tell the truth."

John Ritter
"Don't turn the press against you, son."

Linda McMahon
I'm not a real aggressive person, and one thing he said a lot, that his father always told him, is that whether you're going for a job interview or whatever, walk into the place as though you own it.

Chris Lemmon
"Simple is best. And be as good as you can be at what you do." Those were the pieces of advice my grandfather gave to my father and my father gave to me. My grandfather was a baker, and when my father left Boston to go to New York and be an actor, my grandfather said, "I want to wish you the best of luck, and always be as good as you can, because remember, I'll always find magic in a piece of bread."

4.
Nancy Cronkite Whitney:
Communion

The features were not the same in all,
Nor yet the difference great: but such as is the
case between sisters.

—OVID

Undoubtedly, the most important and interesting interview for
me was the one with my sister Nancy. Although I'm told we
were close when we were children, playing and giggling and
getting into mischief together, I have few memories of that
closeness, for as we grew up, we grew apart. We lived separate
lives, and even though we are less than two years apart, our
interests never coincided, and we have virtually no friends in
common.

There was always an undercurrent of jealousy between us
when we were growing up. I alternately worshiped and hated
Nancy for being prettier, smarter, and more popular, and I felt
sure she had stolen all of our adored younger brother's affections.
I vacillated between arousing her antipathy and needing her
approval, and these emotional extremes kept our interaction
volatile.

Our relationship improved in direct proportion to the distance
between us; it wasn't until I moved from New York to California
that we started to be friendly. Despite this, we rarely had a

conversation about anything important. We had never built a foundation of trust and communication, so we would discuss books or diets. Neither of us had ever mentioned Dad's fame. When I asked to interview her, thinking that her feelings might be hurt if I didn't, I anticipated a strained and uninformative conversation.

I was wrong. I was not prepared for the myriad feelings and experiences our conversation would reveal—the discovery of a communion between two sisters. Not only did I learn a lot about my sister—about how much we differ and how much we are the same—but we also talked about things we had never talked about before and opened the way to a closer friendship.

We sat in the window seat in my parents' country house, watching the wind-ruffled bay as we spoke. Nancy's husband, Gifford, was going for a sail; my parents were in town. The house was quiet, except for their ancient springer spaniel, Buzz, shuffling and panting back and forth, and barking after her random, insistent fashion.

We weren't accustomed to extended conversations, Nancy and I. We didn't usually have that much to say to each other. This was to be one of the longest talks we'd had in some time, but, even so, between bouts of animated dialogue there were lengthy and sometimes awkward silences, monosyllabic answers, and time spent watching the water.

As Gifford was leaving the house, his parting words were, "Tell Kathy the story about when you were a child and used to watch your dad on television."

"Well, Dad really tells it much better," she said after we were alone. "But when I was little I always used to sit in front of the television and scream, 'Daddy, out of the box! Daddy, come home!'" I have heard that part of the story told many times about each of us, depending on which child is present to be embarrassed. "Well, one time," Nancy continued, "Dad explained to me all about how television works. I was just a little tot, and he went on and on about how the airwaves go out. I was nodding and agreeing, and at the end of his explanation I asked him, 'But, Daddy, how do you get in the box?'"

Nancy, who was two years old when Dad began appearing on television, has no memory of the first time she saw him "in the box," nor does she recollect any special awareness of Dad's importance as she was growing up.

Of course, it didn't seem unusual at the time that nobody made a fuss over us or treated us any differently, but when I left that rarified atmosphere of the society we grew up in, I began meeting people who hadn't always known me and who reacted to me not as Kathy Cronkite who lives down the street, but as Walter Cronkite's daughter. Unlike my old friends, the strangers often asked, "Wasn't it very difficult growing up? Didn't people always make a fuss at school?" and all the rest of the questions that made me realize how lucky I had been. Nancy and I agreed that the lack of reaction to Dad's budding fame among our early friends and teachers was probably because at the private school we went to, there were many other kids whose parents were just as important.

"But," she said, in one of her frequent non sequiturs, "I do remember one time lying up in my bed—this is a really bizarre thought . . ." She started to laugh. "It's sort of idiotic, too. Anyway, I was thinking something like, 'God, my dad's Walter Cronkite. I wonder how it feels to be Princess Anne.' Fairytales were my big thing."

"I remember you were always a good storyteller," I said. "Before I could read, you used to read the same comic book to me over and over, each time making up a different story to go with the pictures.

"You know," I said, as I attempted to get back into my journalist role, "as I look at my list of questions here—it's really weird. I was going to ask you what are the first questions people ask you about Dad after they ask, 'Are you any relation to . . .' but they're probably the same ones they ask me. Like, 'Is he really like that?' "

"Oh, yeah—"

"And, 'He seems like such a nice man—' "

"Oh, yeah, they do say that," Nancy agreed, "don't they? But then I always say, 'Oh, sure.' "

"I had a lot of trouble with that when I was going through those stages when you don't always think your father is so nice," I said. In fact, my father really *is* a nice man and so much more than just nice, but part of being a teenager, it seems, is thinking the worst of your parents. But you'd still have to smile and say, "Oh, yes, he's such a nice man," between clenched teeth.

"Oh, but I never did say that," Nancy said. "I was awful when I was growing up. I'd go on and on about how I hated his guts and how he made me stay home and gave me a curfew. I'd just give them the whole rap about what a drag I thought he was." She laughed a little self-consciously and added, "People really thought I was fucked up, I'm afraid."

I asked her if she had ever denied the relationship altogether.

"Oh, yeah! Because I just wasn't into hearing, 'Oh, he's my favorite fan,'" she said, referring to a common swap of pronouns often committed by tongue-tied fans. "A couple of times I just didn't want to get involved, so I said no."

How did she react to those "favorite fans" when she was out in public with Dad?

"I never went anywhere with Dad alone. Oh, when I was young, we went on rallies. We did rather well. Some kind of junior navigators or father-and-children rallies. Couldn't do it now. I've completely forgotten how to work the gadgets.

"And I remember going out to a few dinners with him. Some of the lunches and dinners I've had with him, especially recently, have been very interesting. I remember going to lots of dinners when we had some certain problem growing up. And I remember him teaching me to play tennis when I was younger."

"He didn't teach *me* how to play tennis," I said, mocking our childhood rivalries. "But, of course, I hated tennis, as I recall."

"That might be why," Nancy said mildly.

I do sometimes feel left out when Dad and Nancy and Chip grab their racquets and head for the court, but whenever I think about learning tennis, a vivid and uncomfortable image is recreated in my mind. It is I, a little girl in a little white dress, planted in the middle of a clay court as vast and as blisteringly hot as the Gobi Desert, swatting desperately with achingly tired arms at small white balls thrown at me by an anonymous tennis instructor.

"I remember I was always very bad about doing fear sports," Nancy continued. "And he was very bad about teaching me those. Like when he was first teaching me how to sail on the Sunfish." Her idea of "fear sports" struck me oddly. It was not an expression that would occur to me, but if it did, I might apply it to race-car driving or mountain climbing, not sailing. "I was very young. He'd be heeling the boat over quite a bit, and I'd start to get afraid, and he'd turn around and say, 'Oh, Nancy, you're such a coward!' It really hurt my feelings.

"Ditto when he was teaching me to drive. It might be one of the reasons I still don't drive, because I remember he put me behind the wheel of a car when I was young, maybe nine or ten, and I was quite frightened when cars would be coming in the opposite direction.

"But he was very good at teaching me the other sports that I took to, the ones that weren't fear sports, such as swimming. I remember going swimming with him a lot when I was very young and swimming on his back. He gave me a very good attitude about the ocean."

It was a funny indication of the difference in our temperaments even at a young age. I was terrified of the surf when I was a child, and, although I am less fearful now, I used to feel that Dad was a little disappointed in my reluctance to enter the water. Once through the waves, however, I shared Nancy's joy in riding on Dad's strong, safe back. On the other hand, I remember sitting happily on his lap, steering the car just like a grown-up, while he worked the pedals that I couldn't reach.

"I'm sure," Nancy continued, "because he enjoyed driving a sports car fast, he thought that a nine-year-old girl would enjoy driving a sports car fast.

"I think both Dad and I consider New York a kind of a hellhole and really enjoy being out in the country, enjoy swimming.

"But that's a difficult question. I can think of a lot of differences. . . . I remember when I was living out in the country, and I was telling him how funny the farmers were, how intelligent and what a good sense of humor they had, and Dad seemed to take the attitude that if they weren't well educated, they couldn't possibly be interesting and intelligent."

Once again, I was struck with how different our perception of Dad was. Dad does indeed place a very strong emphasis on formal education and has condemned friends of ours who lack an education despite their other qualities, and he does seem to equate intelligence with education. But I have also seen him stay up late into the night, questioning a Maine lobsterman on the details of his craft and listening attentively to the answers.

"What do you admire most about Dad?"

As always, Nancy took time to think before answering, choosing her words carefully. "I admire his being able to write a very coherent and quite excellent radio show every day. I don't think I could do it. Deadlines freeze me up anyway, as I discovered in my last couple of attempts at college." I thought it was interesting that she would mention primarily his daily radio editorials, which most people are not even aware of, rather than the *Evening News*, for which he is famous. "I admire a lot of his programs when I see them. I admire his work quite a bit, actually."

"His news shows or his specials?"

"Well, it depends. I don't watch the show that often, but once in a while I see something that I really appreciate in a show. I never see anything that embarrasses me."

"Did he ever do anything, either connected with his work or not, that embarrassed you?" I asked, as I had asked most of the people I had interviewed.

"Well," Nancy replied, "I remember one time when I was going to Brearley, and he came and made some kind of a speech. He said something like, 'My daughters have taken up skiing, but I hope they'll get back to studying.' "

I laughed with surprise and recognition. That was it, the incident that had prompted the question in the first place. That childhood embarrassment had so impressed me as the one example of the difficulty of being the child of a famous person that I had made that question part of my repertoire as I interviewed others. I don't remember another thing about his speech, but I can see him standing on the auditorium stage, pronouncing those words with a smile.

"I didn't think that it was very good that he should make such jokes at my expense," Nancy continued. "But I admire a lot of things about him privately, too. I think that he's basically rather kind, and I hope I've inherited that. Don't you feel that way about Dad? That he's basically kind?"

"Definitely," I agreed. "Although we both went through a period of time when we didn't get along with the parents. What changed? What was the turning point that ended the conflict?"

"Well, the fact that I realize that they're getting older and I'm not always going to get the chance to be with them and get along with them. That makes me feel guilty for the times I could have gotten along with them. Like one night at dinner Dad was saying something about how he always wanted to take a bicycle trip around the world with me, and it never happened. It was *too* touching and it almost made me cry, thinking about it afterwards. Because when I was in my teens and I could've been doing things like that, we were arguing instead, just because I wanted to be free."

I told my father about this part of my conversation with Nancy. His eyes puddled as hers had, and he looked down at his plate. "You know," he said, "every time we're together in the country, she asks if I want to go for a bike ride with her."

"Also," Nancy continued, "I used to be resentful because I thought Dad had an interest in keeping me respectable because of his image, rather than because he loved me. Now I think that it was *also* because he loved me."

"Do you think that his image—either his concern with his image or other people's concern with his image—ever got in your way or made people expect something of you?"

"Well, later, among the people I met, it was a definite handicap. Like at one commune I went to, a beautiful Zen place in Hawaii. I was there for two weeks and everything was very cool, and then they found out who Dad was. Immediately they started coming down on me that I wasn't doing enough work and this and that.

"In small towns where I've lived, people would gossip about me. I really can't remember the exact stories, but I'd hear all kinds of stories about myself. It was sort of a poor people's resentment of the rich. It bothered me even more because I was personally poor. It's bad enough if you're rich and poor people resent you 'cause you're rich, but when you're *poor* and people resent you 'cause they think you're rich . . ."

I asked her in what ways she thought Dad's public image is different from the way we know him.

"I don't think there's any difference. Do you?"

"No," I admitted. "I just wondered if you thought there was. A trick question."

We sat suspended for a moment, each waiting for the other to speak. However, this was my inquiry; it was up to me.

"Well. We talked about the lack of reaction to Dad's position among our private school friends, but what about among boys? Did you ever wonder if they wanted to date you because of Dad?"

"No, never," she said emphatically. "When I was growing up I never considered that."

"I never did, either," I concurred. "And people always say I must have been awfully naive. Then you start thinking back over all the guys you've gone out with . . ."

"No, the people I went out with were also the rebellious type, and they definitely weren't trying to get anywhere in the straight world and try to make a score on Walter Cronkite's daughter." She laughed at the thought.

"Well," I said, "to pursue the idea of being used, did you ever feel that perhaps friends were trying to use some power they supposed your name carries—for example, at a restaurant where you can't get a table, and your friends nudge you and say, 'Just tell them who you are?' "

"No."

I was left hanging.

"Actually," she said on second thought, "I do have one friend who has done that a few times. Tried to impress waiters with who I am. I do find that kind of obnoxious."

"Makes me feel like a fool," I agreed. Then we were becalmed again. She gazed at the water and wondered aloud where Gifford was.

"Do you think," I asked after a minute, "that people assume that because Dad is rich and famous, he must have spoiled you?"

"But were we really spoiled? I remember being nagged at a great deal when I started rebelling against doing my homework,"

Nancy replied. To me, being nagged with good cause has little relation to whether or not one is spoiled. "When a person's constantly nagged, punished, harassed, and so forth about failing to do their homework, both at home and at school, it doesn't seem to me as if they're really spoiled."

I never realized that she had gone through that. I always admired her, and, along with the other successes I attributed to her, I always thought of her as a good student.

"But it didn't really take much to be good at it," she demurred. "Just do the reading. Well, I took an interest in it, and I enjoyed doing the reading, and I was able to remember it.

"I loved school when I was very young and didn't have much homework, and I did very well. Then, as I got older and more rebellious, I found more things to do—got a false ID, went to discotheques, or whatever. I can't remember all the things I did, but I found many amusing things to do other than my homework. Then my life really became hell at home. I don't think of myself as being spoiled as opposed to Gifford, whose mother totally dotes on him. Anything that he does is wonderful.

"People say that I'm spoiled, but they only say it to make me angry. I really feel that the parents were quite strict. I remember not being able to go on dates—I can't remember how old I was, perhaps thirteen or so—and it's really true that everyone else was going, simply to movies and so forth, maybe a double date. I remember not being allowed to do that."

"Well, you were the first child, and they were probably a lot more strict with you than they were with me," I said. "I don't remember ever really hassling with them over dates. Either I didn't care to go, or nobody was asking me, or the parents didn't say no. I don't remember which."

"Oh, I remember all that happening."

There was another silence; I took a different tack.

"Tell me about the 1964 political conventions, when you worked for Dad at CBS."

"Well, I never really saw him. That was one thing that was great about it because I had a lot of freedom. I was working late, and he was working late. It was kind of interesting. They sent me around interviewing delegates which was a real shocker, because most of them seemed to be a bunch of drunken fools."

I had worked briefly at the Miami convention in 1972, and it seemed to me that in such a circumstance, one of two things could happen: either they would work you extra hard to make up for your being Walter Cronkite's daughter, or, as in my case, go out of their way to be sure that didn't happen. I was frequently bored and frustrated watching the other teenaged pages, or gofers, doing most of the work while I was told to "Relax, Kathy, John'll get it."

Nancy commented that she felt she was treated just like everybody else. "Well, maybe everyone was very polite to me at that convention because of Dad, but I'm glad if they were polite to me for any reason. I think everybody was very busy. I remember working very hard and the other gofers working very hard, too. Most of them were children of the CBS staff as well."

"Other than the conventions, did Dad ever help you get a job?"

"Well, his friend got me a public relations job," she said.

"Was it hard going into a job under those circumstances? Did your coworkers resent it?"

"Oh, no, I'm sure they didn't," she said. "They were all getting much more money than I was."

"Do you think you were paid less because of Dad?"

"No."

"Did you ever think of going into journalism?"

"Yeah, I did. The last time I thought about it was four years ago.* I wanted to do a series of articles about various communes, the ones that advertise in the *Village Voice*. I wanted to expose them, to write about what they were really like. But my contact, a publisher of an underground newspaper, was kind of a lecher, and I didn't quite want to get involved with him. It had nothing to do with Dad, the fact that I didn't do it."

"You edited for the *Paris Review* for a while, didn't you?"

"Yes," she answered, "except that ninety-nine percent of the stuff was incoherent drivel written by Ph.D.'s in English and supposed to be short stories."

---

* After this interview took place, Nancy started contributing free-lance articles to a consumer newspaper in Manhattan and to the *Waterway Guide*, a publication for yachtsmen.

I asked her about her future plans and whether she feels that Dad's success puts any pressure on her to be successful.

"I don't really think so," she answered. "Because I think everyone wants to be successful, and everyone wants their children to be successful."

"What about fame? You had mentioned pursuing a career in the performing arts; success in those fields is usually equated with public renown."

"I really don't think I'd like that," she answered. "I guess I wouldn't like having strangers and fans coming up to me all the time. And saying all those same old things."

"Wouldn't it be different if you were hearing it about yourself?"

"I get very embarrassed reading about myself. I was interviewed for a local paper once. It was a very bad interview job. They made me sound different than what I really was. That's the kind of thing that would happen all the time."

"What about that movie you were in?"

"It was a lot of fun, but for me it's just something that I could have fun doing and possibly get money out of. It's not a desire to become well known. I have no desire to travel around or that kind of thing. If I were in movies, I would have no desire to go on location. None whatsoever. I'd much rather just swim.

"Basically," Nancy concluded, "I'd like to have a little bit of money so we could live in the country and have a farm. If I wanted to get some sun, I could pull a few weeds, rather than just lying out in the sun, getting a headache trying to read. But it would take a lot of money to find the farm I'd like."

"So any job is basically a means to an end. Is that what you're saying? That anything you would want to do is basically so you can get enough money to be able to have a farm and then quit?"

"Yes," she said. "Farming is work, too. I wouldn't mind raising organic vegetables. Some friends of mine in Vermont had a beautiful organic farm, and I really enjoyed working with them, but they had a lot of capital to start with. They had no tractors, just a beautiful team of gray Belgians, a matching pair, and we'd all go out on the cart. It was just great."

"It's hard to make money on a farm, though, isn't it?"

"Well, I think they made pretty good money selling organic

carrots to Boston. Then, of course, I never saw their account books. I worked on a dairy farm—that was very enjoyable, too. But there wasn't money in that at all."

I remember visiting Nancy on the farm and being amazed at what hard work it was and how well she took to it. They rose before dawn to do chores, and she learned to bake bread and cook the venison that a friend had given them.

"I've never enjoyed anything more in my life, really," she said. "That was the best job I ever had. But the barn burned down, and he was underinsured, so that put him out of business.

"I'm kind of too nervous for the stage and singing," she went on, picking up an earlier thought. "Maybe I could get it together and practice a lot with some other people and do some good work. Sometimes I sing very well, and I might enjoy doing that, but I'm not really sure how I'd do. I wouldn't want to use Dad.

"I remember one time I went to a Grand Old Opry audition in New York. I went using my married name, and I was sort of nervous, so I didn't sing very well. Also, the accompanist didn't know the song and played the wrong note a couple of times. It was a total disaster. But then Dad said, 'Why didn't you tell them who you really are?' This was after I was rejected. 'Because there's publicity value in that.' For some reason the idea completely repelled me. I thought I'd much rather learn to accompany myself on the mandolin, or find other people to sing with, or take up some other avenue."

"I can understand not calling them back to say, 'This is who I really am,'" I agreed, "but would it be so hard to go in in the beginning using your real name? I mean, your maiden name?"

"I never thought of doing it that way because it wasn't my name," she said. "Of course, everybody I've discussed this with thought I was completely crazy on that point, also."

I commented that I could understand wanting to get a job through one's own merit, rather than just because they could get publicity through you, and she answered simply, "Have I told you how I feel about publicity?"

I was struck again by the ways in which we are so different, especially in our feelings toward publicity, careers, and travel, which for me are inextricably linked. I would rather travel than do almost anything; one of the attractions of writing and acting, and publicizing those accomplishments, is that both offer the opportunity to travel. To me, even the personal appearance tours with a dozen interviews a day in three different towns is thrilling, just to get to see different places and meet all kinds of people. I love staying in hotels and getting on and off planes. I love it all.

"I'm frightened in planes," Nancy said. "And I'm frightened in sailboats. I get bored on trains; I get sick on buses."

"And you don't drive."

"I get frightened in other people's cars half the time. But I really like riding my bicycle."

"It does limit the places you can go somewhat," I suggested.

"I get tired pretty quickly on my bicycle, too," she said just as Gifford walked through the door. "Anything else?"

We both tacitly agreed that the interview had to come to an end. I had only one more question.

"What do you say, particularly now that you have a different last name, when people ask you what your father does?"

"Well, I don't like to tell them when they're people I've just met," she said.

"Why?"

"Well, I sort of think that people will like me better if they don't know."

"So what do you say?"

"Oh, I tell them."

We have both mellowed considerably since the day when she beat me about the head with a heavy wooden sap bucket because I wasn't walking fast enough through the sugar maple grove. In fact, just a few days before this interview, she had had a long talk with a friend of mine in which she apologized for "all the mean things I did to my sister when we were little."

He had said, "Oh, yes. I heard about the famous sap bucket incident."

Nancy paused a moment and then replied, "Well, but that time she deserved it."

5.

Images

Mirrors should reflect a little before throwing back images.

—JEAN COCTEAU

Part of growing up is deciding what image we want to present to the world and what actions we must take or avoid in order to live up to that image. That learning and sifting process is complicated by also having to take into account what images our parents present to the world and whether we want to support, deny, or destroy them.

I have always felt it necessary to maintain a public image which would reflect and uphold my father's, regardless of how outrageous my behavior might be in private. But at the same time, I feel limited by it. I am fairly open with my friends; I feel no need to hide my mistakes from people I am close to, but Walter Cronkite's daughter admitting to indiscretions is quite another thing.

My father's image is serious and steady and fatherly, and fatherly he is, indeed. He takes his work very seriously, as is appropriate, but at home he is far from sedate. He is a gregarious man who relishes spinning a one-line joke out into an elaborate shaggy dog story, who opens Christmas presents with a child's

71

delight, who, in fact, approaches every undertaking, recreational or professional, with enthusiasm. He says what he thinks and, after carefully considering all sides of an issue, stands by his beliefs, though he enjoys playing the devil's advocate in an argument.

He is thought of as the most trusted man in America, straightforward, kind, intelligent, and fair, and that image is well deserved. But anyone who has spent an evening with him on the dance floor, or crisscrossing town till long past midnight in search of a good jazz band, or who has seen his infamous mock striptease or heard his throaty and off-key rendition of "Bill Bailey" would hardly apply the word sedate to Walter Cronkite.

Ed McMahon's off-camera image also differs from his television persona, and Linda passionately refutes her father's image as a party-going boozer. "Usually the second or third question people ask is about his drinking. I don't know how to answer that. I don't know whether they want me to tell them how much he actually drinks or what. The way Mr. Carson talks, he'd be at a bar every night all night long, and he couldn't function if that were true. I think most people know that.

"I get very defensive about it because if there's one thing he does do, it's work hard. People think it's just party all the time. They assume he goes in, does his hour and a half, has fun, and it's not work. That's not true."

Similarly, I am always shocked at the naiveté of people who assume that Dad goes to work around six, sits down and reads the news, and comes home.

When I was in my teens in the mid-sixties, there were times when my best friend and I used to sneak out of the house late at night. I kept my spare blue jeans stuffed way back in a corner of the front hall cupboard and went downstairs in my nightgown, so that if I was caught on the way in or out, I could explain that I was just raiding the refrigerator. We would meet and go down to Greenwich Village, where we would hang around with the musicians, smoke dope, and live crazy for a few hours. And just before dawn we would sneak back into the house, tiptoeing up the suddenly squeaky stairs, and slip into bed before the rest of the family woke up.

Once we were safely out the front door and on the way to Astor Place, I would assume my anonymous alter ego, my alias. If anything happened, if we got involved with some weirdo or got into trouble, it would not reflect on Dad. I wouldn't have to worry about anyone bragging that they smoked dope with Walter Cronkite's daughter.

More than that, it was a chance to be just me, to be liked or disliked for my own self. I could talk about things like where I went to school and what kind of music I liked, instead of hearing, "Wow, how does your father feel about . . . ? He must really . . . Do you get to . . . ?"

Under an alias, I didn't feel the pressure, real or imagined, of people always expecting me to be as intelligent, well informed, and politically aware as my dad. I am embarrassed to admit, as Walter Cronkite's daughter and as a citizen of a democracy, that I do not read the newspapers every day. When I am using an alias, no one is surprised by that.

Only recently I accompanied a friend to a semipolitical meeting convened by a mutual acquaintance. The chairman introduced me as Walter Cronkite's daughter and asked me to say a few words about the newsmen who are still missing in Southeast Asia. I was not pleased to be singled out that way; I had come to listen, not to speak, and although my father is deeply involved in that cause, it is one about which I know very little. I have learned in situations like that to say simply, "I do not speak for my father."

When I was previously married and using my ex-husband's name, we had some close friends with whom the subject of my father had never come up. One day when I went over to their house, my dad was on television. It was not his usual broadcast but an unexpected special report, and I exclaimed, "Oh, there's Dad!"

"That's your father? you didn't tell us; why didn't you tell us?" our friends asked indignantly.

I have never been able to understand why some people react

that way. I made no attempt to hide who my father is, but neither had I introduced myself by saying, "Hi, I'm Kathy, and my father's Walter Cronkite."

Of course, there are also people who don't believe you when you do tell them.

When I was in college, a fellow student and I began talking. When I told him my name, he asked the famous question: "Are you any relation to . . . ?"

". . . Walter Cronkite?" I finished for him. "Yeah, that's my dad." He laughed, as though I was joking. "But he really is!"

"I was just kidding," he said. It was a response I had heard many times.

"Yeah," I said, "but I'm not."

When I was unable to convince him, I pulled out my birth certificate to prove that I am indeed Walter Cronkite's daughter. I'm still not sure he believed me.

Upon reflection, I was ashamed of my insistence, and, in a way, that incident was a turning point for me. I realized that it shouldn't, and doesn't, matter to me whether or not someone I'll never see again believes me. The fact that I'm Walter Cronkite's daughter is not what's important about me; I certainly hope it's not the most interesting thing about me.

"One of the toughest things," Jack Ford said, "is breaking down preconceived notions of who I am and what I should be. You just have to be yourself, which is the easiest thing, and either you offend people or you don't. It's something you live with.

"At first it was difficult when I moved from Utah back to Washington, because the focus became much finer on what I did. I became much more sensitive to criticism. . . . People were paying attention to me, and I felt very self-conscious. I felt that there was this mold that I was supposed to fit into. It started out as a terrible experience. There was a tendency to put you in a coat and tie and make you well mannered and tight-lipped. Unsure of myself at that point, I tried to force myself to live up to those expectations. That lasted a few weeks, until I couldn't stand myself. I was very unhappy.

"But you either burn out, or turn your back and walk away

from the whole thing, or make something out of it. I've always been a very independent person. I've always been the son who had to have things his own way and get in all kinds of trouble for it. But in the end I learned my lesson. There's a hard way and an easy way to do things in life, so it's not such a bad idea to listen to people who have been around the track at least once."

Like Jack Ford, Mary Crosby had a clean-cut, all-American image to live with. "I was raised as an all-American girl, except that I'm a celebrity's daughter. I grew away from that in the last couple of years, but not that much. Naturally, everybody has some kind of preconception about what you'll be, about what you are," she said. "God knows what the preconceptions of me are after the publicity I've had lately. I've been getting really weird hate letters.

"Up until last year, I think my image was—not quite Debbie Boone. A very light person, I would say, a nice sweet young girl, not a person with strong feelings. Now, after just that one article about me [in *People* magazine], they probably think that their assumptions were totally wrong, that I'm a 'typical Hollywood kid,' a very superficial, selfish girl. Not to mention a lousy Catholic.

"I was the black sheep of the family. I was a good girl but also very strong and independent. I ran away at age seven. I made it to the driveway. I was furious because my mother packed for me. That happens in every family, but people don't believe it would happen in our family.

"It's good to know what you want," Mary went on. "And to know it young. I think celebrities' kids *have* to, because otherwise they would become so confused trying to live up to other people's images. I'm a private person, but if somebody wants me to smile and look pretty, I will, even if I feel like a bitch that day. That's okay, because it wasn't infringing on my life. A lot of what people see in me is real, is true. 'America's Ingenue.' Well, not quite, but close. What people wanted from me was not hard to give, because I believed in it."

Christie Hefner has a particularly striking image to live up to or live down. "I think there's probably no way I could behave that wouldn't confirm what some people expect or surprise other people," she said. "I don't think people are reacting to *me*, particularly; meeting me, or especially meeting my father, is something of a Rorschach test. What people think about us is more of an indication of what they're like than what we're like. So I just accept it for that.

"When I was invited to participate in a panel at Yale, a couple of students were assigned to give me a tour of the campus. They were very nice, and later one of them said, 'Gee, you're not what I expected.'

"I said, 'Okay, what did you expect?' "

"He said, 'Well, I think I expected you to get out of a limousine and have a couple of Afghan dogs.'

"And I said, 'You're right. I'm not what you expected.' "

Christie spoke of another image problem that many of us have, which is that children of famous people are often assumed to be independently wealthy. Even if our parents are well off, it doesn't necessarily trickle down to us. While recognizing the problem, Christie admitted that it was less acute when she was younger, because she carried her stepfather's, not her father's, last name.

"It's mostly a problem with, say, a political group that will ask me to be a sponsor—a thousand dollars a person for something. It's painful, because it's the kind of thing you wish very much you could do."

The common misconception that famous people are all rich and that their children are all independently wealthy is a familiar theme among the people I spoke to. In spite of the Hollywood life-in-the-fast-lane image of Barrymore, Sr., it would be a toss-up as to who is farther from that King Midas world—John Barrymore, Jr., or John Blyth Barrymore.

"It's been real rough the last eight years," John Blyth said. "I've worked as an usher, a delivery boy, you name it. A friend of mine walked into the restaurant where I work now [as a busboy] and said, 'It's good to see you doing this. You haven't suffered enough.'

"My first impulse was to punch him in the nose and say, 'Don't ever fuckin' say that to me again.' Most people don't believe it.

"There are at least ten separate businesses or corporations making a lot of money off the Barrymore name, and I'm not making a dime. When I first got to New York, I walked into the Barrymore

Theater and demanded free tickets to the show. The first guy I met was the guard. He was totally cool. He said, 'You mean you're not getting any money from this? Nobody in your family gets any money from this? We take in ninety thousands dollars a week here. You mean you're broke? You took a Greyhound?'"

After graduating from high school and attending music school for a year, Linda McMahon chose to spend some time on her own, independent of her father's financial support. "I'd be waitressing or working as a salesperson, and people would wonder why—like they think we have trust funds!" she laughed. "I really resent that. I hate that. They'd wonder, 'Why does his daughter have to be waiting tables?' Because I want to, that's why!"

"I remember during one period when I was on my own and not doing very well," I told her, "people would say, 'Why are you broke? You can always call up your dad and ask for money.' But I really couldn't."

"Mmmm, yeah," she murmured in agreement. "You know if you're ever in trouble, you always have that, so I know that I would never *really* be on my own. In a way, I resent that, because I could never really break away. I'm not going to run away and never communicate with them—I could never do that—so he always knows what I'm doing and how I'm doing, and if anything ever happened, he would be there. That's kind of nice, but on the other hand . . . Did you ever feel like you just wanted to go to Europe or something and just be another person?"

The false image of celebrities' children as having access to a lot of money can have unfortunate results, as Nora Davis suggested. "There's some question," she said, "as to whether that was what my husband was all about. Getting ahead. He wanted to be a millionaire, anyway. He told me that, on seeing who my parents are, his parents said to him, 'Get that girl . . . ha, ha, ha.' Well, he got me.

"But I don't socialize a lot. I don't put myself in situations where people can point to who that is. When people come over, and my mother's vacuuming and my father's working the compost heap, little by little they realize that we all have to eat and go to the bathroom and sleep at night.

"The one thing I cannot do," Nora concluded, "is protect myself from it. There are people out there who are going to swamp you with b.s., and if you believe them, then you've believed them. And if they hurt you, then they've hurt you. I try not to let it worry me. Too much. I've been pretty lucky in that my instincts and my intuition are very sharp, and as a rule I can tell what people are really interested in. And I probably goof a million times."

Polly Styron said she never had any reason to worry about being taken advantage of. "I never got the feeling that anyone tried to be my friend bcause of my father," she said. "We had money and were generous with it. We always had a good time and maybe did things that other kids couldn't do, but I can't think of one friend who tried to be a friend because of that. It's nice to be spared that."

But there were other pressures she spoke of: "I'd hand in a paper and wish I wasn't Polly Styron, because if it was lousy, my professors knew who I was. Often peers would expect that I would do well, too. I would feel that conflict. But I could just be paranoid."

Polly felt pressured to live up to her father's image as a writer; did Lorenzo Lamas feel that people expected him to be the Latin lover?

"I imagine so," he said. "I felt I had to live up to it. 'Reaching deep inside my psyche,' I suppose there was always that question, would I be as good as Dad? Well, I don't know [whether I am]. We'll have to let the people be the judge.

"From what people say, I look like Dad did when he was my age. I have a swimming picture on my wall—I swam varsity, and Dad was a Panama champion swimmer—that was taken when I was eighteen, and I have one of Dad taken when he was twenty-one, and we looked exactly the same.

"Dad always wanted to get out of the Latin lover syndrome. But it worked for him, and it made him a very affluent fellow."

I asked him if it bothered him to be thought of as "Lamas Two," as he had referred to himself.

"No," he replied. "Listen, I'd like to be half as successful as he is."

Mark Vonnegut's father certainly has a bizarre image. "Yeah," he said. "People always want to know: 'What's it like? Isn't it pretty far out?' They think I must be either exceptionally cool or exceptionally fucked up. I just like the way he is as a person. And sometimes, you know, I don't like the way he is. I can get mad at him.

"It was very funny for me in the counterculture situation where people thought my father was a god. That was very strange for me, to feel like just about everybody in the whole world could say their parents were idiots and get everybody to side with them. I would be the lone man out. In the generation gap, I was in a funny kind of bind. I felt a little lonely. Everybody else was complaining about their parents; I couldn't complain about mine."

Mark's odd grievance was a recurring one; we missed being able to complain about our parents freely. It doesn't mean we loved them any less, but rather that we didn't want to be set apart from one of the common pastimes of our teenaged peers. For many of us, being different, standing out from the group, was one of the scariest parts of being who we were.

"My father's fame gave me a certain amount of notoriety which was as much to my detriment as to my well-being," Nancy Sherman stated bluntly. "It made me a little out of the ordinary, which I always thought I was, but it hurt because I was out of the ordinary not because of myself, but because of my father."

When I asked Michael Keeshan how his father's image affected his own self-image, he replied, "I like to think that, for the most part, his is a positive image, that it sets me up as someone who has some kind of credibility, a guy who was raised in an all-American environment, so someone meeting me for the first time knows that I'm not a crazy person. For some portion of the population, you're a 'show biz' kid, but my experience has been that that's a very small portion. Most people think positively towards you, and that's because most people think positively towards my father.

"When they meet you, they have some kind of feeling that something nice happened in their day, and they're going to go home and tell their wife and kids that they met Captain Kangaroo's son. You've got them on your side.

"However, after twenty-six years, it's rare that I enjoy talking about my father's work. There are people I could talk to for hours about it; I get into very philosophical discussions here at the agency on the role of children's advertising. Or occasionally I meet someone in education and can discuss the role of television. I enjoy that kind of discussion. I don't enjoy too much 'What is Mr. Greenjeans really like?' or 'How many people does it take to do the puppets?'

"When I was on the road with my father, of course, I had to be well behaved and dignified and a little gentleman. You'd go into a classroom on your first day [as] Captain Kangaroo's son. The teacher doesn't necessarily expect more from you, but because in theory you're someone special, she's always looking at you, and you're more a focus of attention, so anything you do, right or wrong, gets exaggerated. Until second grade, my mother sent me to school in white bucks, chinos, and a blue blazer. That was in my Pat Boone fetish stage," he laughed.

"But I think children always reflect on their parents. They're expected to be a certain way, famous or not. I am more conscious of that now. I wouldn't want to do anything that was embarrassing to my father, in particular because I'm in a relatively close circle in his acquaintances.

"But I'm also an independent person. I've never been known to lack an opinion or not to speak out on an issue that he may or may not agree with.

"If I had been a dismal failure for some reason, I might have been very conscious that I had embarrassed my father. If I had dropped out of high school at the age of thirteen and started stealing hubcaps and selling them at a profit, maybe I would have embarrassed him. But I didn't do that, and largely because of his influence."

I don't remember my parents ever suggesting that my behavior should be influenced by Dad's reputation or image. The pressure that I felt to perform a certain way, to play it straight and be sure not to cause any scandal, came from within.

On the contrary, Jenny Buchwald said that her father pointed it out to her. "Yeah, he's used that on me. 'What happens if . . .' or 'You really shouldn't do that because of me.' Eventually I began to believe him.

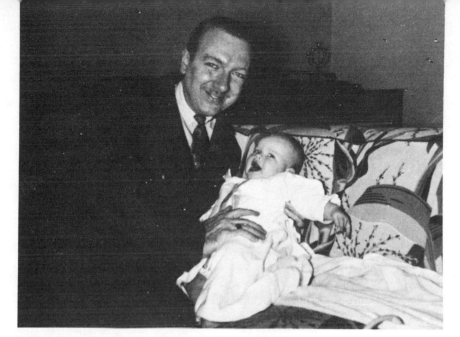

Dad and me, 1951

Dad and me, sailing off Martha's Vineyard, on his boat, *Wyntje*, 1980

A Cronkite family vacation in the early sixties. Left to right: Nancy, me, Mom (Betsy), Dad, and Chip

My husband, Bill Ikard, and me at our wedding, Martha's Vineyard, February 14, 1980

My brother Chip on *Wyntje*, off Martha's Vineyard, 1980

My sister, Nancy, in a recent role in the film *Murphy's Law*, 1980

Rick Armstrong with his father, Neil Armstrong, his mother, Jan, and his younger brother, Mark, 1969

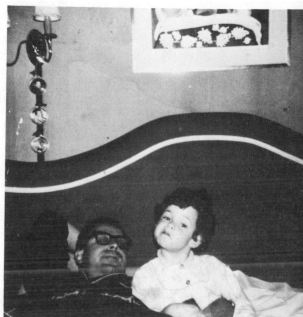

Jennifer Buchwald with her father,
Art Buchwald, 1958

Jennifer Buchwald at Disneyland, 1979

Charles M. Schulz with three of his children: Meredith (*left*), Monte (*right*), and Craig (*foreground*), 1955

Mary Frances Crosby and Bing Crosby, rehearsing for a television special
of Bing's in 1977

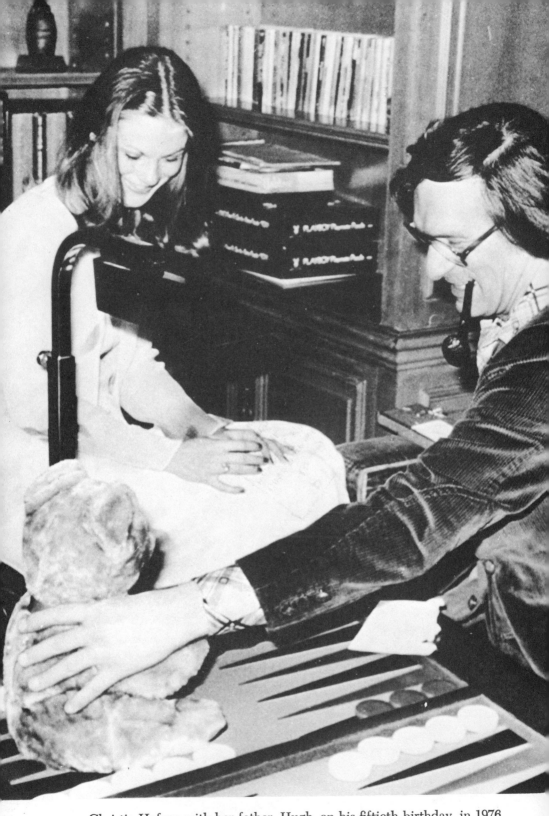

Christie Hefner with her father, Hugh, on his fiftieth birthday, in 1976

Mark Vonnegut plays chess with his father, Kurt Vonnegut, Jr., 1980
PHOTOGRAPH © 1980 BY JILL KREMENTZ

Nora Davis with her parents, Ossie Davis and Ruby Dee, 1980

Ruby Dee holding ten-month-old Nora Davis

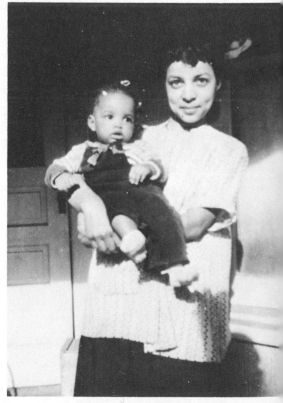

Lorenzo Lamas (sporting a T-shirt made by his stepmother, Esther Williams) with his father, Fernando Lamas, in Hollywood, 1977

A picnic in New York's Central Park in 1972 with Lorenzo Lamas (*third from left*) and his mother, Arlene Dahl (*far right*), his stepfather, Rounsevelle W. Schaum, his stepsisters Raini Schaum and Carole Holmes, and his stepbrother Eric Schaum

Chris and Jack Lemmon in 1980

The Ford family. Back row, left to right: Susan, Steve, Jack, Mike, Gayle; middle row: Betty and Gerald; foreground: Liberty

Arlo Guthrie (*far right*) at Café Society in New York's Greenwich Village in 1960 with (left to right) Joady, Woody, Marjorie, and Nora Lee

The Guthries at home, 1980. Left to right: Arlo, Abraham, baby Annie, Cathyalicia, and Jackie

John Ritter (*center*) with his father,
Tex Ritter, and his brother Tommy,
in Van Nuys, California, 1951

John Ritter, 1980

"At first I thought, 'Ahh, fuck you. Let me do what I want.' Then I realized that it's really true, that it *can* wreck his image, and he's worked really hard to get his image. Who am I to wreck it? I used to smoke joints right out on the street, but then I became more discreet, wouldn't do things in front of people. Also, I don't want that image myself. Anymore. I used to love it, being a big druggie. Now I don't care for it at all."

After all these years of living up to my father's image or not, of trying either to prove or deny who my father is, I have finally learned simply to accept it, to accept people's reactions to it, and even to be amused by them.

Once I was taking a computer class under my ex-husband's name. After one class, the teacher and I were chatting when Dad's unfortunately defunct series, *Twentieth Century*, was mentioned.

"I just think Walter Cronkite's the greatest," the teacher said.

"Yeah, so do I," I agreed. "He's my father." It was the first time I remember my pride overcoming my embarrassment enough for me to volunteer the fact.

"Yes," was the response. "The nation's father figure."

"No, I mean, he's *really* my father."

"Oh, I know," my teacher persisted. "A lot of people feel that way."

"Yeah," I said, giving up. "I guess they do."

6.
Christopher Buckley:
A Literary Tradition

Speak in French when you can't think of the
English for a thing—turn out your toes when
you walk—and remember who you are!
—LEWIS CARROLL, *Through the Looking-Glass*

What's the French for fiddle-de-dee?
                                    —IBID.

I finally caught up with Christopher Buckley at the office of
the *Harvard Crimson* in Cambridge, Massachusetts. We walked
around the corner to a little pub and ordered imported beer.
"Is your first question going to be, 'What's it like?'" he asked
with a smile.

Christopher is tall, aristocratic-looking, and quite charming.
He is so courteous and poised that one almost expects to have
one's hand kissed. This is not to say he is old-fashioned or square;
his humor is wonderfully wry and irreverent, and he sprinkles
his conversation with a discreet number of obscenities, although
he speaks with the same sort of distinct East Coast-intellectual
drawl as his father.

In William Buckley's wonderful sailing book, *Airborne*, Christopher is described as being "introspective, but there are trip
wires everywhere, which bring on the most infectious laughter
in the house."

Although we had not met before the interview, I have since
had the pleasure of getting to know him and have been delighted

to be able to spend time with him. He is an intelligent, genteel, and humorous companion and a good dancer.

I called him at about six-thirty one evening to ask if he would escort me to a testimonial dinner for my father. After we'd spoken for just a minute, he said, "Look, can I call you back in a half hour? I'm watching my old man on television."

"Of course," I said, without thinking, and hung up.

A few minutes after seven, the phone rang.

"Hello, Kathy? Buckley here."

"Oh, hi!" I replied. "Look, can I call you back in a half hour? I'm watching my old man on television."

Christopher is immediately recognizable as a Buckley, and when I asked him whether people he met connected him to his father, he answered somewhat elliptically: "I grew a beard once. Part of it was wanting to grow a beard after twenty-two years of not being able to grow one. I think probably there was a slight disguisement. But it didn't work. I've got a face that rings bells, and Buckley's a peculiar enough name to ring most. Also I'm in, roughly speaking, the same business. So I find I'll be sitting down talking to some radical professor, or, for example, Alger Hiss's son. I had to talk to him about the *Harvard Crimson*. We'd been talking about ten minutes, and I'd been calling him Tony, and he said, 'Do we know each other?'

"I said, 'Oh, no, no, I just called you Tony because you're young!'

" 'No, I mean . . . Do I *know* you?'

"The question's usually, are you any relation to the *Yale* Buckleys? And now, since I have an uncle who went off and became famous for six years, James Buckley, they usually say, 'What branch?' Which I find very displeasing.

"So, as usual, I said to Tony, 'Well, Bill's my dad.'

"He said, 'Oh!'

"I said, 'I don't think our fathers have ever *met*.'

"He said, 'No, but I think they certainly know a lot *about* each other.' "

"Once someone has made the connection, what is the first question they usually ask?" I wondered.

"Lately it's been, 'You must have had a very interesting child-hood.' To which my stock response is, 'Well, I was farmed off to wet nurses. So I don't really know.' You know, you toy around with these things. Only a couple of times in my life have I actually lied and said, 'No, no relation.'

"The very first day I registered for classes at Yale—a terrify-ing day—I was standing in a long line in Connecticut Hall, wait-ing to go through that marvelous welcoming ceremony of having our cards stamped and photos taken. There must have been two hundred people within earshot when I got up to the desk.

"And the guy says, 'What's your name?'

" 'Chris Buckley,' I mumbled.

"He says, 'What?'

"I said, clearing my throat, 'Ugh. Christopher Buckley.'

" 'Buckley? Hold on a second. Are you any relation to the *New York* Buckleys?'

"And, ah, I said no. Because it was my first day at Yale, and I knew I was going to be there for four years, and I just didn't feel like announcing it in front of two hundred of my peers."

"Do you meet people who ask if you're 'any relation to,' and then go into a long tirade about differences of opinion with your father?" I asked.

"About what a fascist he is? Strangely enough, I haven't had a lot of those experiences. I mean, if I ran into Joseph Stalin's daughter, which God knows one day I might, the first thing I wouldn't say is, 'What was it like growing up with a real *killer*?'" Chris said with an exaggerated wink.

"I might try to steer into a conversation about what Minister Molotov was really like, you know. So, with me, most people have not gone on to rampages about what a crypto-nazi he is. Of course, if they said that, I'd counter by calling them a faggot."

I had forgotten the notorious on-air feud between Gore Vidal and Bill Buckley that had climaxed with just such an exchange of epithets.

"Well," he said in response to my fits of laughter, "we might as well have fun.

"I remember one traumatic incident back in high school with an eighteen-year-old senior. Some kid who was a real sweetheart. He was the kind of guy that everyone didn't like. He was from New York, so he knew about my dad. He would ask those kinds of questions, 'Does your father really want to put Negroes in gas ovens?' and stuff. It was easy to tolerate, but he just got nastier and nastier about it. I was a [thirteen-year-old] freshman, and he was a big senior. One day my dad's picture had appeared in the *Times*. He amused himself by scrawling swastikas all over his forehead and giving him a Hitler haircut and a Hitler moustache—which is, as you know, fairly easy to do with any face— and pasted it on my door.

"I remember being very upset; I cried and started to punch him, which was ridiculous because he was a foot taller, and he'd probably beat me up in return. In one of those marvelous moments, another senior came along who was on the football team and liked me. He saw what was going on, because I was holding the photograph and crying and slugging at this guy. He put the other guy up against the wall and told him if he ever looked at me again, he'd be reduced to two pounds of Gainesburgers."

"Did you ever tell your father about that?"

"I never did. It's hard to sit down and really talk about how difficult it is to be his son. He knows. We love each other very much, and I think, partly as a result of that, sometimes we had a hard time communicating about serious things.

"We have a newspaper in New York, and when I became managing editor, the *New York Post* put it on page six, which is their gossip column. Just a tiny, tiny announcement that it was reporting the news from the wunderkind front or something and said that William Buckley's son, twenty-four, was to be managing editor. I don't think they mentioned my name; it was William Buckley's son. It was titled, 'Bill's Boy.' I found out from my mother that it had upset him a great deal. These are the mysterious ways in which we communicate."

"Do you ever expect that 'Bill's Boy' syndrome to stop?"

"No," he said. "No, it won't. There's an old Chinese proverb that says that true happiness consists in a son outliving his father. This is what all fathers want. I suppose the very bad day will come when my dad will not be around. It's a little more difficult posing an 'Are you someone's son' of a fifty-year-old than it is of a twenty-year-old, because when you're twenty, you are a son; when you are fifty and your father is dead, you tend to be your own man. So I imagine in my senescence, if I ever reach it, the question will be, 'Wasn't Bill Buckley your father?' And we will tend to talk about historical appreciations of *him*, rather than what it was like for me to grow up as his son."

"Do you call him Bill?"

"Oh, God, no!" he answered immediately. "Do you call your father Walt?"

"No," I said, almost embarrassed by the idea, "but some people call their parents . . ."

"I don't. I've just reached the stage where I'm calling some of my aunts and uncles by their first names. That goes along with twenty-five years of experience. No. I call him Pup, with a u, because when I was four, I couldn't quite pronounce Pop. Also, my mother's British colonial, so I always call her Mum. So it's Mum and Pup, and that persists. I sometimes call her Ma, which she thinks is very American."

He broke off abruptly and asked me to turn off the tape machine for a second. During the interlude he vacillated about telling me a particular story that he obviously wanted to tell but was afraid might be damaging. I assured him that he could always change his mind later, in which case I would leave it out.

"Sure," he agreed. "Okay, are we on again? I would like officially to apologize to *People* magazine for treating their reporters like total shit.

"My dad had just done *Saving the Queen*, and one morning I was on my way out, and he said, 'Oh, by the way, *People* magazine is coming at eleven, be sure to be here.'

"I said, 'What do you mean?'

" 'Well, I think they want to take pictures,' he told me.

" 'Well, it's *your* book; I think they should take pictures of *you*. I didn't have anything to do with the book.' Oh, what a scene that was.

"He said, 'I think we ought to cooperate.'

"So *People* magazine came with some photography equipment, and I behaved very badly. I refused to talk to them. I posed in a *surly* manner, with my best grimace and beard. They made me look like a real shit. For very good reason. They kept asking me *questions* while we were posing—which I've done since I was four for *Vogue* and *Look* and *Life*. I've been through it before, but at this point I decided that for *all* reasons I just didn't like playing Little Lord Buckley for *People* magazine. So they asked the kind of questions you or I would ask if we were there interviewing William Buckley, and his son happened to be there. You know, 'Are you going to go into journalism when you grow up?'

"And I said, 'I'm already in journalism,' with not a *trace* of humor.

"Then they said, 'How did you like *Saving the Queen?*'

"I thought, 'Well, *I'll* be goddamned if I'm going to answer that,' because I liked it a whole lot, and because I'm not good at making quotes. So I just didn't open my mouth. Five seconds went by. *Ten* seconds went by, and it become *mildly* awkward, and finally my dad, who's brilliant at these things, chimed in and said, 'He thinks it's the best book he's read since *Moby Dick.'*

"Then we walked down to the beach for some surly photographs, and when I divined that they were through with me, I just walked away. I had this *big* scene with the folks who've always raised me, without lifting a hand, to be polite and courteous. I displayed, perhaps, *not* those virtues. God, I almost left home that day. I just felt tremendously bottled up by the whole thing. So therefore may I apologize to *People* magazine for being an asshole."

"I really envy you being able to do that," I commented, "to say no to it. We used to do all that getting dressed up in your Sunday best, going downstairs to have *Good Housekeeping* take pictures of you making cookies with your mother."

"Yeah, which you never did," he said.

"Well, actually we *did* make cookies a lot, but not the way they had us doing it."

"Yeah, yeah, in your best clothes."

"And there's always that urge to say, 'No, *this* is the way I *really* am.'"

"When I was six years old," Christopher related, "some magazine arrived to take pictures of the family of the then-young reactionary who was attracting tremendous attention. I was there, in jeans and grubby. My mom sort of marched me off and suddenly I was dressed in shorts. Not cheap shorts—like gray flannel shorts with knee socks and a clean white shirt. I mean, I really looked like a six-year-old faggot. They took pictures of my dad helping me across a lily pond which was captioned, 'A Helping Hand' or something—an admission that my dad had no better things to do than help me across a lily pond when I was six. A proper six-year-old should have been drowning in a lily pond.

"Then there was another time when I was seventeen. When I was in high school I ran a summer camp for inner-city kids, and I was home for a weekend." Christopher cleared his throat and chuckled. "My father is going to be very upset when he reads this." He laughed. "But anyway, we'd taken some acid. . . ." He leaned into the microphone and said very distinctly: "These were the days *when I took acid*, which *all* seventeen-year-olds did then.

"Anyway, we were going to go off and have a fun time in New York City. You know how history is comprised of accidents. Well, it was a little chilly, and I needed to go home just to get a sweater. So I walked in the front door and tripped over a co-axial cable in the foyer. The place looked like the Democratic convention. There were lights and cables everywhere. The first person I saw was Mike Wallace, for whom I have all sorts of respect. There he was, thrusting out his hand, saying, 'Oh, good, I'm glad you're here. You're on in five minutes!'

"I thought, oh, dear. I went up and found my mom who was getting dressed up for her interview and said, 'I'm not doing this.'

"She said, 'You *must* do this. It's for your father.'

"I said, 'What do I have to do with *Sixty Minutes*?'

" 'It's for your father, change your shirt.'

"I was seventeen, feeling much too old for changing of shirts, and said, 'No.' Well, she won that one. So I changed my shirt, and my friend is sitting down there in the foyer beside himself. We were under certain influences. Anyway, five minutes later I found myself in the hands of the technicians, and Mike was making this big deal about, 'We're just sitting here chatting man to man, forget the cameras, I just want you to make yourself comfortable.' And my field of vision is slinking off.

"An old friend of mine said, 'It's downright impertinent to look at someone's face and hallucinate.' And this was my impertinence at the time.

"I threw myself on the sofa, and technicians are saying, 'Okay, now move your hand over here, now put this hand like that.' It was one of those very posh corners of our house where a lot of leopard skins are coagulated with chinchilla furs and Pekingese and a Rosselini painting on the wall. So I found myself again in the Little Lord Fauntelroy stance. 'Now, wouldn't you be more comfortable crossing your legs?' Yeah, right. So there I was feeling quite unnatural, and the LSD wasn't going away. Then we had our interview. It must have lasted forty-five minutes, because by the time it was over I was in severe, advanced stages of hallucination. Of course, he asked all sorts of questions like, 'Do you like to play sports?' You know, wow . . . sometimes. The question he wanted to get at was, of course, buried in the middle, and it was, 'Do people razz you about your dad?'

"I mumbled about how sometimes they did and sometimes they didn't. Then I beat a real fast exit. I watched the cut on television when it came out a couple of months later, and I acquitted myself decently. I guess no one knew what was up. So that's my Mike Wallace interview."

"That's the epitome of what can happen when tripping," I laughed, "and the nasty circumstances you can find yourself in."

"Like an unexpected meal with your folks," he added. "Inevitably, they serve troublesome food like soufflé, and they always want to talk about *serious* things that night. 'What are you going to do with your life?'"

The idea of having dinner with William F. Buckley while incapacitated by drugs made me wonder what it must have been like going through a radical era with a conservative for a father.

"Well, I went to Yale, and people told me subsequently that I would have had a much harder time going to a place like Columbia, but I think that's probably not true. Because Columbia was a little more radical. I probably would have had a very hard time if I'd gone to Harvard; I would have committed suicide if I went to Berkeley. But Yale was, on the whole, not hard. I graduated from a Catholic boarding school run by a Benedictine monastery in 1970. So I missed the very heavy moments. Before I went to school I took a year off to work in the merchant marine, which is a very good thing to do. Because no one knew me.

"I remember stepping out onto the docks in Manila and passing a black market newsstand and seeing an Alfred Eisenstadt portrait of my family on *Life* magazine. Which was a startling thing to see for a deck boy twelve thousand miles from home. I bought a copy of it and took it back to the boat to read the story. This seaman walked in, and I sat him down with *Life* and said, 'Well, Arvid, you've asked me about my family. Well, here they are. This is my dad, this is my aunt. This is my uncle, and he's a senator—that's sort of a nice thing to be in government.' I could only have done it on that ship in Manila. Nowhere else would I have sat down with *Life* magazine and said, 'Hey! Family scrapbook!'

"But, as far as the radical days, I found out later that my three freshman-year roommates at Yale knew well before I met them that they would be rooming with William Buckley's son. They were cool about it. They waited a decent interval, maybe a month, before starting to ask me oblique questions about where did my folks live and stuff just to prime the pump. But I was never singled out. In those days I kept a very low profile politically if asked for a political view—which I really didn't have so much in those days. They tended to be more liberal than conservative, and I always passed the buck.

"I remember, the party of the right, which is the conservative faction, came around and solicited me, but I told them the truth, which was that I wasn't politically involved, or politically sentient, and to please go away.

"I had something of a problem deciding whether I would join the *Yale Daily News*, because my dad had been about the most conspicuous leader of all time. I had a terrible time the night they announced the introductory meeting. I walked back and forth between my dorm and the *News* building, each time touching the doorknob and deciding I wasn't going to do it, then getting back to the dorm and deciding I would do it. I made about three round trips that night. Finally, I threw myself in and started writing for the *News*, and they were all highly cool about it. There was not a mention made. These weren't radical editors, but they were, you know, your good FDR liberals. They were all absolutely marvelous, and very encouraging. I couldn't write my way out of a zip-lock bag in those days, and they spent a lot of time with me.

"About a month after I joined, I covered a lecture by a professor who had been suspended from Yale for holding down two jobs, it turned out, which is quite reasonable grounds to suspend. They didn't even fire the guy; they suspended him. This was a man of questionable integrity, anyway. It turned out he made money off students by letting them hook into his TV antenna which he had illegally hooked onto the antenna in the dorm. They were just petty things like that, but he was very popular. He was a guest lecturer in this course that was out-and-out gut."

"What is gut?"

"A gut is an easy course, a course you took if you wanted to be sure of getting an A. I think the final paper was: 'Write a three-page paper on how you get along with your roommate,' or something like that.

"So in the second paragraph of the story I said, 'The professor appeared at a session of this course, known to most as a Super-gut.' Well, a week later I was *roasted* in this very Maoist—even Stalinist, I think—mimeo of a newsletter which was put out by the guys who had been taking too many drugs or attending too many demonstrations to graduate, so they were still there.

"They did a whole piece on me. About how neo-nazi William F. Buckley's son is busy slandering Third World activists. And the piece I had written was a straightforward news piece. The only subjective line was the 'Super-gut' reference, and it was for that that I was accused of carrying on this neo-nazi torch. The editor of it was an Indonesian guy in my Spanish class. The next day, mildly furious, I waved this in his face and said, 'Uh, Jummo, did you read that story?'

"He shuffled and said, 'Well, ummmmmm . . . yeah.'

"I said, 'Well, what did I say about the Third World radicals that so annoyed you?'

"He said, 'Uh, it was your whole attitude.'

" 'Well, Jummo, I'm not going to say anything more to you about this. Just get your fuckin' facts straight and just read the piece and then tell me you think I was slandering Third World activists.'

"That was one encounter, but that was really about it. Every now and then in a class a professor would make a comment, 'cause Yale's very liberal. Hugely liberal. Most Ivy League colleges are. Once or twice a professor in a philosophy course, or something, would make a mildly tendentious remark in a lecture which I was attending about 'effete capitalists, like William Buckley,' or something like that. I would never rise to that bait."

"Do you think it was bait?" I asked. "Did the professors know you were there?"

"No, no, not at all. No, I think it was just, you know, standard allusion."

There was one question I had been wanting to ask all morning: "Is there any truth to the rumor that your father went outside the territorial limit to smoke dope?"

"Oh, yes. Well, he wrote about it. It's not a rumor at all. I was not there." He smiled. "He was going to go on *Firing Line* to talk about marijuana. He'd read everything about it, done everything about it except try it. He wanted to do it legally, so he invited his buddies out on his boat, *Cyrano*, and he had a police captain friend of his get some Acapulco Gold and sort of escort the dope to the limit. So my dad did 'the correct thing,' which he thought was to put music on *low* and listen to some jazz, and they all sat around blowing dope. And everyone got *smashed*. Except him. I think, possibly, because he smoked it like a cigarette. Sort of quick in and out. But the report I got was that he was about the only one competent to bring the boat back into the three-mile limit after that little escapade."

"What year was that?"

"That would have been 1970 or 1971.

"The contradiction is that everyone assumes that if you're William Buckley's son, you were raised with thumbscrews and racks. That's the farthest thing from the truth. I was raised the way I would expect Timothy Leary's children to be raised. I had one of those classical educations, you know, seven years of piano lessons which I hated, a horrible French governess who beat French into me. I think the last time I was told to be home by a certain hour was when I was fifteen. After that it was, you know, stay out as late as you want, but call and let us know where you are. It was very liberal. He never whispered a word about where he wanted me to go to college. Which was Yale. Never.

"The one night when I did mention that my aspirations were to go to the University of Hawaii," Christopher laughed, "there was some degree of dumbfoundedness. But I was never told to do a damn thing. Except read."

"What was the biggest hassle you had with them?"

"It was probably over smoking cigarettes. When I was fifteen, I was a pack-a-day man. You see, my dad and I carried on our relationship a lot in letters, 'cause he's very writerly, and I tended to be, also. If I had something serious to say, I tended to put it in a letter. So he wrote me in high school, and this is the only act of discipline I can remember, that if I didn't stop smoking, he wouldn't let me get my driver's license. I was sixteen. But he said, 'And if you do this, I will give you anything you want , you need only to name it.'

"What I needed then was a way of hurting him for this *outrageous* act of authoritarianism, so what I knew would hurt them most would be something like my not being there for summer vacation. So I wrote and said, 'Fine, I will give up smoking'— which I didn't—'and in return for which I want to go to summer school.'

"They couldn't figure it out, couldn't figure out why I wanted to stay at Portsmouth Priory and study Latin and Greek all summer when I could be at home with them. I think he must have thought I was having too much fun being sodomized at Portsmouth," he laughed. "But here again we took that to a draw. It was one of our perfect family compromises—I went on smoking, I got my driver's license, and I came home for the summer. Well, I continued to sneak cigarettes till I was eighteen. I didn't have permission. I think my ma at the age of forty, when she went home to her folks, continued to have her cigarettes in the bathroom."

Not long before I met Christopher, my mother had sent me his father's book, *Airborne*, an exhilarating account of a transatlantic voyage on Buckley's yacht. I got to about page twenty-two and said to myself, "That's it. I want to go." Although Christopher had been quoted frequently in the book, mostly in the form of excerpts from his journal, I asked if he had any afterthoughts about the trip.

"Afterthoughts?" he echoed. 'Yes, I'm delighted to air this, come to think of it. If you read the first chapter, you noticed that it closed with a notation that I made in the logbook. We were out in moderate seas, it was pitch black, fourteen hundred miles from home. It was four o'clock in the morning and I had just woken up, and I was still a little groggy, and we had a rule about safety belts, gotta wear your safety belts. I came out on deck to relieve my father, me and Danny, and I wasn't wearing my safety belt.

"Dad said, 'Ahem, do me a personal favor and put on your safety belt.'

"I said, 'Uh, don't worry, I'll put it on.'

"And he said, 'I *will* worry if you don't put it on right now.'

"I thought, well, fuck you, you know, so I went and put it on and was very surly. And he, marvelously, wrote this little entry in the logbook about how 'In due course the safety belt for the first mate was found and secured.'

"I was *not* in a mood to be amused at six o'clock in the morning in the middle of the ocean with moderate seas, sleepless, so Danny wrote under it, 'Up yours, W.F.B.: Danny.' And I wrote 'Get Fucked.'

"Well, he sent me the first chapter as soon as he'd written it, and it ended with my notation as it had been written—'Get Fucked.' Then he'd had better thoughts about it because by the time it had gotten into galleys he had changed it to 'Screw You.' I remember seeing the galleys and feeling very betrayed. I felt that my linguistic integrity had been compromised.

"I said, 'I didn't write, "Screw You"; I wrote, "Get Fucked."'

"He said, 'What's the difference?'

"I said, 'There's a great deal of difference. "Get Fucked" is more direct, more vehement. "Screw you" is something that *you* would have used thirty years ago.'

"And he said, 'Well, inasmuch as this book will be read by people whose *exclusive* discourse does not consist of *animal* noises, I think that we ought to do the correct thing and go with "Screw You."'

"And I said, 'Get *Fucked.*' To this day, I feel that I got a raw deal.

"But it was a wonderful book. I took the photographs, and he chose ones that I thought were the worst. I'd open to another page and see this photograph of Danny that was so clear that you couldn't tell if it was Danny or Mao Tse-tung, and I said, 'Well, why did you use *this* photograph?'

"It finally got down to him saying, 'Well, it's, it's *my* book, and I want to choose the photographs.' Which is perfectly *valid,*" Chris said with good humor. "I mean, he *did* go into hock up to his eyeballs to go on this trip.

"Those are the only afterthoughts I have. I closed the book with a little, well, I mean *he* closed the book with a commentary from my journal which I wrote in the bay of Cadiz, in which I said that I would ship out with him any day. And that hasn't changed."

"There was one quote from the book that I found interesting. Your father said something to the effect that 'all the years of tutoring you in the art of sarcasm had paid off.'"

"Yeah, something like that. It's funny, the most revealing comments he often makes about me, I read in newspapers or magazines. I remember in 1965 when I was thirteen, he gave an interview to the *Daily News*. He was running for mayor, and I got to school that day and found my classmates clustered around the *New York Daily News* having absolute fits of glee," he laughed. "This was the same piece, by the way, in which our family wealth was put at one hundred ten million dollars—a myth that has persisted to this day, *would* that it were true. But I found everyone *hooting* and absolutely beside themselves, and I ambled over and said, 'What's up?'

"Well, he had been asked to talk about me, and he said, 'He's a good boy, fundamentally lazy, but a good boy.'" He laughed again. "Then I read that Scavullo book, and I think Scavullo asked him whether or not *I* had a hard time dealing with him, and my old man said a *nice* thing, which is that 'Up to the age of fourteen he had a hard time, but at fourteen he learned how to,' I forget the exact words, 'he learned how to outwit me.'

"Every now and then I'll tune in to Merv Griffin, and Merv will be on talking about *Airborne* with my dad and say, 'Well, you know, is your son a good sailor?' or something, and the old man will say, 'Uh, *fitfully*.' "

"Do you make it a point to watch him on talk shows and so forth?"

"I'll tell you something I'm not particularly proud of, but I've probably only seen about thirty percent of *Firing Line*. I read his column religiously and all pieces and now all books, but I don't think I picked up one of his books till I was seventeen. But I'll say this: they say it's a bad time for heroes. I've got no problem with heroes, because I've got one hero, and that's my old man. It's been one long fucking thrill, being associated with him."

"It's obvious that the relationship between you is super, full of respect and love."

"It's a very *oblique* relationship. I mean, he loves me very much, he loves me *hard*. I'm an only child, and that sometimes creates more problems than having a famous father. I just recently got assigned to be the European editor for *Esquire*, so I'm moving over to London.* And this is a *good* thing. It's very exciting. I'm scared shitless about it, but I'll be European editor, and that'll be interesting.

"So he was the first one I called up, and I said, 'Well, what do *you* think?' This is the sort of offer that you really don't have to think about. Except I did because I thought, he'll *miss* me. And, in fact, he didn't say that, but he was very thoughtful about it, and he started going into a lot of stuff about how my literary sensibilities are very American, about how it's much *less* fun in Europe these days than it *used* to be in the golden days of Fitz-

---

* Since the time of this interview, Christopher has decided instead to take a leave of absence from *Esquire* to write a book, although he still occasionally free-lances articles.

gerald and Hemingway, and how I've got an *absolutely* terrific job in New York, *anyway*.

"In other words, he couldn't quite bring himself to say that he didn't really want me to go to London because he wouldn't see me. He's very sweet in that way. I know exactly what's going on. But he never, ever made any kind of selfish request. He's always very analytical. If he sets his mind on something like that, he will come up with an *analytical* argument rather than a personal one, because he knows that I will do anything he asked me to do. For that reason, he never asks me."

"There was something in *Airborne* about if he asked you to do it 'as a personal favor,' you would jump overboard?"

"It was about shaving off my beard. He said at the outset of one trip, 'Do me a personal favor and get a haircut.' And I thought, ka-rist, we'll be out on the boat for thirty days, and you want me to get a haircut. But I got a haircut. He said it lightly, but I took it seriously. But I didn't shave off my beard. I think his comment was that I came on the boat looking like Peter Pan and ended up looking like Charles Manson.

"It's not *tough* being William Buckley's son; it's just occasionally an *issue* with somebody.

"As a matter of fact, the obvious suspicion is that you can get a job at CBS, I can get a job at *Esquire*. My dad had just won a hundred-fifty-thousand-dollar lawsuit against *Esquire* about a year before I got there, so *Esquire* was not particularly in the mood to do him favors. In fact, the guy who hired me told me he had carefully not mentioned to the chairman of the board what my biological encumbrances were. Well, I got a job at *Esquire* because I went to the launch party for the book, *Airborne*, and the editor of *Esquire* happened to be there. It was not a put-up job, but I'd be insane to suggest that there were no connections for me to draw on. In fact, I didn't draw on any connections, but there was a social situation to which I could go, and there was someone there.

"The irony of this is that at the time I was on my way to South Carolina to work for the *Charleston Evening Post* for a hundred and twenty-five bucks a week. But I found myself liking to point it out, like I pointed it out to you; it's an obvious matter of some residual insecurity. Less of a problem since I advanced at *Esquire*, and that's presumably not because you're someone's son."

"Maybe the fact that you're a terrific writer has something to do with it?"

"Well, I don't know. They weren't hiring me for my writing, I think. Well, I don't know. One of the editors who interviewed me—and I went through four or five interviews—said, 'Well, you've grown up with conspicuous people all around, writers and the like. You're obviously not shy.' Which couldn't be farther from the truth. Though there *has* been a procession of famous people. I remember Norman Mailer, poor Norman Mailer, being made to read one of my short stories from fourth-grade composition. And, wonderfully, he wrote on the top of it, 'To Christopher, a fine young writer.' These are things that made me turn turquoise with embarrassment."

"Did you ever go through a period of searching and anxiety about having a famous parent?"

"The time I really noticed, it was a pretty odd day. It was the 1965 campaign, and my dad said, 'Why don't we go out for the day?' Which we never did, we never went out and walked around.

"I said, 'Sure.' As it turned out, it was a day of in the street campaigning, shaking hands, pressing the flesh. I think he wanted to have me along as someone to hold onto. I didn't realize at the time. And it was the day that Pope Paul was visiting New York, and there was a special benediction at Saint Pat's which was by invitation only. So we got to the corner of Madison and Fiftieth, and the sidewalk was barricaded off for the VIPs. We hit the sidewalk when no one else was there, and the crowds were just *horded* over the barricades, viewing this procession which we made alone. I don't know where Walter Cronkite was, but we could have used him.

"And, ah, my God, what a frightening spectacle that was, because almost everyone jeered. Like, 'Hey, Buckley! Yeahhhh. Mumble mumble . . . Rich man! What do you care?' It was *severe*. And he's squeezing my hand and walking down . . ."

"To give you strength or to draw it?"

"No, I think to draw strength, a little battery. He hated doing all that stuff. His campaign was more a campaign of ideas than your run-of-the-mill baby kissing and frankfurter eating at Nathan's Famous. I think that was the first time I was really aware that he was a figure. The rest of the campaign involved a lot of that. Nothing quite like that day, but sitting on stages and being the candidate's family. My heart goes out to Amy Carter."

"Did you ever do anything that really shocked your parents?" I asked. There was a long pause. "Or embarrassed them?"

"Embarrassed them? Things like the *People* magazine incident would have shocked them.

"I was always the kid who never got caught. 'Cause I was a wily little fucker. So they never really had to come down to a police station and bail me out for throwing eggs at police cars and that sort of thing. If you go way back, there were the pedestrian sorts of things where I'd sneak out and stay out all night and then would arrive back at seven in the morning with beer on my breath, age fourteen. I think that shocked them. But I was a fairly respectable son in those days."

"Did you worry about a public image of being respectable?"

"Never a public image. I always just worried about what they would think. If you're at a private boarding school that expels you for getting caught smoking cigarettes, you worry hugely about it. At the time, age sixteen and seventeen, I thought that if I got kicked out of Portsmouth I would either try to fake a suicide to convince my parents that I was contrite or run away. But it would never have anything to do with, 'What would the public think?' Never at all.

"We've had a very free-floating dialogue on marijuana. I remember at some point my mom getting very worried that I was going to get busted, or something. 'You can't, now that you have an uncle who's a senator.' Of course, that didn't cut down on the intake of joints, or anything. But it made me a little bit more careful. I would never have Jack Ford's problem, but it occurred to me that it would make a very nice local story. It would probably even go out on the wire services. In fact, it would definitely go out on the wire services."

"It went on the wires when Jack Ford just said he had smoked it," I pointed out.

"But he's in a much more advanced stage of celebrity. On the other hand, because the old man is conservative, it would then become sort of a point. Even though for seven years now he's been on record favoring decriminalization."

"What kind of expectations do you think people have of you?"

"They're always very curious. Often they'll ask, 'Are you in political agreement with your dad?' I think they expect someone a little more sedate, a little more intelligent. They expect someone who is pretty straight, kind of inward, and, you know, not terribly conspicuous. Someone with no discernible talent. I think that's the expectation of sons and daughters of famous people—that they really are the greatest of hangers-on. This goes for wives, too. The problem the wives of famous people must have."

"But I think there's always the woman-behind-the-great-man idea."

"Yeah, there's seldom the son behind the great man. But I think they probably expect something a little polysyllabic of me."

"I was considering bringing a dictionary today."

"No, no. Of course I tend to lapse into Renaissance Latin."

"Let me ask you about the intelligence thing. I always used to feel incredibly stupid, compared to my dad. I'm starting to shake that feeling, to realize I don't necessarily have to compare my intelligence to his."

"There's a guy I heard of who made a great deal of sense to me, the son of a very distinguished professor at Yale called William Wimsatt. He wrote probably every textbook on Alexander Pope you've ever read," he said with a straight face.

"Wimsatt was one of the new critics," Christopher continued. "He was a tyrant-god of the professors at Yale. Real old school, been around. I think the son's name is William Wimsatt the Third. I'm not sure at all, but he goes by the name of Augie, and he's a motorcycle freak. He's one of the best motorcycle mechanics, and he hangs out at the local cycle joint and is apparently

very happy leading that life. I thought, there's the perfect solution
to one of life's problems which is: What do you do if you're
William Wimsatt's son?

"It makes a lot of sense whenever you hear about someone
going off and doing something entirely on his own terms, unre-
lated. It would be the perfect thing for me to do by this formula,
which I don't quite believe in, but it has a romantic appeal. I
thought of staying in the merchant marine—you know, it's something different, and no one will compare you. Because now people
will, see? I'm already getting a little of that now."

"Do the comparisons annoy you?" I asked.

"Well, they astound me, because there's no comparison at all.
I mean I think he's one of life's great things, and they come along
every century. You don't know the half of what a remarkable
man he is. I'm not just talking about his intelligence, I'm talking
about what kind of a good man he is. And I find myself comparing
myself more to *that* part of him than I do to the polysyllabic part.
We have different styles. And he hasn't left much territory uncovered. I can no longer go out and become a great novelist and
be the novelist in the family. He's done quite a lot, hasn't he? I
could come off and write *Jaws III* or something and be slightly
different. But people will make comparisons, and I've just put
myself in the position where they might. I would love to write as
well as he does and love to speak as well as he does and love to
have that mind. But I'd love to work one tenth as hard as he does
—he's right; I am bone lazy, and his output is sort of legendary."

"You mentioned all his different accomplishments; what do you
say when people ask what your father does?"

"I say he's a writer. Generally, if you say someone is a writer,
they will say, 'Oh, who does he write for?' That will open Pan-
dora's box. Not as many people make the connection with the
name as I would think. Maybe they know it already and just
aren't going to mention it. A lot of times I'll be in an interview,
and it'll be long, and it will get chatty, and I will mention my dad.
Like I'll say, 'He said last week that Mozambique is essentially a
terrible situation.'

"And then they will say, 'Well, you know, I wasn't going to

bring up your dad, but since you did . . .' Which means to me that they knew about it already."

"I find it difficult to say what my father does without eventually being put in the position of saying who he is," I said.

"You're right; it's a little difficult pussyfooting around that situation. For instance, Clay Felker decided at one point that he wanted an interview with Fidel Castro and put me on it. So I said, 'Well, only last week my dad went on national TV and called Fidel the premier barbarian of this hemisphere, but I'll give it a shot.'

"So I called up an old CIA buddy and asked him how he would proceed on this, and he said, 'We'll lunch on it.' So I went to kiss some Cuban ass in Washington to tell them how marvelous I thought their policy on human rights was. They hadn't made the connection yet, but they stipulated that I would have to send them a résumé. Because the cat was not yet out of the bag, and in due course they wanted to know *my* feelings about Cuba, and I said, 'Well, I'm very curious.' Which was true. I sent them an old résumé I'd typed up after I got out of college. Under background it said: 'Father: editor of *National Review*,' which is how I would identify him in any colloquial encounter. I have not heard back from them. So whether or not I'll be scrubbed for ideological reasons, I don't know.

"On the other hand, in journalism it's not a distinct disadvantage. I can't think of anybody who has seen me because I'm William F. Buckley's son. I can think of people who've given me phone numbers of other people because I'm William Buckley's son. But, you know, small, small things. Not like Jimmy Carter's unlisted number. Just like trying to track somebody down who went to school once, and the admissions guy said, 'Well, I wouldn't ordinarily do this, but what the hell.'

"Malcolm Muggeridge currently has an aphorism about it, and that is that there're disadvantages in having famous parents, but the butcher inevitably gives you an extra cut of meat. Except I always get fatty lamb chops."

"What are some of the advantages? What have you inherited from your father?"

"It's easier to talk about what I haven't inherited: a fine mind, his olympian endurance, his goodness, his tolerance—"

"Not many people would associate tolerance with William F. Buckley," I suggested.

"He's very tolerant. I mean, he has time for everybody, even people most people don't have the time of day for. I haven't really inherited any of that. I don't know if you're a born writer; I don't think I was. Hell, I never even read as a kid. I spent most of my time with TV or comic books. So I didn't inherit any great intellectual curiosity, either."

"But you wouldn't be in the business you're in if you didn't have some intellectual curiosity."

"No, no, I cultivated some of it when I got to Yale."

I had been staring all through the interview at the outside edge of his right hand on which was tattooed the slogan, "Fuck off." Finally, I couldn't help but comment on it.

"Yeah," he said. "I actually got a memo from the old man about this. It was about two years ago, and it was something to the effect of, 'Now that you're about to graduate and be a real person, I think it is time, quote, to put away childish things, end quote, and to get your hand fixed.' It's been with me for eight years, and I tend to think if I don't get it fixed within a year, I'll have it the rest of my life.* I've developed certain mannerisms to hide it. For example, if I'm sitting across from some great lady of society at a party or something, I just . . ." He demonstrated how he sits, elbows braced on the table, right hand cupped in left in a thoughtful-looking manner.

"What do you do when you're sitting next to Mrs. Cronkite?" I asked, knowing that he had recently been her dinner partner.

"I'm not worried when I'm sitting next to Mrs. Cronkite," he smiled. "I just figure we can bullshit and be good old folks."

"I remember my mother telling me *years* ago how upset the Bill Buckleys were about their son's tattoos," I said.

"It's a problem. I surprised them with it. I didn't announce that I was coming back from the merchant marine, and they were just *euphoric* to see me. They hadn't seen me in a long time, and I

---

* The next time we met, he had, indeed, had it removed.

hit them with this *real* fast. Because I wanted them still to be euphoric when they realized I was scarred for my life. My dad burst out laughing when he saw it, and the old lady—she tells it much better than I do—'clutched the curtains and her heart and called for rosewater.' They warned me about everything else, you know; my dad had arranged for lessons in self-defense with some pro, so I can kill people now with my hands, and the old lady packed me off with tetracycline and all sorts of antibiotics. The one thing they forgot was the tattoo. And I come back 'tattooed up to my neck.' "

This was obviously a quote from his parents, since my mother used the same phrase in her description. It is also something less than accurate. He has the small 'Fuck off' and one large tattoo covering one bicep.

"I'd show it to you," Buckley offered, "but if you've seen the photo in *Airborne*, you know what it looks like. It's a little weird; it was weird at Yale. I remember taking off my clothes to get into bed the first night I was there and sort of wondering what my roommate was going to think. It was clearly an oddity; I would venture to say that no one else in my class had a tattoo. But I've learned to cope."

7.

Walking the Line

O the mind, mind has mountains; cliffs of fall
Frightful, sheer, no-man-fathomed. Hold them cheap
May who ne'er hung there.
                              —GERARD MANLEY HOPKINS

Mark Vonnegut's schedule as an intern didn't allow much time for interviews. But finally one summer day, I walked up the path to his old two-story frame house on a residential street in suburban Boston. It is a substantial house, the sort that one thinks of automatically as a home, in a quiet middle-class neighborhood.

Mark and his sixteen-month-old son, Zachary, were alone; his wife, Pat, was at work. He walked me through the lower floor of the house with Zak on one hip, showing off his family's art: the dark, almost Renaissance-style paintings of his sister, the cousin's stained glass, a wood chess table expertly crafted by his brother, and his own deeply colored, chaotic nonobjective paintings.

"We all grew up multitalented and confident," he explained on the way to the kitchen. We settled in at the kitchen table, in a windowed corner looking out on the sloping lawn and jungle of trees. Throughout the rather disjointed interview, Zak whimpered and begged crackers and beer from his father, and the mongrel pup, Kent, chewed unremittingly either on my hand or my pants cuff.

I asked Mark whether he had worried about his family's re-

123

action to his writing so candidly about his mental illness.

"Yeah, I tried to make everybody come off honestly but as well as I could. In terms of public relations, I didn't think much about it. I didn't want him to feel hurt. You know, I worried that was going to be a temptation, a natural inclination of a lot of readers, and certainly it was the natural inclination of a lot of shrinks—to zero in on The-Son-of-Famous-Man routine. If I had ignored it, everybody would have said, 'Aha! That's why he went crazy, because his father's Kurt Vonnegut and he can't deal with it.' If I had ignored any topic, I would have had a different life. And it would have been a different book if my father was a used-car salesman.

"I don't think anybody really believed I was writing a book. Maybe towards the end, there. People would say, 'Well, he goes into the study, and as long as you don't hear any screams, I mean . . . Let's let him go to the study and pretend he's writing a book.'" He laughed. "I think my family was mostly happy that I was out of the mental hospital and was able to live uninstitutionalized. You know, I very easily could have been one of the many permanently institutionalized vegetables."

"How did your hospitalization affect your entrance into medical school?" I asked.

"Well, one of my professors is a deeply sick man. His first line to me was, 'I know who you are.'

"I said, 'Okay.'

"He said, 'I don't have any special instructions from the administration or anything. I'm going to treat you as if you were normal.' And later he said, 'Are you still writing?'

"I said, 'Well, yeah, I work on something now and then.'

"He said, 'I mean are you writing about this, here, now?' He was going mad.

"I've learned to be so patient and tolerant. It would be so easy for me to slam these people. But if I just sit there and just sort of nod my head gently, people go on and on, and you really get to see what's in their minds. It's fascinating. I like to see these specimens sort of rave on about their preconceptions [about me]. I suppose it is very insulting, but I really don't take it that way."

He paused and then added, almost to himself, "What a strange man.

"People are asking me about it," he went on, referring to his breakdown, "because they are considering me for an internship. Which is a very precious thing. What I say to them is, consider it a vaccination. I mean, you're taking on these twenty-four- and twenty-five-year-olds—who knows what you're getting? I've had mine. I would say I'm less a risk than they are.

"I know it well, and I know what to do about it when it starts happening. I see it coming many miles away. I think anybody who's never had [a breakdown] is less prepared, less well equipped to deal with it, with life. Anybody who sees himself as totally mentally stable, never go crazy, stuff like that, just is not living in reality. Those people are out of touch. The mind is a very complicated thing.

"You know, anybody can go crazy any time. I think I do have an advantage in that I know a lot of tricks, and, you know, I have a pretty good warning system. I used to do a little test. If I have coffee and start feeling a little wobbly—I don't drink coffee for a while. Once you have a margin of health, you can do anything you want, but just be aware of what affects you what way. They've done the experiments. They can produce paranoid psychosis in anybody with amphetamine."

"One of the things I found so interesting in your book was how frequently your father appeared in your hallucinations," I said.

"I think it was very helpful for me, going through that, to feel that my father was a part of it. I think I put it as 'a voice worth tuning in to.' I think a lot of people in that situation feel, 'Oh, Jesus, if only Kurt Vonnegut were here, everything would be all right," he laughed.

"What I'm saying is that it helped the whole thing feel a little less spooky to me. The whole thing was a little more familiar. Partially, I think, because of my father, and partially because of having studied religion.

"Most people assume that when they hear voices, it's God speaking. I had my questions. If it *was* God, you know, I wanted a little ID.

"The thing is," he said, "if it weren't for involuntary commitment, I would be dead."

The most disturbing encounter I had while working on this book took place in New York City late one evening. S. is the son of one of the leading pioneers in the women's rights movement. He agreed, reluctantly, to be interviewed, but when he arrived at my house that night, he hardly spoke a word. He said he didn't want his name used, and I agreed. He also didn't want me to tape the conversation. And he didn't seem to want to answer any of my questions.

I put away my note pad, my questions, my tape recorder and sat back in my chair. To hell with it. If he just came for a visit, I'll visit. I'll just relax and have a friendly chat and chalk it up as one that got away.

But the man who sat across from me, tense and taciturn, did not invite relaxation. He sat rigidly on the edge of his armchair throughout his visit, as though prepared for flight, looking suspiciously out at the world like an animal in a cave. He had only recently returned to New York from several years out in a rural area where no one knew who he was.

"I'm afraid that people won't accept me for who I am," he murmured, "but who my mother is, what she is. I've been away so long from places where these things become an issue. I wanted to get away from the whole thing and sort things out. I'm still trying to sort it all out."

I asked him how he reacts when people ask him about the women's movement.

"They realize immediately that it's a dead end, because I discourage talking about it. I'm not attracted to girls who are into women's lib. Human relationships are so complex anyway, I don't see where political rhetoric has anything to do with it," he answered.

"What did you think when your mother was starting the whole thing?" I asked.

"At first I thought it was just some lame-brained thing a bunch of women did in the living room from time to time. Sort of like a social club. Later, I went to one of the first big rallies to hear her speak. I thought maybe there'd be a few thousand people there at the most. As it turned out, there were maybe eighty, maybe a hundred thousand people. 'Jesus,' I thought to myself, 'they're serious.' It really blew my mind."

"How did your mother's career affect your decisions about your own career?" I asked.

"I'm a man," he stated. "Look at what my role model is—a leader of a militant women's organization. My father's not rich or famous at all, just an ordinary man. How do I use my mother as a role model? It doesn't make any sense. Not to me. Naturally, a kid would look to the most successful parent as a role model. Look what I've got. I have a lot of problems with it."

There was a long silence. S. was clutching his glass of juice, staring at the carpet. He sat forward suddenly and stared at me as he said, "What it is, is I'm afraid of people using me, trying to get close to me because of that relationship."

"Do you think that happens very often?" I asked.

"No," he replied, sitting back a little. "No, it probably doesn't happen at all. It's probably just my own paranoia. I've even used other names occasionally, just to avoid the problems."

"That's a common reaction, you may be pleased to know," I reassured him.

"Really?" He seemed relieved to know he was not alone in his "paranoia."

We talked for a while about his various activities in the last few years, about some of the careers he's tried, about his education, until he brought the conversation back to his main fears.

"I'm afraid of being emotionally ripped off," he said. "Some days I feel more defensive about it than others. Today was one of those days. I almost didn't come."

"Why did you come?" I finally had the opportunity to ask. "You don't want your name used, you don't want me to make notes. Why did you agree to do the interview?"

He paused for just a second. "I thought maybe you had some ideas on this whole thing. You've learned to use that energy in a positive way by writing a book about it. I thought maybe we could talk and share some ideas," he said. "I'm trying to sort it all out."

I was a little surprised that he had come here to learn.

Suddenly he turned his head away and asked, "How did you learn to live with all the pain? And the rest of it?"

"About thirteen percent of the population," Mark had said, "will be institutionalized at some point for mental illness. And that's not counting the walking wounded who'll never get into a hospital."

After S. left that night, I found my mind drifting back again and again to his gaunt face and haunted eyes. I had interviewed my first casualty.

8.

Arlo Guthrie:
Down on the Farm

It's better to be unknown because of who you
are, than to be known because of who you are not.
— Arlo Guthrie

The day I drove to Stockbridge with a friend to meet Arlo
Guthrie, the Berkshires were veiled by intermittent drizzle, but
the gently rolling hills of western Massachusetts were still a
beautiful sight. We put up for the night at the historic Red Lion
Inn and the next day received directions to the Guthrie farm.

After a few wrong turns and occasional dirt roads, we reached
the Guthries' driveway just as Arlo was pulling up in a four-
wheel-drive van. I had forgotten how good-looking he is. As near
as I could tell, he hadn't changed at all from the old Alice's
Restaurant days. He beckoned us to follow him past the white
clapboard farmhouse to the more recently built "office."

"Well," he asked, once we were settled on the couch with a
huge, wet German shepherd between us, "what are we gonna be
talkin' about?"

"Oh, about how your father's career affected your career," I
said, a little off balance. I was supposed to be asking the questions. "Your public and his, how his fame affected your self-
image when you were growing up . . ."

"I don't know anything about that," he answered.

There was an awkward pause. I had a moment of imagining that the whole interview would consist of such uninformative and dead-end answers, but my fears were groundless; it didn't take long for us to warm up to each other.

Arlo and his wife, Jackie, their children, and their friend George (more than a friend, not exactly a manager, George refers to himself as "secretary—which originally meant 'keeper of secrets'") welcomed us into their home with nourishing good-will. It was the first interview I did in which I felt I was treated like a new friend, rather than an intruder.

We talked until it was dark and then all piled into various cars for a trip to Alice's Restaurant. "Oh, boy! A feast!" Arlo said, rubbing his hands in childlike anticipation while Jackie phoned a few friends to invite them along. "We haven't had a feast in ages!"

It was not the Alice's of the famous song, although it was indeed the same Alice. She had worked her way up from a tiny coffee shop "just a half a mile from the railroad track" to an entertainment complex, including a restaurant, bar, disco, and motel, just down the road from Tanglewood.

Alice gone entrepreneur? Arlo Guthrie sitting at the head of the long white-clothed table perusing the wine list and charging dinner on American Express? It seemed a little incongruous to this child of the sixties, until I thought about how much I'd changed, too. When "Alice's Restaurant" made the charts, I was a barefooted hippie hitchhiking around Vermont.

Despite her seeming success (the new Alice's closed only a year later), Alice was exactly as I'd always imagined her, only emphasized by the classy setting. She joined us briefly, hitching up a chair to the table, cursing Arlo amiably in her husky voice, flicking cigarette ashes on the carpeted floor, and knocking back her glass of whiskey neat.

After we returned to the farm, the kids were bedded down; while we sat talking about the music business, Jackie and George supplied three guitars, and I tried to pick out the few chords I knew while they played. It is an indication of their honest warmth that they created an atmosphere in which an amateur such as myself could strum along comfortably.

Earlier in the day, I had asked Arlo if he had ever thought of doing anything other than music.

"Yeah," he answered. "I thought I'd be a vet, but as soon as I realized that I'd have to go to school, I realized that wasn't going to work out.

"I just never could find anything I could do as well. It's not that I wanted to be a guitar player or a singer, it's just that I ended up doing that the best. And felt most at home doing it. I'm not overly aggressive in wanting to find a place in the world or anything like that. I really don't care," he laughed. "I seem to be happy, so anything to make a living and to stay relaxed is all I'm looking for."

"How old were you when you started working towards a career in music?"

"I never did. I started playing guitar when I was real little— it wasn't any big thing. Just something everybody did," Arlo said. "I discovered one day that a 'C' on the guitar is the same as a 'C' on the piano, and it kinda blew me away. Then I realized what music is, and I liked it, and I kept playing it."

It was not his father or other musicians but Arlo's mother who taught him a few rudimentary chords on the guitar. "She really helped me learn to play more than my old man did. By the time I was maybe ten or twelve," he said, "I was listening to records and slowin' them down and picking out all the notes, and learning from Ramblin' Jack Elliot and other people who were around."

Arlo had grown up in the folksinger subculture. When he was just a child, he would accompany the likes of Ramblin' Jack Elliot on his tours. The family made regular outings to Greenwich Village in those years, taking Woody from the hospital to hear Elliot, Dylan, and other friends who could be found playing for pennies in the park on almost any summer evening.

"Eventually," Arlo said with a trace of nostalgia, "the whole scene there moved into the coffeehouses."

But it wasn't until after high school that he turned to music as a means of support. He discovered while bumming through Europe playing his guitar on street corners that not only would passersby accept his "cowboy songs," but they would also fill his cowboy hat with enough coins to keep him in food and "brew." He returned to the States to attend college but soon decided that higher education wasn't for him and started hanging around the clubs in the Village.

"Basically, I just went to hear other people, but in those days, you didn't just go empty-handed when you went to hear somebody; you brought your guitar and you played with them. So it turned into more people coming, and it just sort of kept going."

Knowing how our parentage is routinely exploited, I assumed that at first Arlo was probably introduced and billed as Woody Guthrie's son, but he denied it, adding, "I didn't have to be [billed that way] for it to be known.

"At first, they probably hired me because they thought I would draw, being that I was Woody's son. And I did. But I don't think people would have kept coming back just for that.

"When I first started playing, the audience I was playing to was totally different from what it is now. They were all tourists who went down to the Village to see hippies. Now, all of those hippies knew my father, but the people I was playing to didn't. They didn't know anything except that there was a lot of hippies downtown."

But even with the fame Arlo has achieved on his own, he cannot escape the specter of his father, particularly when he is asked to appear at a political event as Woody's son.

"I always kind of figured he was more of a social activist than a political activist. He invented his own social structure that he wanted to see happen, so every time he was aware of an injustice, he would invent a right [to counter it]. That was his basic political platform. I think that's what I like about him: that individual ability not to go along with any group, but to think of what's right or wrong on your own, and to go out and join other people regardless of what party they're coming from, as long as they want to get that same job done.

"The idea of coalitions is not a new one," Arlo said. "I think that that's what he was best at doing—convincing people that if you want to get something done, you sometimes have to work with people who don't agree with you on every single issue. You can't ignore something you see happening because of your own arguments, because it doesn't even have anything to do with that. So that's something I learned as a kid, something that I believe in.

"For example, I don't really care what [political] parties support the antinuclear stand, as long as it's supported. I'd just as soon be there with them whether they're coming from an anti-Westinghouse point of view or an antiscientific point of view. It really doesn't matter. I've got my own reasons. I'm not asking anybody to explain his, and I don't always want to have to explain mine. It's enough just to be there and get the job done."

"Who is winning the nuclear fight in Massachusetts?" I asked.

"We're all losing as long as we're all paying for something that we won't get nothing out of," Arlo replied. "I don't think the people in this or any other state want it. California doesn't want it. We're paying in terms of all the electricity rates being increased. [The nuclear plants] may get built, but they won't get used. We don't think it's necessary."

Arlo has been a force in the antinuclear movement, and I wanted to hear his viewpoint, because although the incident at Three Mile Island had not yet occurred, the nuclear battle is something in which I've always been interested.

"Don't you think that once the plants are built, the power companies will say we have to use them to justify the expense?"

"I think that's the position they've taken," he said. "But I think sometimes it's better just to junk it [than to risk the malfunction]."

"Is opposition to the use of nuclear energy your biggest cause?" I asked.

"No, I don't have any causes. I just live in Massachusetts, and I'm opposed to building nuclear power plants here or anywhere else. I don't want electricity from nuclear power plants to be shipped to Massachusetts and thereby put the heat on some other people. So I support the efforts of everyone who doesn't want a nuclear plant near their house, too."

"Most people aren't hip enough to say, 'Well, why should they build one next to someone else's house, either?'" I commented.

"Well, it'll get that way," he assured me.

"I'm afraid it won't get that way until we start seeing some tangible evidence of people dying from it."

"But the point is, we're already seeing that," Arlo explained. "We're seeing it in the increase in leukemia and other cancers. It's not a political choice for me. I don't want them built because they're stupid. It's not because I'm a Democrat or a Republican or a Marxist or a fascist or anything else. I just don't think they're necessary, and I don't want them around."

"In the long run, though, would you consider yourself a Democrat or a Republican?"

"I think basically I'm a constitutionalist," he stated, "if that's a word. I admire the guys who put together the Constitution more than anyone else."

It occurred to me that perhaps Woody had been a political figure who sang, whereas Arlo is more of a singer who is involved politically. I asked him whether his politics were close to his father's.

"I think they're better!"

"Why?"

" 'Cause I'm now, and he was then," he answered with straightforward logic. "I'm not into nostalgia."

"Do you think your *public* image is more political or less political than his was?"

"I think the only image he had was political in a sense, because it was the only commercial aspect of his life for a long time. He didn't make a living as a humorist or as a professional Okie. That didn't do it. I think the only thing people responded to were some of his political beliefs. The first people to pick him up and hire him were people involved in politics. But I'm not restricted to that.

"I think there's a big difference between what my image is and what I actually do. Even the 'City of New Orleans' was called 'a ballad about disappearing Americana,' or something like that."

"Wasn't it that?"

"Yeah, right, but it certainly wasn't political."

"Most people probably think of your music as satirical, funny, political commentary . . ."

"Which is all true," Arlo interrupted. "Except that I think people who have been following what we do for ten years now, anybody who would normally buy my records or go to a show, wouldn't be limited to just that. They'd also be into certain kinds of folk music, certain elements of traditional American music, some symphonic material. They'd think of me more as a singer of contemporary folk songs."

"Is your audience still basically the folky, liberal, political set?" I wanted to know.

"Well, they turned into that. They were going through stages, too. At first they were just poor. Then they became political." He went on adding to the list and chuckling at each new category that came to mind. "Then when they got married, they became progressive. Then they were liberal. Then they were postprogressive."

I wondered if an audience had specific expectations of him because of his father, but he said he had never felt that that was the case.

"Not as a musician, anyway, not in a professional sense, 'cause my old man wasn't a professional. The thing is, he was a professional *person*, but he wasn't a professional musician or a professional singer. He didn't sing very well or play very well. He was a professional writer; he wrote very well. He could easily write a hundred typewritten pages a day. Single space. Both sides! The reason there are volumes of unpublished material is because he was a compulsive writer. But the performing was not the most important thing to him. It was just a means to get across what he was writing.

"So if people expect me to be professional, which means showing up on time, I guess, and being in tune, it's not because of anything that has to do with my old man."

"Is your stage persona very different from his?"

"My stage personality allows me to be more receptive to a greater number of people than my offstage personality, which requires that I get into fewer people."

I remembered a concert of his that I had been at years before in which he had successfully achieved a feeling of intimacy between himself on the stage and the audience below.

"That's really good," Arlo said. "Other people tell me that, too. They say, 'Boy, you sure are the same onstage as . . .' like that's supposed to be some great feat. 'The same onstage as he is offstage. Never changes.' That's supposed to be credible or something. There was that credibility gap for a few years that everybody was talkin' about, talkin' about how credible everybody was. It always impressed me that people thought I was the same [onstage and off]. Because I didn't feel the same.

"How can you be the same? How can you talk to five thousand people the same as you'd talk to two? You can't. You're stupid if you think you can, if you attempt it. *But*. That doesn't mean you can't be just as intimate with five thousand people as you can with two. You just have to find a different mode to do it in. l can't be the same person I am to my kids to everyone in the audience, obviously. Even if I could be, I don't think I'd want that. It's kinda fun bein' a sort of professional schizophrenic," he laughed. "I have even more sides than that. That's only two."

"Do you remember the first song of your father's you ever heard?"

"Actually, I first appreciated my old man when I heard records of him when he was younger, goin' through his hillbilly act. Which was great. It's the most perfect hillbilly act you ever heard."

"It was all an act?" I asked with surprise.

"Oh, I think he was a great actor," Arlo answered, a little ambiguously. "He was born in a real hick town, and it's still like that. Okama, Oklahoma, probably isn't that different than it was sixty years ago. He was able to relate to those people, and yet he wasn't limited to that. He read everything in the world. All these books here were his, and he's written on every page of almost every one. Totally self-educated. Yet, he was able to relate to those people all of that other stuff in his gut."

I asked him if he remembered when he was first aware of his father's fame.

"I didn't know until I was in the sixth grade that my father was a singer and a writer that other people knew about," he answered. "I knew he wrote some, but I didn't think that anyone else knew.

"I was pulled out of public school at the end of fifth grade, and I went into a progressive private school in Brooklyn where all the teachers were cronies of my old man. We'd all stand up and sing songs, and they started singing some of my old man's songs. And I didn't know the words. I only knew fragments of them, because we'd all be singing 'em around the house. I was blown away. I wondered how everybody knew about them.

"And they were all looking at me and saying, 'How can *you* not know the words to these songs, and you're the guy's kid?'

"I said to myself, 'Yeah, well, gee. I *am* his kid, and how come I don't know the words? How come?'

"My first thought was just, 'Boy, I'd better learn these songs.' And I went home and learned them. Just to be like all the other kids. It had nothing to do with my old man; it had to do with me.

"But that was my first introduction to my father being anything more than just some crazy old man. I was stunned."

Did it change his perception of his father in any way?

"It changed my perception of *me*," he said. "Of who *I* had to be. I didn't even know what he did. It was only when I grew up that I read his autobiography and found out. We weren't sitting around telling Woody stories. My mom always figured that I'd find out whatever I wanted to know, and I pretty well have. There's a guy named Joe Klein who's doin' a biography of my old man, and he's got some *incredible* stuff, stuff that's outrageous, and I'm really looking forward to that, to finding out. I had my own vision as a little kid, but now I'm going to be able to find out at the same time as everybody else."

"What about *Bound for Glory*?" I asked, referring to the film David Carradine starred in, based on Woody Guthrie's autobiography. "Were you involved in the movie?"

"When I first heard about it, I wanted to be involved in it. I didn't necessarily want to be acting in it, but I wanted to be involved in the production. But when I read the screenplay," he said, dismissing it with a snort, "I wasn't for making the movie. I would just as soon they hadn't made it. And that's not from hindsight.

"During the production of the movie, I went to visit the set for a few days, but I was never asked to be in it or to participate in any way. Except they wanted to use my name as an adviser, but they didn't want my advice," he laughed. "So I said, 'No!'

"I have different things against it from hindsight than I had from foresight," he went on. "To make a long story short, from hindsight, I think that the character in the movie had no sense of humor, which to me was one of the most important things about my old man.

"He was a very eccentric person. I think somebody who's eccentric is basically somebody who knows how to follow their own instincts. If you crawl out on a limb to do that, then that's what you have to do. Sometimes the branch breaks; sometimes it don't. But you crawl on it anyway, 'cause that's where the fruit is.

"If everyone just went along following their own intuitive sense, I think probably a lot more people would be [considered] nuts. But a lot more people would be happy. Americans have always been eccentric. I think it's part of our culture to like people who are eccentric. We got room here to be crazy."

I asked him to tell me more about his mother. He mentioned her professional life as a dancer and said, "I think I was influenced as much by having a professional mother as by having a 'legendary' father," laughing at the latter adjective.

"They were in two totally different worlds. When they first got together and started combining them, it was great. At one point, my mother and her friends actually convinced him to be onstage with them." He chuckled, thinking of the results. "While they were doin' a dance, he was s'posed to be playin' this song. Of course, they had to have it the same way each time, and he couldn't do that. So he had to relearn all his own stuff to suit them. I think if both people are reasonable, you reach some sort of compromise, you work it out. It takes two people who appreciate the art form," Arlo commented.

"And each other?"

"Well, you have to appreciate the art sometimes before you can appreciate each other. If you don't understand what it is your spouse is doin' in the first place, then what do you really know about him or her?"

I asked him if he told tall tales to his children, or if he wrote them whimsical story-songs like the ones that made him famous.

"Anything that drops the jaw of your kid is worth telling," he answered. "But mostly my kids are too weird. I can't think weird enough for them. They're really strange kids. First of all, they'll believe anything you tell 'em. I told my kids once a few years ago that I rode a frog back from town. And they just said, 'How big was he? And if he was that big, where is he now? I want to see him.'

"And then we had to go look for him. And, 'How would you recognize him?' they wanted to know. It just got stranger and stranger. And then I had to write a song to go with it and every-thing. It was great."

How do his kids respond to his music?

"Oh, they like it, but I think they're more interested in the things they're interested in than in my work. Which is great. I would hate my kids to be fans. And I don't need another critic," he laughed.

"Do they ever get to go on tour with you?"

"Yeah. We travel in a big old Greyhound bus, and it's great. We yank the kids out of school every once in a while and take 'em. We used to put our kids to sleep in the guitar cases; take the guitar out, put the kid in, and go do the show. You should probably interview them." Later I did attempt to inter-view Abraham, the oldest and a very talkative child, who be-came suddenly monosyllabic.

George entered the office annex where we sat, and Arlo looked up to ask if there was enough hay for the cow. I have always wanted to live on a farm in the country as he does, concerned with hay and cows and such, but it's an intimidating fantasy for a city kid with no knowledge of those things.

"Yeah, but you find out real quick," he assured me. "Real quick. This kind of farm works out real good. Nobody knows anything, but we get all these things done.

"Hey, we moved up here nine years ago, and I'll tell you, tryin' to live off the land is hard, very hard. It's a whole lifetime of work. Which is why I thought it'd be good to do it soon. Because if the inevitability of having to do it is really going to happen, well, then, all the more reason to get out there and get some roots planted so your kids will at least know what to do. I think my kids are gonna know a lot more than I ever knew, just because they were born here.

"I think one of the great things about thinking in terms of inevitability is that it motivates. Not that it ever is a reality, but it sometimes helps to have an illusion to motivate you. Just like a kid. Babies don't just sorta get up and start walkin' around. They live under a definite illusion that they can walk. If they didn't think they could walk, they wouldn't try. But living under the illusion prepares their mind for the eventuality, the *fact*, that they can. I think that's partly true of any endeavor. I think that you have to start by being deluded that you can do it," he laughed. "Once you accept that you can, then you learn that you are, and then you no longer require the illusion."

Was it his father's career that inspired him with the illusion of being a singer-songwriter?

"Somebody asked me something like that on TV once. It really put me on the spot. And it suddenly occurred to me in that spot that I *was* his son, and to deny it for my own purpose would be stupid. The interviewer kept asking me, 'What is it like to follow in the footsteps of your old man?'

"And it suddenly occurred to me that I wasn't following in his footsteps [just] because I'm his son and doing what he did. It suddenly occurred to me that where I'm going there aren't any footsteps. If there were footsteps, it would be a hell of a lot easier. But what I do, no one has done. Because no one's been me.

"So I rather enjoy it. Now I think of it as your parents and ancestors layin' down before you. At some point you fade into the picture, and if you end up doing the same thing they did, well, I think you can probably do it better in terms of how you feel about it than somebody who just tries to jump into it.

"I remember when I moved up to the country here after livin' in New York [City], I didn't know about pipes freezing or rocks in the field and tractors and horses. I didn't know anything about any of them things. I didn't know the names of trees or birds or nothin'. It was like living in a world that was totally alien to me.

"That's not true in what I do; I know what I am. When I go to do a show somewhere, especially if it's a benefit or a political thing, I'm standing on pretty firm ground. What I say and what I think and what I feel have weight, not just the weight of one life; it's got the weight of a lot of lives.

"I think that's important to have. I think it's important for our kids to have."

I asked how he felt about his own kids carrying on that tradition.

"The real question is: 'What is the tradition?'" Arlo answered. "Is it a tradition of playin' music, or is it a tradition of bein' a certain kind of person? I think that's the most important part of fitting into that tradition. It's not what you do but who you are. And yeah, I want them to carry on the tradition of knowin' who they are."

But what about carrying on the tradition of social commentary through music or otherwise?

"Let's simplify it: music is a vehicle. It's always been a vehicle. It doesn't matter whether it's classical music or folk music or disco. It's a vehicle for something. What it's a vehicle for is more important to me than what the music sounds like. In that sense, I go along with what my father felt about it, because that's what he felt. But you cannot then compare the two kinds of music and talk about *that* being the link. Because that's not what the link is. The link is what the music's supposed to convey. What is it talking about? What is it dealing with?

"It deals with a lot of different things," he answered his own question. "'It deals with outlaws and inlaws. It deals with life as we know it. Sometimes it's silly; it's kids' stories or kids' songs. Sometimes it's heavy and deals with things that are in a way oppressive. It could be anything. So when you ask what it is that I want my children to inherit, that is what I would like them to feel. I don't care if they're into music or a carpenter or an architect. They don't have to be anything; they can be a bum if they want to, as long as the thing they're conveying by doing is important to them."

"What would they be conveying by being a bum?" I asked,

partly joking and partly wondering if he thought there could indeed be a purpose to the vagrant life-style that Woody had sometimes led.

"They would be conveying something like the wealth of the world didn't mean that much.

"I like being up here in the country," he went on. "Getting out of New York City. I think it's good for my kids. Something got lost that I feel responsible to reintroduce into this family."

"What do you mean?"

"There are certain things that I lost by growing up in New York City, which were alien to both sides of my family! All of the creation that's around, being able to look at the stars, and stuff like that. That was a real big treat for me in the summertime when I was a kid. In order for me to be able to help my children have that foundation, some kind of relationship with the world and people in it, I want to be comfortable, and I want to be able to point things out to them that are important to me. So here I'm able to do that.

"I think that's the only responsibility I feel. My old man and my mother did the best they could in those circumstances to do the same for me. Basically by saying, 'This is who I am. Aside from being your mother or your father, this is who I am. And you're gonna find out who *you* are, and when you find that out, come and tell me, and we'll sit down and talk about it. But I can't be somebody else for you, and I don't want you to be somebody else for me.' And I think that's a real good relationship to have with your parents.

"Like with my kids. I play two different kinds of music. I play music for myself, and I play music for other people. Two totally different forms. It could be the same song I'm playing, but it means two different things at different times. The first thing my kids have to learn is what the difference is. 'Cause if I'm playing for me, you can come bother me, interrupt me; that's okay. But if I'm working for somebody else, don't bother me; this has got nothing to do with you. When I'm onstage, you can't come running out, and if I'm rehearsing, I don't want to be bugged.

"At the same time, I gotta make myself available for them. But they gotta know who I am and what I do in order for them to have that same feeling that it's all right to say, 'This is me,' to their kids. To say, 'I'm going to be me; you find out who you are.'

"And I think it's their responsibility to learn [when I can be interrupted]. I don't want to go around putting up signs saying, 'This is this time, and that's that time.' They're supposed to be able to know that because they're my kids. And they do. And they expect the same thing from me. I don't want to bug them when they're doing stuff that's important to them, with their friends, unless it's something that I consider more important. And I have that prerogative. 'Cause I'm bigger," he chuckled.

"I think that the most valuable thing that I learned from *both* my parents was that they were *them*, and I had to grow up, as hard as it was or as easy as it was, with them bein' them. That meant I had to get used to my mom bein' real picky in the house—you know. 'Clean up your room!' and stuff like that," he said, imitating his mother in a falsetto voice. "And I had to do it. It also meant that I had to be loose enough to deal with my old man, who'd go to the store for a pack of cigarettes and show up in L.A. three weeks later. Just got lost, y'know. All the hurts that that inflicted or all the pleasure that it gave, it didn't make any difference, because that was them."

It was well after midnight when we were led back up the hill to the annex to sleep. George showed us how to work the sauna, helped arrange a makeshift mattress on the floor, and bade us goodnight. I lay looking up at the rafters, thinking over my visit with Arlo.

I had observed with envy a peaceful, rural life that has always attracted me. I saw that dedication to work and success need have no conflict with family and farm. I learned that a laid-back attitude such as Arlo's can enable one to attempt the forging of a new life-style with little foundation; that a rural family tradition can spring from an erstwhile urban family; and that a city kid can successfully go country.

Although initially reluctant, Arlo revealed himself as a man without pretensions, open, pure; a man who puts a premium on staying relaxed and on getting along with people; a man who likes the simple things, yet has inherited a legacy of social consciousness and conscience. He believes in God and in a strong family unit—a contrast to the erratic and eccentric behavior of his own father in his early years. He is generous with friends and strangers, and enjoys seeing other people enjoying themselves. He lives life to the fullest, and although he is laconic, his eyes dance about the room as others converse.

Most important were Arlo's attitudes about his parents. Perhaps the hardest lesson to learn is to accept our parents as people, as who they are, and that we can never truly assimilate our parents and their success or lack of it until we can do this. But at the same time we must, like Arlo, have the self-confidence to recognize that "there are no footsteps," that the way we are making is unique and valuable.

I also learned a lesson about parenting. Perhaps even more difficult than our acceptance of who our parents are is our acceptance of who our children are in their own rights, and I would guess that Arlo's support of his children for who and what they are is a powerful step in helping them to understand who and what he is.

He seemed to have all the answers; he seemed to have somehow achieved a peace with himself, his parents, his children; he seemed comfortable living in partnership with the earth and comfortable also with both his father's fame and his own. His parents had affirmed who they were, had allowed him to be at ease with who he is, and he expected the same of his children. How simple it sounds; how difficult to achieve.

Consciously or unconsciously, it seems that Arlo has taken up his father's fallen sword—that special ability to communicate through song—and has tempered it into a plowshare suited for the atomic age. He is tilling fields his father never dreamed of. But the message in Arlo's music and what Woody had to say are basically the same: let's make the world a better place to live in for everyone. And that is what he lives by.

9.

Fame and Success

Celebrity is a comic distinction shared with
Roy Rogers' horse and Miss Watermelon of 1955.
—FLANNERY O'CONNOR (from her letters)

There is one very important distinction between the famous
and their children, and that is the matter of choice. We are
sometimes thought of, or at least treated as, hangers-on, groupies
almost, who "use" their connection with the well known.

A friend of mine dates a recognizable actor, and one day when
I was talking to her about my book, she said, "In a way, you and
I have a lot in common—that whole thing of being associated
with someone who's famous, of going into a restaurant, and all
the attention's on them. . . ." But, I pointed out, the difference
is that she's there by choice, and I'm not. I cannot choose who
my father is, and he had his career long before he had me.

"Ever since my dad first mentioned doing this interview, I've
been thinking about the whole idea of fame," Monte Schulz said.
"I mostly connect it with people from Hollywood. That's the most
transitory fame and notoriety.

"As you get older, you start to develop prejudices, and here's
mine. It's when you get somebody on the Johnny Carson show

because they're well known—they've been on television or some-thing—and they're answering these questions about politics or theology or parapsychology, and their word is taken as gospel because they're well known. Just because they're famous, it doesn't mean they know anything. And just because they're famous doesn't mean they *don't* know anything. I'm not really even interested in the whole concept of fame. I think it's inter-esting to measure a person through what they've achieved, rather than by the fact that they're well known. But most people don't care about the achievements, they care about the fame."

Michael Keeshan said, "I'm always competing with my father because I would like to do as well in life—not financially, not success, not fame—but I would like to have done as well in a business or social environment as he has. And yet be well ad-justed and not feel I've sacrificed anything getting there. I don't want to work to the extent that I give up my family. I don't want to hurt anyone else, or step on any toes, or stab anyone in the back on the way up. I think that if you start out with the intent not to do that, you won't do it, and you'll get to the top anyway. There are a lot of people who think that the only way to get to the top is to do all of those things. Those people seem to fall off the ladder halfway up."

"I don't respond to anyone else's definition of success," Jack Ford said. "It's so personal, I don't think it makes any difference. But there is an external [as opposed to personal] success. There are a series of events you go through in a day's time, and each one of those little events could be described as successful or un-successful, and I do think about those. But I also have a tendency to say, 'What's done is done, and there's nothing you can do about it now.' People who worry about goofs, and I fall into it occasionally, are crazy. Why worry about it? There's nothing you can do about any of it, except go out and do a better job next time.

"Oftentimes people ask how I deal with everyone thinking of me as Jerry Ford's son. It's not hard for me. I'm proud of my parents, and I think a lot of it has to do with the way they brought us up. There was never any intention to pursue stardom or to achieve public recognition. It was total devotion to doing a good job; if people appreciated it, that was great, and if they didn't, you still have the satisfaction of having achieved, or of trying to do the best to achieve what you set out to do.

"You don't grow up with any pretense, or even acknowledgment, that there is anything special. It might have been third or fourth grade before I even realized that everybody else's father didn't run for reelection every two years."

"The first time I saw my dad at work," Debby Erhard told me, "I was actually sick. It was in Aspen, where he was doing a guest seminar. The auditorium was just packed with people. And my dad was up front. People were on the edges of their seats, waiting for him to say what they wanted to hear. I felt like I was special. That's my dad! All these people here are looking at my dad!"

Monte Schulz talked about *his* father's work: "Dad doesn't share The Strip too much with the rest of the family; I think he feels that everyone takes it for granted. In fact, I almost think he feels that we are annoyed by it at this point, maybe thinking, 'Well, Dad's famous, so what, it's not our fame, we're not famous.' I just feel proud of him for being that accomplished.

"People always ask, 'Is there any relation between any of the characters and any of the members of your family?' I used to tell [them]. The truth is . . . we used to be. I'm not going to tell you who's who, because it doesn't apply anymore, so it would be kind of distortion. Some of us were fragmented personalities, and others were composite personalities. Some of the characters aren't even in The Strip anymore. One of my sisters was one character, and then one of my younger sisters grew into the character. I can't see my brother as being any of the characters. I'd say I was closer at one point to Linus, but now I see Linus as being a sort of naive character. Linus is the religious one of the group. He's supposed to be the one that had the sanity, who restored some order to the situations, but not anymore. He's sort of fallen by the wayside. He's not that applicable anymore.

Applicable to Dad, that is, not necessarily to society."

One person who asked to be anonymous said, "I think what screws up the kids of the famous is that they never learn the 'street smarts' that got their parents where they are. Particularly in show business, the parent comes from a poor background and learns street smarts—that is, unorthodox means of self-preservation—to help him get to the top and stay there. Then he resolves that his children will never have to suffer the same indignities he was subjected to.

"So the kid is overprotected; everything is taken care of for him. Then when the parent dies, or the kid suddenly gets out into the world, he's defenseless. He becomes a victim. The people around him pick him to pieces, and, not having any street smarts, he can't deal with it. It happens to a lot of us."

In *The Enchanted Places* Christopher Milne wrote of his father: "He had pressed on to become a famous writer and here was I staring up at him, filled with resentment. Other fathers were reaching down helping hands to their sons. But what was mine doing? What, to be fair, could mine do? He had made his own way by his own efforts and had left behind him no path that could be followed. But were they entirely his own efforts? Hadn't I come into it somewhere? In pessimistic moments . . . it seemed to me, almost, that my father had got to where he was by climbing upon my infant shoulders, that he had filched from me my good name and had left me with nothing but the empty fame of being his son."

Susan Newman commented, "There have been films that are atypical Paul Newman movies, that he's wanted to do. I don't know whether it's partly lack of courage, but I think it's valid when he says, 'The general public will not accept me in this part, and if I do this, it will hurt the film.' Well, if *he* can't decide to do whatever the hell he wants to do, then who can? I remember that as being a really frightening moment, that with all that great fame and success, someone's still got you by the tail."

"I'm proud of him for the way he always tried to do a good

job," Bela Lugosi said of his father's work. "Even though . . . a lot of pictures he was in were not very good, that didn't deter him from trying to give the best performance he could. Usually the only redeeming feature about some of those films is his role."

Bela talked candidly about the degeneration of Bela Lugosi's film career and later life. "That's affected me, because a lot of what's been published has been uncomplimentary, and I'm sensitive to that. He was a fellow who lived life to his fullest. His ups always seemed to be higher and his downs lower, because he was such a dramatic person. In life, as well as on the stage. I'm witness to a lot of good times with him; he had a good life. He had some problems, too.

"I've come to have a lot of respect for him in several important areas. For one, no matter what the difficulty he was in, he always somehow had the will and spirit to keep trying to dig himself out.

"Don't forget—when he decided that he was addicted to drugs and that that was bad, he committed himself. This was at a very late age in his life. He must have been close to seventy. That's very hard, physically. No one made that decision for him or talked him into it. It was strictly on his own. He was subjected to horrible treatment, because that kind of thing wasn't in vogue when he did it. I think he was very brave."

Lorenzo Lamas said, "The best way to deal with things is not to deal with them at all, to just let them happen, to let them flow and be natural. If you start worying, that's when you get your mind all messed up. Just let things happen, and take each day as it comes."

Chris Lemmon echoed Lorenzo's sentiments, but with more direction. "The best idea is just to do what you think is right. It's *got* to be that to maintain a semblance of sanity, if nothing else. Because it *is* a hard fact to deal with, that you're a famous person's son, if you want to make it hard.

"I think that every child of a famous person faces it in one way or another; it's a question of how it's dealt with. You can either make it bad news, or you can simply realize what the situation is. If you're smart enough to realize that it's all your own doing anyway, you can either take it the easy way or take it the hard way. I have a nice apartment, a nice amount of money coming in that I make myself, and I also happen to have a father who's a genius at what I'm trying to be good at. What, am I going to complain?"

Mark Vonnegut told me, "I think people do expect the sons and daughters of famous people to be enormously screwed up, but I don't know what's so great about having a failure as a father. The whole thing has taken a bum rap. Out west, you have a lot of people whose parents' fame is contrived, and incredibly at odds with the public and private people. It's screwed up the parents, and the kids are screwed up for that reason. The whole thing's a hype, anyway. But if your mother or father is genuinely gifted and industrious, what's the problem?

"I think it's embarrassing to live in a culture that makes people live famous. I think it's embarrassing to be part of an economy that pays people, stars and others, unreal sums of money to be unreal things to other people. I think that's profoundly embarrassing.

"If any teacher gets on Zak because of his name, the teacher's going to have some broken legs, you know? I think famous parents should be a little more sensitive to the pressures on their children and really nail people who mess around. I think a certain amount is unavoidable, but I hope Zak and I will be good friends. He'll know who I was, so other people won't be telling him who I am."

"So many people become successful and don't understand why," Nora Davis said. "They have no idea why people adore them, and they don't wish to be adored like that after a while. Then they're afraid if they deviate at all, they'll fail. They're not themselves anymore. They're whatever it was going to take to be *out there*. I don't want to be that kind of a person, no matter how I feel swept into the mainstream of acting. I always want to have a part of me that goes home from that. I'm a family-oriented person, and I hope that I can integrate the two, because I'd hate to think which one would have to go if I had to make a choice. My mother always said that being an actress is one thing, but that at the end, when you're too old, or they don't want you anymore, or you're played out, it's nice to have a family to turn to and lean on, to reminisce with, and not end up an empty star."

10.

Jack Ford:
A Time in the White House

Be silent and safe—silence never betrays you.
—JOHN BOYLE O'REILLY

Jack was surprisingly accessible to me and willing to be interviewed, and I naively assumed that that meant he was willing
to talk. But Jack knows well the politician's game: say as little
as possible while appearing to say a lot; answer only those questions you want to, and divert the others into subjects you want
to discuss; smile, joke, and charm the interviewer so he or she
won't notice that you've avoided the issues; and when cornered,
smile, nod, and say, "Could be, could be . . ."

I interviewed Jack early on in the progress of this work, and
whereas I had interviewed very few people, he had been interviewed by many. He knew from the start that he had the upper
hand.

"I am very, very practiced in the art of the interview," he
warned me. "I know all the right stories; I know how to say the
right things; and I know how to be copy."

We met in his office at *Rolling Stone*, where he worked at the
time. It was after hours, and his one small room was the sole
light in the darkened building. He sat in T-shirt and shorts, with

his feet propped on his desk, lounging back in his chair, seemingly at ease. Although I had lists of questions, as we were setting up the tape, there was one question repeating in my mind.

I blurted out, "What is it really like, living in the White House?"

"Ah, the famous question," Jack laughed. He pretended to reach into his desk. "Here, I have a tape that answers that."

I was surprised when he went on to tell me what it was like:

"Although you always have to be aware of the tours [Jack said], you have a lot of privacy once you go up the elevator. The biggest problem was having friends over. A lot of my friends got to the point where they'd say, 'Hey, I don't want to go through the hassle of security at the gate, security at the front door, security at the elevator.' I'd have to know what time they were going to be there so I could call up and tell each one of the [security] stations. Very unspontaneous. Our house in Alexandria had people just flowing through.

"That was probably the hardest to get used to. With close friends, it could be a lot of fun; but it's difficult with friends who are not quite so close, because they are in awe of the whole thing. It takes a great deal of effort on your part. Even today, in some cases, they're afraid to take the first step, so you have to make a great deal of effort to instigate any friendship.

"When my father became President, I was in an extremely isolated situation. I was working as a ranger in Yellowstone, no radio or TV. The pressure that was building up for Nixon to resign was a million miles away. Those people in Montana and Wyoming just couldn't care less; the weekly newspapers carried more about whose cow had calved out—that was front-page news. I was on my day off, and I'd ridden out about twelve miles to this good fishing spot. I'd just happened to take my two-way radio, and all of a sudden I got this radio call, 'You'd better come back.' They didn't say why.

"I started to ride back, thinking maybe something had happened to my family. I was rather pissed that these people wouldn't tell me what it was that instigated this sudden trip back. When I got back to where my ranger station was, this helicopter appears, and I transfer from my horse to the helicopter and, at the airport, jump on a plane and fly back to Washington. There is only one flight a day to Salt Lake City from West Yellowstone Airport, and then you catch a flight to Chicago and then back to Washington. All commercial flights. At Salt Lake City, a very good friend of ours there who used to be an FBI agent was getting on the plane with me to make sure I got there all right. I almost missed the last plane out of Salt Lake City, because they insisted on searching me for security checks, and I'm telling these people, 'Hey, if I miss this plane, I will not make it back in time to see my father sworn in as President of the U.S., and you're going to hold me up on this security check?' Fortunately, I made it. I remember sitting in the airplane, and the pilot put the Nixon speech on the airplane PA system. It was when I heard that speech that I started to conceptualize what was happening.

"When I got back to Washington, I jumped off the plane, borrowed a suit from a friend, and went to the swearing-in ceremonies. My instinct was to sit in the last row, but when I went to the back of the room, somebody said to me, 'No, there's a seat up front.' And you walk past these powerful people, chief justices and senators, and you sit down. And the moment after the swearing-in, when my father spoke, is when it really sunk in as to what happened. I've heard it said, something to the effect that there was a great sigh of relief on the part of the American people. Whether it was because Nixon was gone or Dad was in, I don't know, I'm prejudiced, but I sensed for the first time the real transition of power and the realization that my father was now President.

"Realize that I was totally isolated and had no preparation for it. I went to bed one night and woke up the next day and he was President. There was no election, no primary, no running, none of the buildup that would prepare you for it. After the swearing-in ceremony, we went back to our house in Alexandria where I grew up, and my sister Susan and I went out to McDonald's to get some dinner. She had secret service at this time, as well as my parents, because she was on the SLA list that they found when the building burned down in San Francisco. So I guess they probably followed Susan. But it really didn't seem all that different, because I went back to the house that I grew up in and had a meal that was very typical. In fact, I didn't get secret service protection for probably another two or three days.

"I went back to Wyoming about three days later, with the secret service, none of whom could ride or pack a horse. My job was backcountry patrol, so I would take my horse and a pack animal for my supplies, and I would ride the backcountry for a week or so. There were twelve secret service guys, three a shift, and each had a shift supervisor, and I had to get up two hours earlier to saddle every one of their horses. And then they've got a slew of equipment, so that's two more horses to pack. So after going through that for two more trips, I said the hell with it, I'll go back to road patrol in a car. There's no way I can get rid of them, so I just have to accept the consequences.

"I went back to Washington for a little over a year to work on the campaign. That's when the biggest effect on our relationship came into play. At that point, I was old enough, and we had built a relationship to where he would listen to me. I had the feeling that I could have an impact, that he was open to suggestions. I mean, people spend a lifetime trying to get the opportunity to say a few words to the President, and I saw this guy every night at dinner. I suggested his original amnesty program, which I took pride in. I wasn't the only one, but I pushed it very hard. I pushed him to run for President. You don't walk away from a situation like that, forever wondering, what if I had or what if I hadn't. At least, that's the way I try to look at my life. I never like to turn down any opportunity, because I'd hate to wake up ten years from now and say, 'Gosh, I wonder what would have happened?' Here's an opportunity to try to achieve one hundred times more than he was ever able to achieve in his previous position. If that's your career, unless you're really faint-hearted, you're not going to walk away from it. It's like an actor saying, 'Here's the biggest part in my life, but maybe I'm not big enough for it.' Well, he'll never make it anyhow. Otherwise you say, 'The hell with it. I'm going to give it my best and see what happens.'

"It's a very intense thing. Every moment of your life was public, and there was no way to hide glaring failures or glaring successes.

Going through that public exposure of those two emotional extremes, and making it through both of them, you realize that life is not really so important and so serious. Well, it's like I said, life is either a good experience or a bad experience.

"If I were to die tomorrow, I could die in a certain amount of peace, because I learned to enjoy life and realize that success and failure are not the end-all to things. I feel comfortable that I could get up and walk away from everything right now. Or if it all fell down, if the paper went out of business or I lost my job, my life would not be at an end. Certainly, those experiences at the White House helped me to reach that idea. Going through the disappointment of losing the election, I mean, God, what could be important compared to that, you know? What could I do that would ever be as important as playing a role in deciding the fate of an election of the most important position in the most powerful country in the world?

"But, in fact, I took it pretty well; I was surprised. On election night when I got home, I had already detached myself from what had happened in the campaign. I was satisfied with myself that I had done a good job, I had done everything I could possibly do, and I went to bed very comfortably that night at eight o'clock. I knew I was tired, and I wasn't worried about the election. I'd voted—that was the last thing I could do. It was amazing; I was at peace with myself."

11.

On the Darker Side

I am always in favor of the free press but sometimes they say quite nasty things.
　　　　　　　　　　　　　—Winston Churchill

Jack Ford has developed a philosophy of peace and acceptance
of his life. But it is one that many journalists seem to feel is
atypical. For example, shortly after Scott Newman died, UPI
wrote the following article. It was titled, "Tragedy in Starland,"
and read in part: *

> The death of Scott Newman, son of actor Paul Newman, from
> an accidental overdose of drugs and drink, is *one more ex-
> ample of that running tragedy*, the troubled children of
> Hollywood stars. . . .
> Many stars' children have turned to drugs as an escape or
> in attempts to seek their own identity. Some of them took
> their own lives deliberately. . . .
> *No matter how much love and attention, not to mention
> possessions, are heaped on the young of the rich and famous*
> many of them feel personally inferior when compared to
> their famous parents.

* Italics added by author.

> *Those who do not take their own lives or accidentally*
> *overdose* frequently are victims of psychological, mental and
> emotional problems. Scores of such young people undergo
> therapy. . . .
>
> For the most part, *the history of celebrities' children* [is]
> *written in the divorce court records and on police blotters*,
> detailing fights, auto accidents and bouts with drugs and
> alcoholism. . . .

The article ends on what may have been intended to be an
upbeat note:

> There are exceptions to be sure. . . .
>
> Jane and Peter Fonda have established themselves apart
> from their father. . . .
>
> Desi Arnaz and Lucille Ball's children, Desi, Jr., and
> Lucie, have brought pride and joy to their parents, as have
> the offspring of Ozzie and Harriet Nelson and many others.
> Liza Minnelli is a superstar in her own right but appears to
> be following the personal ups and downs of her mother,
> Judy.

In an era in which the subliminal messages about the roles of
women in TV commercials, or of blacks in situation comedies, are
analyzed and protested, the messages that the children of the
famous absorb from such articles as these are frightening. We are
told that, although love and attention, not to mention possessions,
are heaped upon us, we are destined to escape into drugs or death
and be plagued with divorce, auto accidents, and fights.

The only way to redeem ourselves, one infers, and to bring
pride and joy to our parents, is to enter their professions. But
even that is not enough. We must also *succeed* in their professions
at a level equal to that of Jane Fonda or Liza Minnelli, a level of
success that few performers ever reach, whether they are children
of stars or not. Nothing less counts.

Every day of our lives we have to contend with this, with even
supposedly responsible journalists lumping us together as
pathetic, psychotic failures. Can you imagine what it is like to
read those descriptions of what my life is supposed to be? Can
you imagine how it feels to know that this is the opinion many

people—strangers—have? That readers will accept an article as true and that there is no way to fight it, no way to say, "That's not me. That's not who I am"? How does Christina Crawford, who according to her autobiography lived a childhood of abuse and denial, feel when she reads that all her problems are due to her feelings of inferiority; after all, according to the implications of the article, her famous mother plied her with love, attention, and possessions, didn't she?

The misconceptions perpetuated by the press undeniably bias the way the public sees us and therefore the way the public relates to us. Magazines which include in their year-end list of pet peeves, "Kids-of who *insist* they're making it on their own"; article writers who always ask if it helps or hurts and then inform the reader that you either "admitted" or "denied" it; and periodical covers explaining, "Why Celebrity Kids Can't Act: Stumbling in Their Parents' Footsteps," all contribute to our negative image. We are portrayed as hangers-on, dilettantes with no talents of our own.

"Most children of celebrities," one such article proclaimed, "have everything they need to make it in show biz. Except talent . . .

"It's really too bad more starkids don't become skibums or turn to other similar professions in which they might be able to make a meaningful contribution."

I am still baffled by the viciousness with which certain writers attack us. Each time a new piece of slander is written, after my rage has subsided, I am left wondering, "Why?" We are all aware of how words can be twisted, how description and commentary can make the most innocent incident sound sordid, but *why* anyone would want to take this attitude will always baffle me. Is it jealousy, or a mean spirit, or some grudge against our parents that would lead someone to describe a beautiful antique dressing gown as an "old ragged housecoat"? It may be another way of saying the same thing but with quite a different intent, and quite a different effect.

How do we deal with the interviewers and article writers? Well, some of us give no interviews at all; some of us don't care what is written about us as long as they spell the name right, as the old saying goes; and some of us just do our best to be cautious and try to shrug it off if we fail.

Jack Ford said, "I'm a pretty shy person basically, but I've learned not to be. You either step up and say your piece, or people put words in your mouth for you. So you'd best get your two cents in while you've got your chance and hope they don't misquote you. You're going to get burned one way or the other, so you might as well get burned getting your piece in.

"I don't see myself as a genius," he said later, "but most of the people who've interviewed me are not very bright. There are a few exceptions, where you run into people who are as good at interviewing as I am at being the interviewee. Stimulating conversation suddenly bubbles out of me, and that's when you really get turned on."

When Neil Armstrong walked on the moon, his son Rick was only thirteen—too young to be interviewed but certainly not too young to be photographed.

"The press was outside, waiting to pounce the minute you stepped out," he remarked. "It got really annoying to have them take twenty thousand pictures of me as I was—very dramatically, I'm sure—bringing in the paper. Now, that's front-page stuff," he said ironically. "I guess they have their jobs to do, but to this day, I do not like people with cameras.

"Almost all the press there really got on my nerves. Nothing personal, of course. They were just so pushy all the time; they wouldn't allow any privacy. Any time I wanted to go anywhere, I had to take all these backwoods escape routes to evade them."

Mary Crosby also learned to deal with the press as a child but grew into it gradually. "Growing up as you did, as I did, you learn to say the right things very young," she told me, "and honesty doesn't necessarily come into it. Lately, I've really gotten into honesty, and I really *don't* like to lie. If someone asks me a question, I tell them the truth, whether they like it or not.

"But at the same time," she went on, "I've learned how not to give them anything, whether it's the truth or not, that they might turn around; I've learned how to make myself invulnerable to attack.

"Because Daddy was such a private person, I learned from the word go that if I should ever have problems, they are private, and they are not to be written on the front page.

"When Daddy was interviewed by Barbara Walters and said that he would never speak to his children again if they lived in sin, I was doing publicity for a dinner theater. On every talk show that came around, I was asked what I thought. I warded that off beautifully. I said my father is a very wise man, and he's lived a lot, and he believes strongly, and I respect his judgments. I didn't say I believed in them; I said that I respected what he felt, as a wise person and not only as my father.

"It was very hard for Daddy, because he was painted into a corner. Barbara Walters is a b . . ." she hesitated . . . "a barracuda. They were on live TV, and Daddy had to give an answer. He was very upset about that interview. He believed it, *but*. He probably wouldn't have followed through on his threat, knowing my father.

"I've fought him before on things. He would tend to paint himself into a corner by forbidding you, saying, 'I will not let you do this,' rather than, 'I would rather you didn't do this.' Then if you would go and do it, he would be forced not to speak to you."

Several of the people I talked to expressed a certain paranoia caused by so much of their families' lives, thoughts, and actions being a matter of public record. Over and over I heard them say, "I'm very suspicious of people who walk in knowing all about my life, and I know nothing about theirs." An extension of that problem was described by Linda McMahon in talking about her parents' divorce.

A divorce is a painful ending of a relationship and a splintering of a family. It has always been considered prevalent among performers, but it is no less hurtful for the people involved. It should be a private matter. Insensitive reporting can only compound difficulties.

I have often wondered if the news media had ever actually *caused* a divorce. It would be difficult for some people to read over and over in the checkout-stand tabloids the fabricated romances and juicy rumors about one's spouse without beginning to suspect they might be true.

"A lot of my friends have gone through divorces [of their non-famous parents]," Linda said, "and it just wasn't the same. People have asked me questions that I wouldn't dream of asking someone, not even a really good friend. Just because it's publicized, they feel that if everyone's talking about it, you must be talking about it. You know—'Is your father seeing anyone? Is your mother seeing anyone?' People can be very insensitive."

I am frequently horrified by the callousness of some members of the fourth estate, but never more than at their determination to turn private tragedies into three-ring circuses. It is admittedly a fine line they walk in their mission to inform and enlighten the public, but is the public really served by close-ups of the weeping widow and bewildered children? One of my greatest fears, the one aspect of being the child of a famous man that will be worse than any that have gone before, is the way my father's death will ultimately be handled. I am afraid of hearing the news of that event on a TV bulletin, and every time the announcer says, "We interrupt this program . . ." I freeze. I am afraid of not being allowed to grieve, of having to wear a public face, of cameras and microphones being thrust at me and intruding upon me; I am afraid of having to walk to his funeral through a gauntlet of shoving fans.

"I remember one woman," Nancy Sherman said of her father's funeral, "hugging me and breaking down, and even though I had done my crying earlier, alone, I broke down again. That night on the news, I wanted to see what they'd said about my father, and all of a sudden I see myself standing there in tears.

"Is there no privacy in life? I thought it was very sweet how they interviewed Steve Allen and Monty Hall and David Steinberg, I liked that kind of thing, but showing people in tears, whether they knew I was his daughter or not . . . And there are people who just come around to famous people's funerals to see who'd be there. Even a distant relative showed up, just to see what celebrities would be there."

*   *   *

There is another danger in too much publicity: because we are in the public eye, we are most vulnerable to threats, and there are an awful lot of wackos in the world projecting their fantasies onto public personalities.

Sometimes Dad brings home some of his "nut mail"—a large amount of it from little old ladies in or out of the loony bin who think he's sending them secret coded messages in his broadcasts. Some of them confirm plans to meet him at the plane; one even offered to pack him a suitcase and bring it with her, to avoid suspicion on his end.

My favorite was the woman who wrote and apologized for all the crazy letters her mother, the poor old dear, had been writing for years, referring to his secret messages and promising to meet him. "But she's in the home now, safe and sound, where she'll no longer have these delusions about your broadcasts. After all, Walter, darling, we know the messages are meant for me."

But although we would laugh over the letters he brought home, I wonder how many more there were that we never saw, that were hidden away or maybe turned over to the police. What about the more dangerous fantasies? For every harmless little old lady, how many frighteningly serious crazies are there lurking on the other side of the TV screen?

In the mid-seventies, there was a new national pastime. After the skyjacking fad began to wane, kidnapping came into vogue. Paul Newman, for one, didn't allow his children to be photographed when they were young for fear of abduction.

People in the news media in particular were taking precautions to guard their families after the kidnappings of an editor of the *Atlanta Constitution*, a Florida disc jockey, and the daughter of a Taft Broadcasting executive. Then there was the kidnapping of Patty Hearst.

At the height of the Hearst episode, various ill-advised friends would make jokes, saying, "Hey, we could kidnap you and . . ." Some people consider that kind of thing amusing, but I didn't think it was very funny. Kidnapping seemed a frighteningly real danger to me. I was very paranoid in those days and am still a lot more cautious than I used to be. Someone knows where I am at all times—my route and my approximate time of arrival. My phone is unlisted; my address is a P.O. box across town.

I remember a few kidnap threats when I was young, but I didn't really know what it was all about at the time. We were carefully protected from the fears, the dangers, but in later years I reasoned it out—the messages from the school secretary not to leave school alone that day, that my mother would come to meet us. For the rest of the week, Mom or the maid would walk me to and from school, all of three blocks.

There were some days when I would leave the house in the morning and see two trench-coat types lounging across the street, watching closely and sometimes nodding when they saw us. It never frightened me at the time, mostly, as I've said, because I didn't know what was going on.

Although children are often protected from the specifics, they usually know when something unusual is in the wind. Polly Styron was nine years old when her father's most controversial book, *The Confessions of Nat Turner*, was published.

"I was aware of the fact that a lot of people were calling my father a racist," she said. "That didn't make sense to me, because I knew that he wasn't a racist, and I knew that that was a lot of trouble for him.

"I didn't personally come in contact with any kind of attack," she continued, "and when he's writing, he's a fairly nervous person anyway, so the atmosphere in the house didn't change dramatically. But now, when I talk to my parents about it, I realize that it was much heavier than I knew. When he lectured, he would get attacked by blacks in the audience. He'd be completely misunderstood."

Hugh Hefner has had his share of threats as well. Christie's own phone may have been tapped when her father "was the victim of a politically inspired drug investigation," but, for the most part, she, too, was shielded from any hint of danger. She recounted one frightening incident that occurred when she was flying out of L.A. to visit her father.

"When the plane landed, before they opened the doors, the stewardess came on and said, 'Christie Hefner, please report to the rear door.' Guards greeted us and put us into one of those little golf-cart-like things. They whizzed us through the front door to a waiting limousine—which was not unusual because *Playboy* owns a limousine service—and the driver said, 'Why don't you wait in the car, and I'll get the baggage?' And I thought, 'Boy, this is terrific service . . . I have never been treated so nicely. They've really spiffed up their act.' We got into the car, and I started leafing through some newspapers that were on the seat, and there was a headline: TWO STABBED AT HEFNER MANSION. It was an awful, awful moment.

"Some people had broken into the house the night before and got into a fight with some of the security guards. One of the guys, in fact, was in the hospital for some time with a punctured lung. It was not that long after the Sharon Tate murders, and there was concern that it could have been that kind of crazy vendetta thing. But it turned out that it was just vandalizing."

In spite of strict security, recent years have proved how frighteningly vulnerable the President can be.

"But you know, it didn't faze me," Jack said. "It fazes me more now than it did then. It was just sort of part of the job. As I look back on it now, I realize, hey, somebody was seriously trying to kill my father. But then, I never really believed that anyone ever would. I fear more for things that might happen to Susan . . . than I do anything.

"But those kinds of things you just can't worry about. It's like worrying about earthquakes. You could have yourself nuts here in California worrying about earthquakes."

I asked him if he had ever had any personal threats.

"They don't tell you when you're threatened," he said, "unless you're obviously aware of it. I was always pretty adamant with my secret service not to be oppressive. They were very good about it, and they tried to hang back. But one time during the campaign, an older gentleman came up and started talking to me incoherently. Then the guy handed me a big envelope, closed. I couldn't figure out what the guy was saying, so I just took it and tried to move away. Well, in about five seconds the secret service took it, which is their normal process. You're not supposed to accept anything from anyone. Later on, we found out this guy had a history of threatening public figures. In fact, he had been committed to a mental institution on several occasions for attempted threats on public figures. He was just a wacky guy.

"They never told me what was in the package."

Political violence is not always physical violence. Nora Davis' parents, along with many others, were blacklisted during the McCarthy era, and ever since then, she said, "They've lost work because of their principles. But [my father's] never been a Huey Newton. He's always been very diplomatic to get the point across. He's outspoken when you ask him, but he doesn't volunteer, so I don't think he's found objectionable politically, like a hot potato. He's in the public eye an awful lot. My mother tends to shy away from politics in an open way, though behind the scenes she's very supportive and involved. But I don't think she's in as much danger as my father.

"We've had life threats—because of their political activities, not because of their involvement with people such as Malcolm X and Dr. Martin Luther King, Jr. . . . Oh, yes. Oh, yes, I've been afraid."

"How do you learn to deal with that?"

"You don't," she said simply. "Especially in this country. I remember my father was involved with Angela Davis, and when she first came out of prison, they brought her here. She had bullet-proof screens around her, but *he* didn't. I remember his secretary's husband, who was a policeman, warning us what to do in case of shots being fired. As I said, you do not get used to it, because someone could threaten him tomorrow. I don't go to pieces, but I'm afraid.

"During the sixties and the early seventies, it was worse. Especially with that Malcolm X thing, it was *bad*.

"I sat and watched on Phil Donahue the young Nazi and the young Klansman the other day, and it reminded me *never* to let my guard down. *Never*.

"The one thing that helps me to deal with it is that I respect my parents a great deal. I know they're not going to live forever, and they are willing to stand up for what they believe in. And this is another piece of advice they gave me: never have so much to lose that you can't stand up and be for real at the right moment. We all have a life to live, and I can't be selfish and say, oh, no, don't go out, stay here with me. If he should be killed doing what he believes . . . I can't . . . So I try to look at it that way, and meanwhile I'm scared."

12.

John Ritter:
Two's Company

He who joins in sport with his own family will never be dull to strangers.

—PLAUTUS

Between John Ritter's television series, *Three's Company*, the various specials he was appearing in, and his honeymoon, it was not easy finding time for an interview. With the help of his public relations man, Larry Frank, we finally arranged an appointment for early one morning. I met Larry in front of the Ritters' new English Tudor house in an elite section of Los Angeles, where we spent about fifteen minutes ringing the bell, banging on the door, and asking each other where they could be. Finally, a sleepy voice called, "Who is it?" When Larry identified himself, John's beautiful and charming bride, actress Nancy Morgan, opened the door in her nightgown and invited us to have a seat while she went to wake John.

After a certain amount of confusion, coffee making, and so on, we were all finally established at the kitchen table, with the puppy stumbling around our feet and the tape recorder running while we chatted. John was gradually waking up, and I was being drawn into a performance in which he skipped from off-the-wall humor to serious reminiscences to bizarre flights of fancy and back again, without missing a beat. The unexpected pratfalls that are part of his routine on *Three's Company* were replaced by the verbal equivalent, with unusual twists to simple stories. Sitting at the table, his physical comedy was limited to mugging that may have been, for him, subdued.

As Nancy made breakfast, we made small talk. Somehow, we got to talking about beards.

"I had a beard in college, the first time," John said. "I was a sophomore, I guess, and we did *Macbeth*. The only thing I had going for me was my beard. I'd never had one, and it came in really well, and I was so impressed with it that I didn't act. Someone would say, 'I saw you in the play.'

"I said, 'Forget the play. How's the beard?'"

Then John gestured at the shambles of half-unpacked boxes and puppy-chewed debris strewn around the barely furnished house. "See, I like the house the way it is now. Other people like to fiddle with things. Not me. This is *it*!"

"Maybe," someone suggested, "you should get some chew toys for the dog."

"We have five hundred things for the dog to chew on. We have socks and balls and toys. We've got one of Nancy's little cousins tied up in the back room. We let the pup chew on his feet," John said.

As the laughter was dying down, John pulled himself back to reality. "I was talking about Shakespeare. I did Caliban, the monster [in *The Tempest*], and that was a really fun show for me. A lot of the purists came to see it. It was at the Shakespeare Society, and they thought, 'This isn't Shakespeare!' because I added a lot of stuff. One reviewer wrote that I played it like Quasimodo's idiot brother. Which I really liked. It was a little bit like that. Like a half-wit Quasimodo. With a little bonnet on a big monster head. One long eyebrow came across my forehead. I've been wanting to do that on *Three's Company* and they said, 'Not this season.' But what can I tell you about my dad?

"You know what's interesting, Kathy?" he continued. "I did this thing called 'The Singing Cowboy Rides Again.'"

He told us about the show which he had just finished, combining old footage of the cowboy films of the thirties and forties with interviews that he conducted with Gene Autry, Roy Rogers, and the like. "I got to complete a relationship with my father's work," he said. "They took a picture of me with Gene Autry on one side and Roy Rogers on the other, and when I saw it, it broke me up. God. I was going through all these considerations like, 'What will Roy think of me if I just start sobbing wildly here? Maybe I should sort of say I'm moved. Maybe I should keep my mouth shut and pretend it doesn't affect me at all.'"

"Had you met all those people before?" I wanted to know.

"I met them all when I was a little kid," he answered. "I remember when I was about eight, we all went over to Jimmy Wakely's house, and I brought some little toys to play with while they talked. So we all sat down at this big table to eat, and they started to say grace. After grace was over, my father pulled me up and said, 'Wut do yew think yer doin'?' I was reading a Daffy Duck comic book during grace. He really did not like that. Anyway, it's a big funny story to Jimmy Wakely. 'That ol' boy on *Three's Company*,'" John said, imitating Wakely's voice, "'his father spanked him because of Daffy Duck.'

"It's so circular, here's Roy Rogers watching me on television. I mean, *Roy Rogers!* I watched *him* on television. He came up to me and said, 'Y'know, John, I liked that one on *Three's Company* where you sat down on that parakeet. That really cracked me and Dale up.'

"They would tell me stories about my dad. Rex Allen said, 'Your father would be on tour, and I'd find him standing in front of two big piles of underwear and socks. He'd be pickin' something out of one pile and go, "Well, that's clean an' that's gotta go to the laundry. . . ."'

"And Rex said, 'Tex, what are you doin'?'

"He answered, 'I bin on the road too long.' I love stories like that.

"He's performed in every state and almost every city. And all through Europe and Asia.

"Dad was incredible. He could knock us out, traveling. I got a sense of who my father was when we went to these rodeos and the Calgary Stampede with the Queen of England and chuck-wagon races. I got in touch with his greatness by touring

America with him one summer. My brother and I were thirteen and fourteen, and it was great. We went to Las Vegas where he opened the Showboat. It was a country-music club which now, I think, has bosoms and stuff and chicks. 'Showbuxom is my life.'"

"Did you ever advise him on his music?" I asked.

"Well," John answered, "he would play little things and say, 'How do you think your contemporaries will like this, son?' He really included me and my brother. Never in his financial affairs. He always said, 'We don't have anything, son.'

"And my mom said, 'Don't worry about it.' So between Dad going, 'Poorhouse,' and Mom going, 'Everything's fine . . .' Actually, my father was right. And my mom was wrong.

"When I grew up, we were on a ranch in Van Nuys. It was real rural. We had a lot of chickens and a rooster and fifteen dogs and three horses and cats and a big barn and stables and what do you call it, a corral and a big hen house. I lived this kind of a fantasy. Dad would have these cowpokes working for him, and Mom would be working, too. I used to dream about that childhood thing. A very peaceful place for me. My father was always sort of impressive and my mother, too. She is very glamorous and very bubbly and totally takes care of people. In fact, when my father died, my mom took care of everybody at the funeral. Then, every night I would go in, and she would cry on my shoulder, and I would sort of take care of her.

"But my dad . . . I was always hip to his popularity. One time, when I was young, we were at a restaurant, and we had a little black girl with us, Jeannie, who was a cousin of the woman who took care of me. And this drunk came over. Now, drunks have always scared me, and they still scare me, because whenever I saw a drunk it would be a big guy and wobbling and not knowing what he's going to do. He said something, and Dad was trying to be nice, and then he said something about the little black girl and sort of touched Mom. Dad jumped up and smashed him in the face, and the guy went sailing. Literally, one hit, knocked him out. And I applauded. It was [like Dad was] the same guy that I saw in those movies beating up Charlie King, or something. And he was embarrassed.

"He'd go out drinking and playing cards with other musicians and actors. Then he'd come back, and he'd ride and play and do bits. And we always called him Tonto, 'cause he had long hair in the back for, uh, movies. He'd put on shaving cream, and he'd come out, and we'd think he was Santa Claus, and he'd peek around and play with us. It was just as I started getting into teenage things that I went through a period of, 'Come on, Dad! Gosh, he's so embarrassing.'

"I remember one time I was about sixteen, and he came out and said, 'Well, your mother asked me to talk to you, son.'

"I said: 'What's wrong?'

"He said, 'Well, you spend a lot of time with this little girl Cathy, you know, and your mother says she wants me to have a little talk with you about sex.'

"And I said, 'Well, Dad, if there's anything you want to know, always feel free to come to me.'

"He thought that was so funny. And he said, 'No, I mean, you're young, and some little girl might think your father has some money. And I don't. But they may want to sort of take you for a ride, you know, and say that they're pregnant and they're not pregnant and get some money from you, and you'd have to sell your baseball mitt. You just use that little tallow whacker of yours for peein' through for a while, now.' Tallow whacker!

"I knew there were some girls who were interested in me not for me . . . but it had nothing really to do with my father. You have to remember that growing up in Los Angeles, Tex Ritter is not on the tip of everyone's tongue every day, you know? He's really famous in the Midwest and the South and in the rural parts of the country. In fact, when 'Nashville Skyline' came out, Bob Dylan said it was okay to like country and western music. 'And here's my good friend Johnny Cash to write my liner notes and sing "Girl from the North Country"' . . . and then all of a sudden people said, 'God! That Johnny Cash is great!' Well, Johnny Cash, you know, was great long before Bob Dylan was around. But I love Bob Dylan for doing that; he gave a tip of his hat to country-western music.

"But I got through many days, or many weeks or months, and

no one would mention my father to me. Then someone would say, usually an older person, 'Your father Tex Ritter? Oh, I loved him.' It never got in my way, or anything."

"What about during the late sixties and early seventies?" I asked. "Those periods of turmoil when we were all real rebellious, anti-Vietnam and all that? Your dad was involved with Nixon and some rather conservative politics."

"*Huge* arguments," John said. "Huge. We would have fights all the time about political things. And he was sharper, so he could usually pin us down. 'Cause he had the facts, and he knew his history, and we were sort of emotional. So for Christmas I gave him an autographed copy of *Soul on Ice*. I had written in it, 'Dear Tex, you're gonna get down in this world, you muthafucka, signed: Eldridge Cleaver.'

"He read it and said now he understood where he was coming from a little bit.

"Then years passed, and I realized that on so many things my father would take the opposite view of whatever my brother and I would say in a discussion, just to pick our brains. You know, like a Socratic dialogue. And that was really good for us. Sort of little mental exercises."

I asked him whether he was ever tempted to deny his relationship to his father.

"No," he said, "because anybody who knew my father, even some of the radicals, just loved him. His thing was through the music. Once one of my closest friends, who was involved with People's Park and all the stuff up in Berkeley, came to Nashville, and he had known my father for a long time but not really close, and he had gotten into the guitar. Of course, the songs he was singing were not the songs my dad was singing, like 'Free Joe Hill,' and all of that. But they sat down together, and it was the most amazing thing, because, through music, here was this sixty-year-old country-western singer and this twenty-year-old student radical singing a folk ballad.

"Dad really never was self-righteous, you know; he'd always listen. But he got in some hot debates with some friends. George Wallace came to him and wanted him to support his campaign, but Dad wouldn't. He said George Wallace had a Napoleonic complex.

"Anyway, if anyone said anything bad about my father, no matter who they were, I'd stand up for him. It was sort of an unwritten loyalty in our family; you know, we can knock each other, but nobody else can.

"My dad had always been glamorous to me. He was who he was in real life as he was in the movies, pure and honest and good. You know? Really sort of a hero, and he'd wear cowboy clothes because that's what he wore. He always did. Except for the evening gown."

John's timing was exquisite. He had lulled us into feeling secure with his seriousness and, at the last moment, pulled the chair out from under us.

"I remember way before first grade," he went on, "whenever that was, getting excited because Dad was going to go sing 'High Noon' on the Academy Awards. That's the first thing I remember him doing—'High Noon.' I had to go to sleep at seven, or whatever it was, and I was furious that I couldn't stay up. Dad said, 'Well, let 'em stay up.' I think I snuck down and watched it, 'cause I remember him doing it. And they won that night.

"I literally worshiped my father. I would watch my father a lot when he wouldn't think I was watching him. I learned how to open any door of our house quietly, and I would watch my father sleeping. That fascinated me. I'd look at this big guy just sort of vulnerable in his little bed, snoring. I'd go over and sit on the side of his bed and look at him. There'd be times when I'd just maybe have a book, you know, and I'd sit in a chair, and I'd just look at him. Just being with him, you know. And he'd go like this"—he demonstrated his father waking up and showing surprise—"'Good goddamn son. What are you doin' here?'

"And I'd say, 'Just lookin'.'

"And he'd say, 'Oh.'

"I was scared of my dad when I was young, because he was so big and so powerful. But then I got in touch with his tenderness, and we'd have incredible talks. When I was around thirteen, fourteen, fifteen, I was pretty wild—hanging around with my teenage friends. I thought we were hot shit. We got in some trouble.

"Well, it wasn't anything like doing drugs or getting drunk. It was just my own little internal acceleration. I was just moving too fast and didn't have many values, or anything. It was running with the pack and trying to gratify myself as fast and as quickly and as cool as I could, just like all of my friends. Then different things started to happen; I met a girl friend, I got involved in things in school, I had talks with my dad, and things started to matter more. It ended up really bringing me closer to my father. I asked him, 'Do you love me? I really sort of have to know that.'

"He said, 'Yes, I do.'

"I said, 'Well, I'd like you to say it every so often, because I'm really insecure.' I'd read a little *gestalt* and seen *East of Eden* and James Dean. And God! If his father had kissed him, he wouldn't have had to do all that.

"One time Dad said, 'Well, now, y'know I'm going away for a long time to do this big tour, an' you're gonna have to take care of your brother and your mom.' He wrote me this really neat letter and signed it, 'Love, Dad.' I wrote him back ten pages, pouring out my heart to him and saying, 'I love you.' It was all in that letter. I was waiting. Finally, I asked Mom, 'Did Dad get the letter yet?'

"Mom said, 'Yes, he said it was wonderful.'

"I said, 'What else did he say?'

"Mom said, 'That was it.' I wanted a review.

"Then he wrote me another letter back and said, 'Now, son, here's a check, and I want you to do this and this . . .' and so on. 'By the way, I really liked your letter. You said some good things, and it really meant a lot to me.' That was it. And I sobbed. He didn't realize that. I guess when you have children, all of a sudden they'll say something, and you'll look and see they've grown, and I guess it surprised him. There I was, asking for more. And he gave it to me. And I cried. I wasn't into being James Dean. I had absolutely no pride when it came to wrenching as much love from him as I could. And attention.

"We would sit and talk, and he would tell me of his insecurities, tell me secrets. And I would, too. He *liked* to dress up in women's clothing," he joked.

"No, that's not true. Mom did, though.

"My mom thinks I can't do anything wrong."

Once again he had switched from serious to insane to serious, almost leaving us behind. "Well, anyway, she comes from total support. My father was very taciturn and stoic and not into expressing his emotions, but Mom is totally into saying, 'I love you,' many times a day. When I was on the Little League team, she ran the concession stand. 'Jonathan's up! Uh, oh! Strikes out . . . That's all right, love!'

" 'Shut up, Mom. Okay?'

" 'That's okay! Smile! Smile! Stand on first base and smile! You look so good when you smile.'

" 'We're losing. What do you mean, smile?'

" 'Just smile! It sparkles the field up.'

"My dad, on the other hand, came to about two games and put it in his act. I made the major leagues somehow when I was nine years old and I wasn't supposed to. I was terrified. These guys were fast pitchers, twelve-year-old pitchers, and I would just stand there, hoping for a walk. My father did a whole routine in his nightclub act about 'Jonathan stands up there and waits for a walk, and when he gets a walk he just stands on first base and tries to act like a ball player. And one time I came to the Little League game and everybody was screaming, "Jonathan got a hit! Jonathan got a hit!" ' And Dad said, 'Next year if he gets a hit, I'm going to run for governor.'

"I said, 'That's not funny!' That killed me. I said, 'Dad, why did you have to do that?'

"He said, 'Well, because it's funny. I don't mean it, son. You know I really love you.' So what I did was, the next year I became really good. I was first baseman, a big power hitter; I was one of the fastest pitchers in the Little League. I had a pretty good knuckleball.

"I said, 'Why don't you put that in your act now, Dad?' I made the all-star team and figured that was what I wanted to do. My father was real supportive of that. He just didn't want me to be an actor. And I understand what he said now.

"He talked about when he was doing *Green Grow the Lilacs* on Broadway, and Franchot Tone was in it and Lee Strasberg would come and they would talk about the Group Theater. You know, in the thirties. And they said, 'Well, how 'bout it, Tex?'

" 'Well, I don't know.'

"They said, 'It's a real neat thing. Come on, you can be in some plays.'

And Dad said, 'Well, you guys are talkin' about method.'

"And they said, 'You understand what we're talking about?'

"And Tex said, 'Yeah, when you guys go on and do a sad scene, you think about old Aunt Rosie's goose that died . . . brings up all that . . .' And he was an out-of-work actor in New York, and he didn't want that on his son. And then he'd go onstage, and he'd say, 'You know, my son told me he wants to be an actor. Goddamnit, I don't know where I went wrong. It looks like I'll be singin' "The Boll Weevil" till I'm eighty.'

"He always felt like a lot of people do, that acting wasn't a real man's occupation. And that's that kind of era. He should be doin' something with his hands, doin' a real job instead of acting. You know, people say; 'I'm an actor.'

"And they say, 'Well, dear, that's nice, so am I. But what do you do for a living? I'm an attorney.'

"There's times when I'll see myself on television, and I'll go: well, what does it really mean? What is the big contribution? Was it worth it? My father didn't want me to throw my life away on this sort of pipe dream. I finally had to convince him that I was really committed, and also I couldn't do anything else . . . at all . . . very well. It took a long time. When I was in college I started acting. I shifted from psychology major to drama, and he was worried about that. He was in Germany entertaining some of the American troops there when we went over to the Edinburgh Festival to do *Zoo Story*, which was a one-act heavy drama, and a thing called *Feiffer's People*, based on the writings of Jules Feiffer. We did it at the State Department-owned America Haus, which is a little refuge for Americans and cultural exchange things. The audiences loved it. And Dad really was moved. He had a long talk with me later and said, 'Well, ya got a little twinkle there in your eyes, son, so I sorta support you, but you gotta learn all about the sets and everything.'"

"When you were growing up and people asked what your father did, what did you say?'

"Well, intention is nine-tenths of communication. Content is one-tenth. And if people ask me, 'What does your father do?' or, 'Who is your father? What is he up to?' then I tell 'em.

"Or I'd say, 'Well, he's a singing cowboy. He was a cowboy star.'

" 'What's his name?'

" 'Lash LaRue.'

"You know, and they'd go: 'Oh, yeah?' In fact, when Nancy met me, she had to learn not to laugh when I'd put people on. But I've been interviewed by certain people and even just asked questions by regular old people who I cannot be truthful to. I won't lie, necessarily, but I will put them on, which is sort of lying. A newspaper guy who was told to get pictures of Nancy and me for this thing in London said, 'Why are we taking pictures of you?' He didn't know.

"And I said: 'Well, it's because I'm inheriting my father's business. My father, in America, is the potato chip king. His name is Laura Scudder; it's a girl's name, but, you know, it's all right . . . he's the huge potato chip king.'

"Then we were in front of the prime minister's house, Ten Downing Street, and the bobbies wanted to know why we were taking pictures of the prime minister's house. And the photographer said, 'Well, I was called by UPI to take pictures of Mr. Ritter, here, because of his father.'

" 'Father? Who's your father?'

"The guy says: 'He's the potato chip king of America.'

" 'Oh.'

"But . . . I finally told the guy, and he was a little embarrassed. Sometimes I just cannot be serious. And I've gotten into some trouble with it. You know, it keeps me interested. I just like to joke.

"But you see something in print which is a joke, and a lot of times they say"—and he quotes in a deep, serious voice—" 'John suggested to Suzanne and Joyce to go up north for some wild

Mazola parties.' Doesn't quite make it. Not quite how I said it. And also ABC . . . I did this joke about, you know, 'Show business is my life.' And they wrote in my bio, ' "Show business is my life," observed John Ritter.' So I have to watch that.

"It took me a long time to get used to myself acting on TV, and I remember what it felt like when I did it, and then to see how I come off, or what I look like, is very interesting. It took me a long time to get over the 'That's what I sound like? I sound like this, and I look like Puddy.' Then I see myself on talk shows. I've gotten over the nervousness of 'Hi, h-h-h-hi, Johnny, I'm so nervous,' " he said, miming chewing his nails. " 'That camera? Hi!' Anytime a camera would cut, I'd go, 'Hello!' and a couple of people would giggle. So I cannot run that routine anymore.

"There was one time on Mike Douglas where I saw that he really didn't care about the interview. He just didn't want me to block his cue card, you know? I started to get very giddy. It wasn't worth it for me to share, so I just played.

"Nancy gave an interview for me in Houston. Little Nancy bailed me out. She gave an interview with this very hostile guy." He turned to Nancy. "Can you give an example of how he did it?"

"Oh, he was from *Women's Wear Daily*," Nancy told us, "and he was totally a jerk. They told him to interview all these people, and he couldn't care less about any of them, didn't know who anybody was. So he comes up, and he goes, 'So, who are you?'

"And I went, 'Nancy Morgan,' " she said with a deadpan expression.

" 'Nancy . . . Nan . . . how do you spell it?' " She imitated the reporter writing very slowly. " 'What are you here for?'

"I said, I'm pinch-hitting for my husband, John Ritter, who was unable to come.'

"He said, 'Could you say that again, slower?' "

"Right there I would go for the big laugh," John said. "I'd go like this, 'What have you done?'

" 'Well, I've successfuly completed electroshock therapy at USC.' I mean, I love that. Those are the guys, Kathy, that's the kind of stuff. You were asking about intentions? If you just want to do the time and get through your job and stuff like that, then

I have to keep myself amused, or I'll just go, 'I don't want to talk to you.'

"My father did a Stanley Siegel Show when he was in Nashville. My dad didn't quite . . . like him. And yet my dad charmed him. Stanley Siegel said, 'Is it true, Mr. Ritter, that you've done a pornographic movie?'

"My father said, 'Well, it wasn't pornographic, it wuz, uhh, soft core, *and* it wasn't me.'

"And he said, 'Who was it?' and it was Lash LaRue. Which I thought was very funny, with a limp whip. And Dad didn't want to say it on the air. And Stanley said, 'Which cowboy star is it?'

"And Dad said, 'Well, I'd rather not say. It's none of your business, now, is it, son?'

"Strange man," John commented as a rather rough-looking figure passed by the French doors which opened onto the patio. "Must be the gardener."

"He's tied up Nancy," Larry threw in. "Does that man mean anything to her?"

"It's all right," John replied. "He lets her go after a while. Nancy never talks about it, though. She needs her strength for the iron maiden later on.

"But, uh, Dad was always putting stuff out there for people," he went on in a normal tone. "Always working. The most important thing in his life was my mom. And the most important things in my mom's life were me and Tom."

It seems to me that with famous parents there are a couple of pivotal points. One is when you realize that the parent's fame affects you more than you think it does, and the other is when you realize that it really affects you a lot less than you think it does.

"I think it's a continual expanding and contracting. It comes up whenever I hear his records on the radio, or somebody mentions his name or talks about him or comes up to me. That's when you know he's not just the normal guy on the street. Sometimes it's annoying when it stops me from getting from one place to another, sometimes I'm fascinated, sometimes I've really heard it before but I like the way they're saying it. Intention is nine-tenths of communication, but I don't think I ever take it for granted—oh, I'm sure I do, though, I'm sure I have.

"When I was little, I was a real smartass. When somebody said, 'Well, little Jonathan, are you and your brother Thomas going to follow in your father's footsteps?'

"I'd say, 'No, we don't have a long enough stride. Our legs are just too . . .'

"Or they'd say, 'My! How you've grown!'

" 'Grown what?' "

"From what I know about your father," I said, "it seems like his primary values were his family, his country, and his God. Did you take those values as your own?"

"Sort of filtered them through my perceptions. But, in a way, yeah. I used to romanticize and say, well, I'm Edmond in *Long Day's Journey*, and there's an older brother, and there's Mother who's very, very crazy, and my father's very strange. Not really; I'm really Tom Winfield in *Glass Menagerie*, my brother's handicapped, my mother's like a man, and my father's never here. Not really; it's more like the *Donna Reed Show*. But the values that my father had of God, country, and, uh; what was that other thing? Family. I'm not a Methodist like my father was. I have sort of a *liberal* protestant view of life, where what's very important is a way of relating to people through the most important thing, and that's through love. I mean, that's why we're doing this, as John Lennon said on the Tom Snyder show. Tom Snyder said, 'Well, John, why do you do it all? I mean, why do you do it?'

"And Lennon said, 'You know, Tom. The same reason you do it. To get a little more, you know what I mean?'

"He said, 'What?'

" 'Get a little more. You always want some more.'

"He said, 'Money?'

" 'No, Tom. Not money. You know what I mean.'

" 'Oh, you mean pussy or something like that?' And what Lennon means is just get a little more love. We don't have to do this and knock ourselves out. As far as God goes, the way to feel divine is through connections with other people, and all that. I'm not that into organized religion, but my father was. As far as patriotism—I was really angry at the corruption in gov-

ernment and the hypocrisy. I was so against the Vietnam war,
and my father was for it until he went to Saigon. Then he said,
We gotta get out of there. It's just like Sodom and Gomorrah.'
But he wanted an honorable withdrawal. But now we have to
go through years before 'patriot' becomes an easy word for our
generation to say. It really sticks in my throat. But I get homesick for America, like when I was in Europe, and during my
honeymoon. I loved Europe and everything, but I really love
America. Mostly I love California. It's my home. People say,
'Would you fight for your country?' Well, I'd rather talk them
out of it.

"As far as my family goes, that's very important to me. And
I consider my friends my family. I'm like my father in a lot of
ways. I literally worshiped my father. There were times when
I was really jealous of the public. I wanted more time with him.
He was away about half my life on tour or doing radio or going
to Nashville. But when he came home, we didn't go out much.
He really loved the family. Now that's happening with me.
Nancy and I have created our own little family here, and that
really is important to me. The family unit."

I asked him in what other ways he and his father were alike.

"Well . . . well, the spurs. Wearing the spurs to bed, I guess,
jumping on Nancy and saying, 'Go, White Flash! Go!' . . . That's
all a lie," he said, quite unnecessarily. "How do I think I'm most
like him? Well, I don't know. Sometimes Nancy will do some
thing that I think will be really neat or charming or adorable,
and I will laugh, and that laugh that I will hear myself do is a
little chuckle that my father did. I never laughed like that until
I met Nancy. It was before I married her, but it was the kind of
really sort of amused, very happy little chuckle that my father
would do with my mother. You know, when I make love to
Mom, I mean Nancy, I, uh, no, I think I'm getting giddy now."

"You're also under arrest," Larry interjected.

"Under duress," John replied. Then, returning to the point:
"I think I'm more outgoing than my father. I have more of a
business sense than he did. There's this story that his business
manager told me. He'd come back from a seventy-city tour or
something, and there would be like eight or nine or ten checks

that would be in his pockets that bounced from one-night stands he'd do. And they'd say, 'Well, we'll get our lawyers on this and sue them.'

"And Dad would say, 'Oh, don't bother with it. Hell, who cares? Those promoters couldn't get the tickets. I didn't draw enough. So don't worry about it.'

"They'd say, 'No, we've got a check for twenty thousand dollars. . . .'

"And Dad would say, 'Well, hell . . . it's all right.' I mean, he was constantly like that. He really put business way down on his list of priorities. My mother and I and brother always wished that Dad would just get it together a little bit more.

"Having business meetings really doesn't interest me, either, so I have people do that. I really love to act, and I really get to play a lot. They take care of that. Now if Dad would have had people representing him, like I do, he would've had more security. I think I've learned about that.

"At first, I was very hesitant to have a public relations person. That's a little bit of my dad's thing about keeping it small and keeping a low profile. He really wasn't flashy; he really liked to go in the back door; he didn't like special treatment. And I've inherited a little bit of that. But also I can choose to play the game. But when I play the game, I go: 'Hi, Army! It's real nice to be here,'" he said with exaggerated insincerity. "And I get away with that because I'm 'that crazzzzzzy cut up, Jack, on *Three's Company!*' Because I'm not Hutch or Starsky, I get to be funny in public, and I get out of a lot of things that way.

"What are you saying?" John suddenly asked Nancy, who had been trying to get his attention. "Are you teasing me behind my back?" He started to go on with his thoughts but turned back to ask, "You okay?"

"Yes, I'm fine," she said. "I'm just waiting for our toast."

"Oh. Oh, that's what I read in your face. I said to myself, 'That's a toast look.'

"But, uh, whether we like it or not," he continued, "no matter who it is, we become our parents in some ways. The more you try to resist it, the more you become it. If you don't resist it, you become it anyway. It doesn't matter. I can hear my dad in my brother's voice or my mom in my voice, or I can see myself doing some of my father's things. And I see my father in me. When someone comes up for an autograph, sometimes I'll go: 'Where are you from?' Or make a joke. And I would see how that would put people at ease. I really have sometimes re-created impressions that I saw my dad do."

I asked him what else he had learned about dealing with fans and fame from his father. "Well, I learned, I guess, all of it from him. That what's really important is the relating, the relationships, not the accoutrements that come with it. In other words, all the bullshit. See, my father really loved the people. He would sit and talk to good old boys, you know. When my father died, people would come up to me and give me little tributes. Things like: Your father changed my life; your father told me the best piece of advice; your father was a father to me; he saved my marriage; he started me in this business, I owe everything to him. People I've never met before. He really got off on the interaction. He loved performing, but he didn't like the glamour."

"When you got into acting, did you go through that thing about using or not using his name and influence?" I asked.

"Well, that was never really an issue. I never brought it up. You know, 'Hi, John Ritter, father's Tex Ritter, "High Noon," you know?' I never did that because going out for an *Owen Marshall*, it doesn't much matter that my father sang 'Rye Whiskey.' 'Yeah, I'm Tex's boy. Did you ever see *Arizona Days* or *Dusty Trails* or *Rainbow Over the Range*? Yeah, that's my dad's film.' Most people think of my father as a singer, rather than an actor. He really didn't 'act'; he was just himself and things that were comfortable. Get the plot out of the way so we can kill and ride and kiss and sing and do all the action stuff and do a big joke. My father had a lot of soul. And a lot of innate timing. None of the singing cowboys thought they were actors. They all thought they were singers, personalities."

"Do you sing?" I asked.

"Not at all. But I've been made to sing a couple of times."

Toward the end of the interview, I commented that at this point, he is probably more famous among contemporaries than his father would be.

"Am I?" he asked, sincerely concerned.

"Certainly among people our age."

"It's weird. Somehow, if I believed that, I wouldn't like myself very much—even though it may be true, because I know in my head that *Three's Company* is watched by millions of people. But he's my father, and he'll always be better than me. Yet, when I'm doing my thing there, I don't think about my father. When I start to sing or when I sign autographs or something, I can relate that to what my dad did, but not the embarrassing things I do in front of a camera. He was proud. When I was on *The Waltons*, he could really identify with that. He loved that show, so he would get real happy. The last time we were together, when I was leaving Nashville . . . the last time I saw him . . . this lady came up to him, as fans always did, and said, 'Tex, would you sign this?' Then she said thank you, and I looked at her little face, and she was so into it.

"And then, as we were walking, another lady came up to me and said: 'Aren't you the guy on *The Waltons*?' I said, yes, and she said, 'Could I have your autograph?' I signed it and turned so she would see Dad, and she looked at him and said, 'Excuse me . . .' and just walked on. Dad loved that. He loved that. And that was the last time I saw him."

13.

Fans

It was the usual "zoo tea." You know, we eat—
the others watch.

—Princess Margaret

Like John and Tex Ritter, my father and I are very proud of
each other's accomplishments, but I am not always as tolerant
of Dad's fans as John is of his father's. I love to eavesdrop when
I overhear someone talking about Dad, and I do so without fear,
for I have yet to hear anything negative about him. But it is
only conditionally enjoyable when people compliment him to
my face.

When I am eavesdropping, I can enjoy hearing the fans'
opinions and then leave or return to my own thoughts or conversation. But when someone speaks to me, I am not free to
walk away. Some days I am in a hurry or in a bad mood. I want
to place my call or have my check approved or make my reserva-
tion without hearing the familiar, "Oh, are you any relation
to . . . ? I'm his biggest fan; my mother watches him every
night; I know you've probably heard this before, but . . ." after
which, they proceed to tell me one more time.

As Michael Keeshan said, "It gets hard to smile; it gets hard

189

to be polite, [to say] 'Oh, thank you, great, super, I'll tell him you said so.'"

I saw the fans from a new perspective when a very close friend started traveling around the country with me, doing interviews. Although we had discussed fans and my feelings about them, he had never before realized the impact they have on day-to-day life.

With all our tight connections and slapdash scheduling, we had to stop at every ticket counter and every car rental desk while the agent expressed admiration for my father.

Perhaps there is an adjunct to Murphy's Law that says, "Fans will demand your attention most when you are least able to give it." That might be one explanation of why so many anecdotes about fans are set in airports.

Jack Ford mentioned, "If I'm waiting for a plane, invariably, at least one—and maybe more—people come up, just pick me out [and ask], 'Now, aren't you Jack Ford?' Walking down the streets of New York, it must have happened four or five times in the space of a week. And you figure on the streets of New York, you can get away with anything. I got to the point where I can pick out the people I want to talk to and the ones I don't. If I don't want to, I just say, 'Oh, I think you've got the wrong person.'"

Do they ever criticize your father to you?

"No," he said. "They may be thinking bad things, but you don't come up to someone and shake their hand and say, 'Your old man's an asshole.'"

One feels the pressure always to smile and be polite, to say, "Oh, yes, yes . . . Well, I'll be sure to tell him . . . Yes, that's so nice of you." Sometimes I blush with pride, but some days I'm just not in the mood to be gracious.

"Oh, yes," Nora Davis agreed, "and I have to hear about my father's play, and then I have to hear about *Raisin in the Sun*, and then I have to hear about all the things that they *think* he was in that he was *not* in, and I have to say, 'Oh, thank you, thank you.' Because it's so much trouble to argue with people who are going to insist that he was.

"But it doesn't bother me that much even now, 'cause I realize we gotta do it. Because they're your public, they support what you do, and they come out to see you, and this is a big joy in their lives. Usually, my parents are very generous about it, but there *are* moments . . ."

Francesca Hilton also subscribed to that *noblesse oblige* philosophy but expressed it in her unique style: "Sure, fans come," she said. "So what? Those are the people that keep the stars going. I used to have a good time [with them], but I'd always bust them because they would ask for pictures 'for their kids,' and I knew it was really for them. I'd ask, 'What are your children's names? Is that your name, too?' I don't know what the big deal is. I don't know if I'd want to go through it, give up all my privacy. That's very hard. But that's a decision you have to make when you decide to become a public figure. You have no choice, and if it gives other people pleasure, what's the big deal?"

The Keeshans didn't have the recognition problem as much. Michael explained, "I think in the early days, my father's makeup looked very different from my father in person. So we could go almost anywhere and avoid the recognition. He was twenty-seven years old, I think, when he started the show, but as we grew up, he grew into the makeup—his hair got longer, he started to gray, he grew a moustache of his own instead of makeup—at the age of forty-nine, he's beginning to look a lot more like the Captain.

"Occasionally, someone would recognize him. Most often, it was a parent who brought a child over and introduced him. But out of makeup, my father was very reticent to acknowledge he was Captain Kangaroo. He wanted to maintain a sense of illusion for the child and felt that it was counterproductive for him to be an actor in the mind of the child, that it was better that he always be Captain Kangaroo. It's the same reason he doesn't let kids on the set with cursing stage technicians and problems that shatter the whole illusion [where they'd see] that Mr. Moose isn't really a moose; he's this guy behind a counter with a puppet on his hand. I think that other performers have tried to maintain the illusion, and I like to think that it's particularly critical for him. To the extent that he wasn't recognized, he didn't try to be recognized. In fact, if a child was introduced to him in the old days, he would more often than not say he was a friend of the Captain's, and he would be pleased to convey his best and see if the Captain would send a picture, or whatever. And I appreciated that."

Linda McMahon remembered the first time she was aware of the power of her father's recognition. "It was when we had a summer home in Avalon, New Jersey," she told me. "Every year we used to take about twenty kids and go to the boardwalk, the Steel Pier, all the rides and everything, and all of a sudden, this one summer, there were people crowding around for autographs. I was so mad. I was so mad because this was supposed to be our night, and it just wasn't working out well. I remember just standing back and watching people talking to him and being jealous," she said, sounding almost surprised. "It was like they were infringing on my time with him. I still get mad sometimes. I guess it's just the mood I'm in at the time, but it still bugs me sometimes. It's just the invasion of privacy that I'll never get used to or like. It's expected when he's out on the road working somewhere, you know it's going to happen; but if it's a family thing and you're spending time with him and then all of a sudden it happens, I get very jealous."

Fans appear to feel in some way that they have a right to the time and attention of their idol, and, to some extent, they may be justified. If one has no desire for public attention, one should choose a different field. But I cannot comprehend the feeling that they also have a right to the celebrity's family, and it is easy to understand the child's jealousy toward the fan. The fan's possessiveness is in direct conflict with the child's sense of ownership of his or her parents.

I heard a poignant episode that occurred when Avery Schreiber and his young children were on an outing. When some fans rushed up to him, shrieking, "Oh! I love you! I love you!" his child turned to him and asked, "But how can they love you, Daddy? They don't even know you."

It is annoying never to be assured of an uninterrupted talk or of time alone together. In the most secluded Bahamian cove, people row around us in circles to photograph "Uncle Walter." Fans ought to realize, but don't, when and where such behavior is appropriate and when and where it is not.

People seem to feel that the star is public property, that because, for example, the star is in the fan's living room every evening on television, they have some sort of connection. It is only an illusion. You don't have to hang a tea towel in front of the screen when you undress; your idols don't know, or possibly even care, that you fell asleep in the middle of their show. They don't know you. You may feel that they are part of your family; maybe in a sense they "have dinner with you every night," but that doesn't mean that they feel that *you* are part of *their* families.

The most terrifying example of a fan's total disregard for the object of supposed admiration was told to me by Nancy Sherman. Once again, it took place at an airport.

"My father always had asthma," she told me, "and he had a bad asthma attack in the airport in Chicago. He could barely breathe. They called the ambulance, and he was leaning over on a railing, holding himself up, and a woman came up and said, 'Can I have your autograph?'

"He barely gasped out, 'I can't breathe!' They literally thought he was going to die.

"And the woman said again, 'Can I have your autograph?'

"He said, 'I can't—I can barely stand up.'

"And she said, 'Look at this! He's so famous he doesn't even want to give out an autograph!'

"There's just no privacy," Nancy continued. "You can't go anywhere without being recognized. Sometimes it's fun to be recognized, but sometimes . . . Shortly before he died, he was still getting recognized but not as much as he used to, and people would come up and say, 'I remember you—weren't you somebody?' People don't realize. If you don't remember, why bother him? 'You *were* somebody, weren't you?' And he'd say yes. He was always very polite to them. He'd give anyone an autograph, and he'd go out of his way to be nice to people."

People don't realize, Nancy had said. They don't realize that you are human, with the same human feelings that they have.

The fan in Nancy's story was unusually cruel; more often, one meets with simple rudeness. I remember one old woman who scrambled and elbowed her way up to me for my autograph. When I returned the scrap of paper to her, she screwed up her face and held the paper up to the light and then turned back to me to demand, "What does this say? That's not your name!"

I apologized for my illegible writing but assured her that it was indeed my name.

"For every nut, there are some genuinely sweet people out there to whom your signature means something. As long as it's not a check they put in front of me, I don't mind signing," Nora told me. "I spoke at some graduations, and all the kids just had to have my autograph, and it just tickled me to death. But I think you get your fill of it, you know? It's just like doing a play: after the umpteenth year of it, you'd be a little bored."

But then there is the other side of fame—the joy and satisfaction that can come from knowing that you've really touched someone's life.

"Kids always liked my father," Nancy Sherman told me. "They loved him so much. We'd always hear about them learning to speak by singing along with the records. They couldn't get most of the jokes, I'm sure, but they would sing along. One woman wrote and told us, 'My child has been autistic for years, wouldn't talk and couldn't talk, and started talking by listening to these albums and is now singing along.'

"Or, 'My daughter's blind, and the happiest thing in the world to her is listening to your album.' We would get a lot of these letters about kids. I remember my mother being in tears. My father really had a miserable life, and he wanted to make people laugh."

Although I am beginning to achieve a small measure of public recognition, it still comes as a shock to me when people know who I am. The other day in Macy's, the saleslady who took my check grinned and said, "That's a familiar last name," a fairly common remark.

"Yes," I responded with an automatic smile. "That's my father."

But she seemed not to have heard me as she said, "I enjoyed you so much on 'Kids Are People, Too' and 'Dinah!'" She went on to critique my performance, adding as an afterthought, "I watch your father, too."

I asked Mark Vonnegut how he perceived the difference between his fans and his father's fans.

"I think my fans are easier to deal with. My father's fans think they're enlightened; my fans are over the line and frank about it. I really think that's a big difference. It sounds funny, but—my fans *know* they're crazy."

14.

Following in Their Footsteps

Mark my footsteps, my good page,
Tread thou in them boldly.
Thou shalt find the winter's rage
Freeze thy blood less coldly.
—"Good King Wenceslaus"

The topic that evoked some of the most volatile reactions from the people I talked to was the prospect of following in their parents' footsteps. Choosing a career is one of the most important decisions in life; it is doubly so when a parent has celebrity in a particular field. You are under a public microscope—conclusions will be drawn whatever you decide.

Christie Hefner made the point well when she was talking about style. "I have found that on the days when I wear a suit, somebody will say in an interview about me: 'Obviously reacting to the very glamorous, sexy women in the magazine by dressing very conservatively . . .' and on days when I wear a more frivolous dress—because I wear whatever I am comfortable wearing—somone will say, 'Trying to compete with . . .' They will interpret whatever they want to interpret."

When a friend of mine who teaches journalism at a local college asked me to speak to his media class, I suddenly realized how my father felt about not having finished college. My first reaction to the request was the same as his had once been: "What can I say to a roomful of college students when I dropped out myself?"

I tried unsuccessfully to write a speech but finally gave up and called Dad for advice. He suggested one of his own tricks: when in doubt, make a few opening remarks, and then throw it open to questions from the audience.

As a result, the dialogue turned out to be much more interesting than any speech I could have planned and, I'm sure, more satisfying to both audience and speaker. But one question stopped me cold:

"Do you think that the reason you chose acting as a career was to establish your identity publicly after living all your life only as Walter Cronkite's daughter?"

I answered truthfully that it had never occurred to me before and took the next question. But it has occurred to me many times since. There is a variety of reasons why I chose acting as a career. It fulfills every part of me—intellectual, emotional, and physical; it is a logical as well as a creative pursuit, combining the two spheres to arrive at a carefully built spontaneity. It affords me the opportunity to travel, to explore different life-styles, different patterns of thought and behavior, even different careers through the characters I play.

My career decisions could not have been uninfluenced by my father's fame, but, more importantly, I know my decisions were influenced directly by the kind of people my parents are: curious, adventurous, interested, and intelligent. Because both my parents are writers, I've grown up with a respect and a love for words, for the power of words and the beauty of words, which may have led me toward both writing and acting. But all the excitement I derive from my profession does not mitigate the deep response I felt when I was asked that one straightforward question.

Why? What indeed gives us that drive to compete with our parents' fame? How much have I fooled myself that my father's fame hasn't affected me?

"I frequently wonder," Susan Newman said, "whether I chose to become an actress out of my own free will. Or was it something that was around me my whole life, so that I'm not making the decision as a free agent? I don't know, and I probably never will know.

"I imagine there comes a time when you've passed a certain level that you have to say, 'I've achieved it on my own,' or you drive yourself crazy. Someone once said to me, 'You want to be an actress? Holy God, Susan. Do you know you're going to be compared to this and you're going to be compared to that . . .'

"I had never really consciously sat down and thought about it, but when I did, I was overwhelmed with paranoia. My friend said, 'A normal young actress starting out would be thrilled to death that one day she's going to be the seventh supporting actor on *Welcome Back, Kotter*. Your frame of reference is putting that accomplishment way down here somewhere, and what your parents have achieved is way the hell up here, intangible territory.' How many actors are there who are as famous as my father? There are twelve or fifteen of them, at the most. It's sort of like living up to the Joneses, but the Joneses are your own family. Whether or not you reckon with it consciously, it keeps coming up in your life. I think it's a tremendous burden."

"The main difficulty," Polly Styron said, "is that constant success hanging over you. How each individual deals with it, whether or not they're going to make it, and whether it's all right to be successful, is a question of the individual. I went through that, too. I remember once we were driving somewhere in the car, and my daddy was talking about some book that my sister had read. (My sister is incredibly well read. At age twelve, she really had read everything.) I remember feeling overwhelmed and saying, 'Well, I'm just going to fool you all and become a jock.'

"I felt I couldn't compete; if I failed, that would hurt my pride, so I just pretended I didn't care anyway. But then I thought, 'Well, maybe I'll be a writer.' Suddenly it was all right to admit that I was interested in books, and it was okay that I hadn't read everything. It was just a personal way of coming to terms with what I wanted to do on my own. I always did really well in English classes—and I always intended to—but I felt I could never live up to how bright my sister was or let anyone else think that I was trying to be intellectual. I went through a period where it was painful for me to write papers in school. I don't know if it was because I thought every word had to be perfect or if it's an inherited trait. It so happens that that's how my father writes, too. Maybe I was affected by being afraid that what I was writing was going to be bad, more afraid than a person who didn't have a writer for a father."

When I talked to Bela Lugosi, Jr., I had a hunch that he, too, would have liked to have followed in his father's career, but when I asked him why he chose not to try acting, he responded, "People who are actors have to talk people into giving them jobs, and I didn't want to have to do that. Not only that, but assuming I wanted to do it, I doubt that I have the talent. Then I would really be under the gun. I'd be compared to him all the time. I'm compared to him less being in a completely different field.

"I guess I took the easy way out; that's one way of looking at it. People have tried to get me to appear in pictures. But I've never really been tempted. For one thing, since I have no training, I really wouldn't exhibit much talent, so I'd only have one shot at it.

"It wouldn't really be consistent with my image as a lawyer. So I've just told most people a price that's high enough, cash in advance, that we've never gotten beyond that point," he said with a laugh. "I think what my father told me and passed on to me affected my choice more than his career," Bela went on. "He thought it would be good to have a profession, for the independence it gives you. Also, I was very impressed by his learning and knowledge, mostly self-taught. He had a very inquisitive mind; he was always trying to learn something. If something came up, he would research it. But as far as his career is concerned, I think that it probably steered me away from acting. It made law an available option, because anything but acting was available."

"But why law?" I asked.

"It was really a process of elimination. I worked all through school in quite a few different jobs, which allowed me to find out what I liked and what I didn't like. The field kept getting narrower, until finally there wasn't much left to do but take the Law School Aptitude Test. Which I did. But I didn't have any lifelong ambition to be a lawyer. I'm very fortunate that the choice I made put me into something I really like. I think being a trial lawyer is as close to being an actor as any other profession is."

Jenny Buchwald has also chosen not to follow in her father's footsteps. In fact, her choices are about as far as you can get from the Washington literati. When I asked her what she wanted to do with her life, she replied, "I always have these crazy ideas—like I want to be a truck driver someday, go across country. Even just for three months. 'Cause I love trucks, and I love CB's, and I could have my dog with me and take pictures. I told this to my mother, and she flipped out.

"My father said, 'Calm down, she's not going to do it.' That's the difference between them: my mother listens to me and believes me, my father doesn't.

"I love to try out all different things. You've only got one lifetime on this planet, so try it all. In Vermont I was a deejay, the only woman jazz deejay. I enjoyed that a lot." When pressed, Jenny finally admitted, "Actually, I love teaching. I taught photography my last semester at school, and I learned so much. People my age respected me. They'd come up and ask me questions, and that made me feel really good. Made me believe more in what I was doing. And in me."

I asked Monte Schulz if he had ever considered what would happen when his father stopped drawing *Peanuts*.

"I think The Strip is funny only because it's *his* sense of humor. No one else could do it. I can't even sign my name the same way twice. Actually, my sister, the one who lives in L.A., can draw Peanuts characters. If she'd stuck with it the last few years, she could easily take over. She was very good. We all tried to; God knows, my brother and I wanted to. We wanted to be cartoonists. Of course, that's natural. But you know, we were no good. Even Dad had to admit we were no good. I could never do The Strip, because we just don't have the same sense of humor.

"The key to The Strip is that what fifty million people think is funny, he thinks is funny, or vice versa. That's why, even though it's a strain for him to maintain The Strip every day, he doesn't have to worry, 'Will they think this is funny?' If he thinks it's funny, that's good enough, because everyone else is going to think it's funny. If I did it, no one would think it was funny."

Christie Hefner may not be imitating her father's sybaritic life-style, but there is no doubt that she is the heir apparent of Play-boy Enterprises. She told me about her beginnings at her father's magazine.

"I was free-lancing for the *Boston Phoenix* and *Oui*, but after about a year I thought, this is a lot of fun, but I don't feel I'm using my mind very much. I want to find a job that's creative but also analytically challenging. Free-lance writing tends to be lim-ited. At that point, relatively out of the blue, my father said, 'Why don't you come to work for *Playboy* and see if there isn't something here that interests you? It is a business that is at its core publishing, and that's what you're interested in, but it's also a business company, and that's more complex and analytical than just writing.'

"There was no pressure in the sense of, 'If you don't want to stay, I'll never speak to you again,' and I felt it would be an interesting experience, regardless. So, in November of 1975, I moved back to Chicago and came to work as special assistant to the chairman, my father.

"I think he was charmed by the fact that I almost became a bunny once, but I think he's much more excited by the fact that I'm working in the company in a position of management and responsibility."

I had to ask the obvious question, although I knew she must have answered it many times: had she ever considered posing in *Playboy*?

"No, but I've never considered posing in *Vogue*, either," she replied with well-rehearsed intonation. "You have to take it in that context. They used to ask that in the sixties. It was sort of one of those watershed questions. If people who worked in the NAACP were white, they were always asked, 'Would you let your daughter marry . . . ? How much do you believe?'

"Someone once asked my father, 'How would you feel if your daughter posed for *Penthouse*?'

"He said, 'I'd be awfully insulted that she hadn't posed in *Playboy*.'"

"I won't work at something I'm not happy at," Linda McMahon told me. "I'd rather waitress. Whatever it is, I think maybe my dad has passed this on: whatever you do, strive to be the best you can. Maybe that's why he can play the second banana as long as he has; he loves it. He looks forward to going to work, which is more than a lot of people can say. I can't imagine living with a father who goes to work dreading it. I worked as a production assistant on *Midnight Special* for a year. I thought I wanted to do something behind the scenes. It was a good experience, but the people you had to deal with, the musicians and rock stars! After that year, I realized I just have to do something where I'm helping someone or doing some kind of good for humanity, no matter how insignificant. But I've tried a lot of things, and I haven't come up with anything yet. It'll probably be teaching, but, then again, I'd want a half dozen things on the side."

The one thing she is certain of is that she will not be an entertainer like her dad. "I was gearing myself to go into performing, but even just giving recitals at school, I used to throw up for half an hour. It's just not worth it.

"It was very depressing to realize I'm just not a performer. I don't think I've inherited that, whatever that is, to want to go out in front of a group of people. I just know it's not for me."

Although Lorenzo Lamas was brought up in a show business family and acting was, as he said, "always in the back of [his] mind," it wasn't until recently that he was bitten by the bug.

"I've always had this great love for animals," he told me, "so I decided to be a vet. I got into all the colleges I applied to and decided on the University of California at Santa Barbara. I had my bags all packed, but there was this question in my mind about whether I was doing the right thing. 'Twenty years from now, when I have my great office in a nice medical building and I'm wearing my white lab coat, checking out a cocker spaniel, am I going to wonder what would have happened if I'd tried it? Just tried it?'

"So I had Dad sit down, and of course he goes like this: 'Lorensso, I see there's some kind of *problem*. Do you want to talk about it?'" Lorenzo had imitated to perfection his father's accent and deliberate delivery.

"I said, 'Yeah. I'm not sure I want to go to college.' This was a *week* before I was on my way to Santa Barbara.

"He said, 'Ah-ha. Well, okay, tell me honesty now, Lorensso. We're not gonna fool aroun' here, okay? Because I'm behind you with whatever you wan' to do.' And he always has been. He's a very fair guy, and I love him. He's my best friend.

"And I said, 'I want to be an actor, I think.'

"Long pause. *Long* pause. Thinking back to how hard it was, he said, 'Oh, schit. Now, do you realize that only four percent of the actors actually make a living? Did you know that?'

"'Yeah, I know, but it's in my heart, Dad. I think I want to give it a try,' I told him.

"Another long pause. Then he said, 'Okay. Let's get you in a good acting workshop so we can know if you can act or if you're going to stink up the theater.'

"So I studied for four months, and then I got a part in *Switch*. So I guess it was meant to be for me to be Lamas Two, to carry on the tradition."

I always thought that choosing a career must be even harder for my brother because he is a male, and, even though we have made some headway in the last few years, journalism has been associated more with men than with women. So I supposed that he had grown up under a barrage of, "Are you going to be a journalist just like your dad, Chip?" He must get awfully tired of it; I know I do. Chip told me that he had had one article published in his high school paper. "I don't remember what it was about," he said, "and it was mostly rewritten by the editor anyway, but I loved the headline."

"Oh, what was it?" I asked.

"I don't remember, but it was perfectly lined up."

Recently, Chip told me, "What we have to deal with more than Dad's fame is his ideal. More important than who or what he is, is what he feels about what he does. He is extremely idealistic [about journalism]. He thinks it's the most important thing in the world to society at large. It follows that anything else you'd do would be frivolous and unimportant.

"However," he continued, "as the night follows the day, anything we would do would be important, because we are important to him as his progeny."

Dad has always wanted one of us to go into journalism. Practically every time I'm with him, he asks why I don't pursue a career in broadcasting. As my own interest grows, each conversation is a little more serious.

Most of these conversations take place on one of our family trips, possibly because that is when we have the most peaceful, uninterrupted time together just to talk. On one recent trip, we talked for the first time about the specifics of the idea. I emphasized that in no way would I be interested in doing the news, partly due to lack of consuming interest and partly because I feel strongly that newspersons should have a strong journalism background, a degree, and newspaper experience before they tackle the television medium. I do not believe in "pretty people" reading the news off a page, written by someone else. Dad, of course, agreed.

"But what about interviewing? Talk shows? That's what you'd be really good at," he suggested. "Why, I've heard you interviewing almost everyone you talk to." He was right. I can hardly have my shoes repaired without finding out all about the processes involved and the biography of the shoemaker.

"All right, Dad," I finally admitted, "I *would* be interested in that. But what am I supposed to do, with no background? Apply for a job by saying, 'Hi, my father thinks I'd be a great interviewer'?"

"Yes," he answered.*

My one experience in broadcasting had been a couple of years

* Some time later, I did in fact get a job as an interviewer—luckily without having to use Dad as a reference.

earlier when I fell almost by accident into a job at a CBS-affiliated television station, working for the local entertainment editor. I was hired as a research assistant and was promised that within a few weeks I would be doing interviews and field producing.

Imagine, then, my horror when, at the end of my second week on the job, I was told that one of my new duties was going to be taking the boss's shirts to the laundry. And this is supposedly liberated 1977?

Well, I stewed about it all weekend, and on Monday I gathered up my pitiful cupful of courage and marched myself into his office. I told him that I was very sorry, but I felt that I had been hired as a research assistant, not a maid, and that he would have to make other arrangements for his laundry. To my surprise he said, more or less, okay. I was off the hook.

Later that day, my dad called me at work as he did regularly, simply because he was so excited that I was working at a TV station.

"Oh, hi, Dad!" I greeted him loudly over the long-distance wire.

I didn't hear what Dad said next, because my boss was shouting from the next room, "Don't tell him about the laundry!"

15.
Jack and Debby Erhard:
The est Family

"Contrariwise," continued Tweedledee, "if it was
so, it might be; and if it were so, it would be;
but as it isn't, it ain't. That's logic."
—LEWIS CARROLL, *Through The Looking-Glass*

My opinion of the *est* organization and the people involved
in it improved considerably after my contact with Brian Van der
Horst, the public relations director for *est*, and with Jack and
Debby Erhard. I anticipated a conversation that would be almost unintelligibly confounded with *est* jargon and a hard-sell
"why haven't you taken *est*" attitude. I was wrong. Although
Jack's answers were echoes of *est*, Debby responded with her
emotions. I felt a better rapport with Debby's open, communicative, down-to-earth sweetness, but found both of them very
charming.

We met at Franklin House, Werner's residence and personal
office, a beautiful Victorian San Francisco townhouse. Inside, it
is immaculate, decorated in browns and beiges of largely natural
materials, wicker and bamboo judiciously mixed with antique
leather and wood. There were dried *saguaro* cacti reaching to
the fourteen-foot ceiling and an ancient Buddha in the foyer.
African, Haitian, and Portuguese statues and artifacts had been
gathered here, among them centuries-old Philippine "talking

vases" and a ten-foot-high fertility statue from Africa. The effect was at once comfortable and formal. Even the toilet tissue had its ends tucked into neat corners as in a fancy hotel, presumably by one of the many *est* volunteers who function as household as well as office staff.

We settled in the den, a book-lined room with antique desk, fireplace, and armchairs. I chose a big old wing chair, upholstered in denim. Debby and Jack sat opposite, with Brian unobtrusively to one side. Debby was dressed in a V-neck T-shirt and stylishly cut jeans. She gestured gracefully with her delicate, expressive hands as she talked and frequently had to brush her loose blond hair out of her unmadeup girl-next-door face.

Jack sat at the third point of the triangle. His thin face and dark coloring reflected his father's, but his hair is curlier and his face a little smoother. Both children share their father's clear eyes and slightly smiling mouth.

An *est* volunteer brought coffee and tea on a tray as we made small talk, feeling each other out.

Jack, who is nineteen years old, is the third child of Werner's first marriage. He is a sophomore at Claremont College, "leaning towards drama and literature." He has appeared as an extra in *More American Graffiti*, and when I asked him his plans, he said that he thought he'd like to be an actor. There is no doubt that part of the *est* mystique is due to Werner's flair for the dramatic, and, later in our conversation, Jack admitted that he may follow in his father's footsteps after all.

Debby, eighteen, is a freshman at Mills College, studying languages and interested in law and government.

"At one point in my life," she said, "I really wanted to be a trainer [for *est*]. Now my sense is that I won't, but it could change.

"I think that I have something to offer. I don't know exactly what it is, but it will in some way contribute to *est* or to what my dad's doing. I think my father has something up his sleeve for me already. I'll probably go into government and maybe in some way support *est* and my father."

Debby was six months old when Werner left his family and she grew up not knowing who or where he was. Although he had started *est* sometime before he returned to claim his children, they had never heard of Werner Erhard or his organization.

"My sense of my father was that he wasn't alive. That's what I had thought for all those years, and I never questioned it. So when I heard he was back, it was a total shock," Debby said.

"My reaction was totally different," Jack said. "I was very, very aware that he was alive. We'd heard all the stories about him leaving, and so when Mom said he was back, I thought, 'That creep!' For a little while, I operated off all the notions I had about him, the stories I had heard.

"We met him at my grandmother's house, and on the way over I realized that all that stuff no longer held any ground at all. It was like he'd never left. Yeah, I was jumping for joy."

"That was in 'seventy-three. January thirteenth. I will never, ever forget that," Debby said in a soft voice. "I have a very clear picture of the first time I ever laid eyes on him." She stopped for a moment, remembering the scene as tears filled her eyes. "Getting me choked up," she murmured. "We came out to California to visit every summer. We moved out here—two years ago?" she asked Jack. "No—three summers ago."

"No," Jack corrected her. "Four summers ago."

"At what point did you take the *est* training?" I asked.

"I did that the first summer I came here. I took the teen training," Debby responded. That was the summer immediately after her father had returned.

"Did you take it at the same time?" I asked Jack.

"No. I held out," he said. "I had absolutely no dislikes or regrets or resentments toward the training or anything that went on in it, and then they *told* me to do it.* And I said no. Just out of the fact that they told me, not because I didn't like the training or the way people were that come out of it. So I didn't do it the first summer; I did it the next."

"What changed your mind?"

"Dad asked me, instead of telling me to do it," he said simply.

In 1977 and 1978, one could scarcely pick up a magazine or attend a party in California without being confronted with con-

---

* It should be noted that in the *est* philosophy, the conjunction "and" is preferred over "but."

troversy over Werner Erhard and *est*. I wondered how Jack and Debby reacted to the swirl of sometimes negative conversation. Were they ever tempted to turn around and set someone straight?

"Yes," Debby started to say, "I remember—"

"It's never malicious," Jack interrupted, as he did frequently to assure me that the world is full of nice people who think only the best of Werner and *est*. "I've never come across anyone who was hostile about it; I think it depends on the rumors they've heard.

"Sometimes you're with someone for a while before they make the connection, and then they definitely shift in their approach to you. Most people in *est* are awestruck: "Produce a miracle! Levitate! Something!' People outside of *est*, particularly if they've heard some things they didn't like about *est* or Dad, are a little more calculating about observing what you do and how you dress. Checking you out, making sure. But they're pretty good about it. I don't think I've ever run across a person who wasn't acquainted with it."

"I have one thing to add," Debby said tentatively. "A couple of years ago, I felt that people don't love me for me; they love him. You know, that Werner's my dad, and that's all they care about. I think I've grown out of that and into taking it as an opportunity, to bringing people closer to him. That's the difference now—people don't have the really big shift in the way they rap to me, because I'm more centered. I'm more clear about my relationship to him and what that means."

"What contributed to your ability to see it a little bit better?" I asked.

"For one thing, just the growth of the relationship with my father. I have always felt inferior to my dad, that he knew everything and I didn't know anything. I've grown, and now I can actually sit with my father and have a discussion with him and feel that I'm equal to him."

I told Debby that I had gone through exactly the same thing, only ten years later. She and I have fathers who are looked up to as fountains of knowledge and wisdom, whose every word is taken as gospel. My God! Who wouldn't grow up feeling inferior? There is a traumatic moment in everyone's life when they realize that their parents are not, after all, infallible. But when your father is Walter Cronkite or Werner Erhard, this common discovery takes on the proportion of cataclysmic heresy.

I remember vividly the first time I knew he was wrong. The dinner conversation had somehow worked around to dolphins. I had studied them recently yet sat silently picking out the flaws in Dad's discourse, afraid to dispute them openly. Millions of people in the United States believed his every word; who was I to question it?

Dad wasn't the cause of my silence; my own self-doubt was. That barrier fell away when I began to establish myself, my own career and income and life, apart from him, when I began to believe in myself and rely less on his approval, when I had enough self-assurance to be able to risk challenging him and to risk being wrong.

We converse as peers now and learn from each other, although perhaps I am still disproportionately thrilled when he responds with, "Why, I never thought of that," or, for example, when he called me to ask my opinion of newspaper reporting versus the electronic media for a speech he was writing on that topic. I'm sure he was pleased to learn that I am now acquainted with both.

I asked Debby if her father could learn from her as well as she from him.

"Oh, yes. Dad's business is people, and I'm sure he's learned a lot about how people get their stuff together in relating to us kids. He's got quite a variety to learn from—a whole range of ages and a lot of different personalities."

Jack has worked for *est* every summer since his father's return. Although he told me earlier that he planned to be an actor, he admitted, "After I do my thing my way, I'll probably be a trainer."

Did he think it might be difficult being a trainer and Werner's son?

"No, actually it makes it a lot easier. When Dad and I stand next to each other—when I have my hair cut a little shorter—we look exactly the same. I think people like it that I look a lot like him. It brings them a little closer to him and gives them a deeper experience of who he is. It enhances our relationship."

"Don't you think that if you were to become a trainer, people would tend to put a little halo over your head that may not belong there?" I asked.

"For sure. People do it all the time *now*. But I can usually represent my family fairly well. I've never had to worry about disappointing him or anything like that. It's fun. It's a challenge."

Neither of the Erhards worried about disappointing their father. "I know that my dad wants me to be the best that I can be," Debby explained. "He doesn't ever want me to let *me* down. I think the only way I've ever let him down is by letting myself down. I've definitely done that."

"Jack, you said earlier that you think you look a lot like your father. Are you a lot like him in other ways?"

"Certainly, that's the direction I'm moving in. I don't see a role model that I would prefer over him. Since he is where I'm looking to be, I feel that it's a good idea to imitate him. At one point, all I did was imitate Dad. It began as imitation; it actually became a context of my life."

"Isn't there *anything* you'd do differently?"

"No," he answered. "Absolutely not."

While Debby agreed that her father was a model of what she'd like to be, she admitted that for a long time, like many people, she has struggled with whether to do things her own way or to accept her father's guidance.

"Now," she said, "in my relationship with my father there is a basis; it's not my way or his way. It's just The Way. I trust him absolutely to guide me, because I know that I don't know where I'm going or what I want to do. And, yes, I'd definitely like to be able to contribute in the way he does.

"The main thing is to tell the truth. It's not always easy. In fact, I spent the last week really getting clear about what it is that I haven't told the truth about. Today I discovered the *only* withhold I have from my father. And I'm communicating that to him. It totally empowers me when I tell the truth."

"To become his partner is the way," Jack interjected. "It's silly for us, his family members, not to be his partners. If he's got to deal with all the 'Did you get A's, did you do this, did you get all this stuff done?', if all the energy is spent there, then we're always at zero. Like if I get B's, that's a negative point, and then, every once in a while, we get to go above the line, nurturing and empowering.

"I'm very aware of where my relationship is at. I'm very aware of what condition it is in. If it's about cleaning it up, or about nurturing each other and making contributions."

Although I cannot accept the need to keep score on a relationship, still, I admired Jack for even being aware of his relationship with his parents at all. Most teenagers merely tolerate their parents. Even after those early tumultuous years, how many of us really consider our relationships with our parents? How many of us *work* at those relationships, keep track of whether they are working well or are cluttered and difficult, and put some thought and energy into how we can make them better?

"That's what I can see that we as children can do," Debby said. "To share that with our friends."

"I did a family seminar down in Los Angeles about a month ago about teenagers and their relationships with their parents," Jack said. "A lot of my friends, if I can get them to start talking about their relationships with their parents, they become very clear that that is what their life is about. And they become their parents. They're very clear that they love their parents and that they want to have a relationship with them that works."

One of the common complaints of children of well-known people is that they don't feel free to express their sometimes negative feelings about their parents in public, or even to their peers, for fear of tarnishing the parent's image. Jack and Debby avoided this problem by having nothing negative to say. But I still wondered whether they felt pressured to keep up a front.

Debby said, "I think the public demands that we fit their pictures. I would think they'd expect Werner's kids to have integrity, to look nice, and to tell the truth and be open with people; and I want to fit that anyway."

"Absolutely," Jack agreed. "Being appropriate. As long as I'm appropriate, I have nothing to worry about. Though sometimes my ideals are *not* appropriate.

"Raz [Ingrasci, one of Werner's assistants] was talking to me about having a character instead of being a character. Like I'm a jar, and the character is a marble in the jar, instead of me being the jar, being the character. Okay, and having a character, you can develop and change it.

"At one point, I would wear very vogue clothes, scarves, and all my collars and sleeves were turned up. That was inappropriate."

I didn't see why it was inappropriate to be stylish.

He tried to clarify. "People look at me and see my clothes and forget that there's somebody there. My clothes should accentuate who I am; I shouldn't have the clothes out there. It should be me out there—nicely dressed and well groomed."

I decided to change the subject. I asked how Werner's public persona differs from the way he relates to his family at home.

"Dad's in the public eye a lot," Debby said. "He's got his way of being in the world; none of it's a front or anything. It's just that he doesn't lay himself totally wide open. So when he's into the family, I think it takes awhile for that to disappear.

"He's out a lot. I've gone on trips with him. When we come back and we're doing things that just daddy and daughter do, there's a shift. I've only experienced it a few times. That's exactly when I'm his daughter. There's giggles and playing, and it's just outrageous. It makes being the person a lot easier. You know, that's like the spice, the sweetness in life."

Jack leaped once again to his father's defense, asserting that his father "really gets real" with people and "has them become a part of him." He did, however, point out one of the differences between public and private appearances that I had never thought about before.

"There's a bit more variety in the things we talk about," he said. "There are things you just don't talk about in public. People get offended."

I suspect that this is true whether or not one's family is in the limelight. Certainly, it is true in my family. Neither the intimate affection and playfulness nor the boisterous zest which comprise the best of our family occasions would suit the evening news, to say nothing of the political discussions, dirty jokes, gossip, and off-the-wall humor that are also a part of our daily private conversations.

"I don't derive a whole lot of pleasure out of the typical father-son relationship," Jack went on. "I mean, there seems to be a little bit of, pardon my language, shittiness in father-son relationships. You know the typical thing, the understanding that your father won't call you on your act and you won't call him on his act.

"I love being around my dad, and we have a great time. I love to go sailing with him, and flying, and things like that. I like being around him when he's around other people, because it gives me more of an experience of who he is and how he's relating to other people."

Like Debby, I have always felt that there is a special sweetness in the father-daughter relationship that is not experienced between men and their sons. I can only guess at the reasons: that the power struggle inherent in that male relationship constricts the affections; that men feel more comfortable expressing their tender side to their little girls; and that macho pressures are less. I do not presume that these are necessarily the factors affecting Jack and Debby, but we talked about the differences between each relationship.

"There's something that I think is only true with daughters," Debby said. "I don't think that Dad could share with Jack what he shares with me. That's not to separate him, that's just the way of the world."

"Do you think fathers have more expectations of sons than of daughters?" I asked.

"Oh, no," she asserted. "Not this one. He expects everything from all of us."

"From everybody," Jack added.

"See, I just want to make sure that my experience of my dad came across," Debby said. "I know there's a lot of room in my relationship with him to expand. I think that our relationship could become something very positive and something very powerful in the world.

"I have this fantasy that I could be able to learn what it is that makes our relationship so great and be able to communicate that to my friends and to other kids, to let other people know that you can actually have a relationship that isn't full of terrible things. I just want people to know that all they need to do is be honest and say all those things that they don't want to say. I told my mom horrendous things that I thought I'd never tell her. And after all that stuff is gone, there's just lots of love and lots of time to play. You can go out and do what you have to do; you don't have to worry about all that other stuff.

"I just want to say, I love my father a lot. As much as you can, I guess."

16.

Amy Wallace:
Collaboration

Distringit animum librorum multitudo.
—Seneca

I visited Amy at her Berkeley bungalow, decorated with a jumble of knickknacks, old herb jars, and European marzipan figures, a style that she described as "Early Toy." Amy and I curled up on the floor with a cup of tea, and after catching up on news of our alma mater—from which I had graduated by the time she had arrived—I asked her about her current projects.

"I am currently one quarter of the *Book of Lists, Two*," she said. "My mother's joining us on this one."

"And the dog?" I asked, referring to the famous Wallace writing clan joke.

"And the dog," she laughed. "Also, I'm thinking of reviving and publishing myself a book that I wrote four or five years ago when I was eighteen. It's a sort of Goreyesque alphabet book. I'm not sure whether it's geared towards debauched children or debauched adults. Or both.

"I also wrote a children's book. That one didn't sell, either. It was a fairy tale, and it was just the wrong time for a whimsical and fantastical story. Four or five years ago was a time of hard-hitting reality—you know, ghettos and menstrual periods—and it was just not the time for winged horses."

"How did all this come about? Did you always know you were going to be a writer? How did you start working with your father? Did you write that first book with the idea of getting it published, or just for yourself?"

"Well," Amy stopped me, "I'll start prenatally. . . . Oh, I have to stop being so silly."

Although Amy and I had gone to the same school, we had never spent any time together; we had never talked girl talk and giggled together as we were doing now, and I enjoyed it. As we went on, we realized how close our experiences were with our contemporaries and with our parents. We were building a friendship through our surprisingly easy rapport.

We talked a great deal that day about the closeness we both felt to our families, a closeness that seemed unusual among our friends. We had shared similar conflicts, growing up as rich kids when it was much hipper to be ragged. And Amy and I discussed our writing at length. It was one of the first chances I'd had to compare notes with a contemporary who was also a writer.

"Well, then, how did it all start?" she picked up where she'd left off. "I don't know. I just always grew up in an environment with writers, and I think I always just assumed I would be a writer. I wrote prolifically when I was little.

"I was very into fairy tales. I had one traumatic incident in grade school: I was writing an epic fantasy in class, and my fourth-grade teacher, Mrs. Johnson—I still remember her name—ripped it out of my hands and said, 'If I ever catch you writing again while I'm talking, I'm going to tear this up!'

"I just kept on, because my parents were so supportive. But I was shocked by that, that she was so enamored of her own voice that my not listening was such an affront to her. Then, in sixth grade, Mrs. Sussman decided we'd all write a poem for Law Day —this was in public school—and I wasn't contributing. Mrs. Sussman said, 'Amy, you usually contribute so much. Why aren't you speaking out, dear?'

"I said that I didn't believe in our country's laws, especially draft laws, abortion laws, and so forth. She started to cry. She broke down in front of the whole class.

"Years later, I found out that she had called my mother and said that she was very upset that such a young person should have such things on her mind, that childhood was a time of joy and lightness, and how tragic it was that I was thinking about wars and abortions.

"Then, for a year, I went to a school in Los Angeles for traumatized children of Hollywood stars. For a long time it had been a school for kids who were wacked out by having rich and famous parents, but it was just converting into a regular private school. I wasn't a traumatized child, at least to my parents' eyes, but they'd heard this was a somewhat reliable school.

"The kids all had Porsches and drove into Beverly Hills on their lunch break, smoking pot and taking cocaine. That was when I was a rabid marijuana smoker, but that was about the extent of that. And I didn't have a Porsche."

"Did you feel deprived?"

"Oh, no!" she responded emphatically. "Not in the least bit. I was in a period of denying such material things. I was very much a hippie. All the other kids were from prominent L.A. families, whether in business or the arts.

"But I didn't like L.A.; I never have, that much. I wanted to break away from my family; I wanted to live in a rural setting. So I asked my parents if they'd send me away to school.

"We looked at one in Arizona—Verde Valley—and they wouldn't accept me because they said I was too arrogant. I think it was because I told them I'd rather not play competitive sports. We looked at some other schools that ranged from very druggy and kind of degenerate to slightly alternative but largely disciplinarian. Woodstock Country School in Vermont fit right in the middle. Also, it was in the most beautiful environment of all of them, and I just fell in love.

"My mother was quite heartbroken at seeing me go away from home. My brother was away, and that was a hard thing for her. When I got there, I was very Californian—extremely friendly and sort of anxious to make friends and share stuff with people. It was my first experience with eastern mores, and people thought I was kind of weird, too outgoing and cheerful. I would invite people to come smoke pot with me, and apparently you just didn't ask someone you'd never met before in this environment. I guess there was a whole etiquette to being new that I was breaking.

"People were fascinated that I didn't have a tan. There was one other girl from California, who had a tan and blond hair. And surfed.

"One of my first boyfriends there was hostile to my background and to my father being famous. He was half hippie and half intellectual snob, you know, which is very popular at a certain age. He thought my father's books were pulp writing, and he was very nasty about it.

"This was the first time I'd encountered this, and I really didn't know how to respond. I pretended to agree, and even talked myself into agreeing, to be accepted. So I went through a period of thinking my father was a schlock writer. In fact, the little of his work I'd read, I'd liked, but I went along with popular opinion. At that time I was reading exclusively Proust and Camus and Rabelais.

"Well, I feel very differently now. I'm almost a little embarrassed at how I felt, but it was part of rebelling against my parents and being accepted by my peer group. Certainly, the hippie environment had a lot to do with it. It just wasn't okay to make a lot of money and be famous.

"On the other hand, I was very proud of him. Other people would say, 'You know, your father's a marvelous writer, and I admire him so much. He's given me so many hours of enjoyment.' I was constantly getting these two different messages. I still do, only now I can handle it a little better," she laughed. "It certainly was confusing at the time.

"My brother had an upsetting experience in a college writing class. I don't know whether the teacher knew who David was or not, but he picked Irving Wallace as an example of popular pulp writing, dissected it, and trashed it. David was humiliated and angry, embarrassed in front of his friends. So he got out of writing and into filmmaking for a while. He needed to have an identity separate from that of the family. He started to use Wallechinsky [the original family name] at that time."

"How did your parents help you through that period?" I asked.

"I don't think I really talked about it much with my parents for a while. I was not communicating with them too well. We used to talk about money, about how it was to have money. A lot of the problems I had were because my parents would send me expensive presents at school, and there was a lot of hostility. Even though you had to be pretty wealthy to go to that school.

"I still like to do a lot of my shopping at thrift stores—there are great finds there—but at that time I would shop there exclusively. Deliberately. Much to my parents' consternation."

"I know," I laughed. "I went through the same thing. But I remember once when I was (foolishly) hitchhiking, and I got picked up by a man in dirty overalls and a pickup truck. I was wearing sandals and patched blue jeans and an old army jacket or something, and he said, 'You can always tell the rich broads when you pick them up, because they're the ones dressed like bums.' It was a very strange revelation to me about what I was doing. That it didn't work."

"Didn't fool anybody, right?" she agreed. "Yeah, I think a certain amount of that is true. My mother was always trying to get me clothes and I just wasn't interested. . . ."

"I have a standing joke with my mother about that," I said. "She was always trying to take me shopping for decent clothes, saying, 'Come on, you've *got* to have a dress to wear.'

" 'But, Mother, I *have* a dress,' I would complain, refusing to admit that one crumpled, calico, ankle-length skirt might not be appropriate for all occasions. Even now as we set out to shop together, she teases, 'I know, you *have* a dress. . . .' "

We laughed and chatted about our favorite ragged clothes, the blue jean jackets and patched shirts that we had clung to as fiercely as a child to its bear, and then Amy brought the conversation back to the conflict between her hippie values and her affluent background. During the years that we attended Woodstock Country School, the school was run on a year-round full-enrollment quarter system, in which one was expected to do something constructive during whichever quarter one chose as an off term.

"A lot of kids would go off and go into other structured situations," she said, "but I would come and live in Berkeley with David and some friends in a communal situation—six people in a one-bedroom house. My mother wouldn't even set foot in the door. She still pales when she thinks of it. Everything about my life-style was more or less repugnant to them for a period. But I wouldn't want to live there again, either.

"I was younger than most of them, and they were all being poor hippies, and again I went along with putting down my family. I was not aware of the way I was behaving, but as I look back on it now . . .

"There was one girl I had some conflicts with in the commune. I guess she decided I wasn't doing the dishes enough or something, and she made some crack, like, 'Well, Amy's used to having a maid.' I was very hurt by that, that she couldn't come right out and say, 'I'd like you to do more dishes.' I would think, these people are very angry about the fact that I can always turn to my family if I'm in a crisis and that they're supportive of me.

"A lot of people I know have been alienated from their parents and have never really developed that relationship. I think they're jealous that I've been able to maintain a closeness with my parents."

I knew exactly what Amy was talking about. In earlier years, many friends complained about my ready acceptance of my family's wishes and my willingness to give up going to a big party in order to spend the weekend in the country with my folks. Some of them had good advice about not letting my family rule my life; some of them who came from families that never spent weekends together may just have been jealous. At least, they stopped complaining when they were invited along.

"In the last few years," Amy continued, "I've created friends who are not going to be taking gibes at my background or family, who are going to be supportive. Before, there were people in my life who were judgmental or critical of me, and I didn't realize that maybe they weren't the best people for me."

"Do you think it may also be because you're starting to make it on your own?" I suggested.

"Oh, yes. Of course, that's changed everything," she said. "That's caused hostility from some of my friends, too. There are people who were my friends who aren't any more. And that's really mutual. Some of them didn't acknowledge that I was working, that I had two careers of my own. I was doing extensive psychic work and making money at it, and also writing. The focus was on, 'You have a rich family; you're not having the experiences we're having; you're not suffering.' It's like there's some sort of rule that poor people or people who are struggling are better people. You can't maintain an intimate relationship when there's that kind of hostility."

"How did you first become interested in psychic work?" I asked.

"Well, when I got to high school, I had some more bad experiences with writing teachers and started writing less in class and more privately. I was going through that period, as my brother had, of needing to do something that was my own."

Amy's budding interest in naturopathic medicine led her through acupuncture and herbal medicine—what she termed "the so-called holistic healing arts"—to Berkeley to study. On a whim she went to a psychic reader and discovered that it was not just mumbo jumbo. "He didn't predict my future; he didn't read my past lives; it was very down to earth," Amy said.

"So one day I called my parents and said, 'I want to go to psychic school, and the tuition is a thousand dollars, and will you put me through?'" she said, laughing. "I had never intended to go to college, and I think my parents were disappointed. You know, how do you tell your friends your daughter is going to psychic school?

"But they said okay, which I think was really admirable, wonderful, and brave. Under the circumstances." After going through the intense eight-month course at the Berkeley Psychic Institute, Amy turned down an offer to teach there to start her own classes in her home.

She advertised readings and healings solely by word of mouth and soon found herself booked for months in advance.

"So I've found something on my own, and it was from that base that I was able to get back into writing again," she explained. "And enjoy it.

"One of the great values my father raised me with was, 'Be your own boss,' one of the great freedoms of life. It may not be true for everyone, but I certainly was inculcated with it, and it feels right to me. It's real nice to work with my family," she said. "It's difficult, sometimes it's very aggravating, but, really, I feel very lucky.

"I think my brother put it better than anyone else. 'Even when we were fighting, at least we always talked.' There was always communication there."

I asked her how she started working with her family.

"It was about the time when I was feeling uncomfortable about being associated with my father's fame, and the last thing I'd ever imagined was that I'd ever write a book with him. There's a psychic dictum that what you resist, you become. My father had written *The People's Almanac* with my brother, and I had worked on it some and enjoyed it. My father liked my writing and one day approached me and said, 'How would you like to write a book together? I wrote one with David, and I'd like to write one with you.' I was eighteen at the time, and he had not seen a great deal of my writing, and I think that was daring on his part. I said I would. It was really moving."

I was touched to hear her tell it—and a little jealous. I would love to be able to collaborate with Dad on something. I would like to be able to give back to him some of the support that he has always lavished on me.

"Ever since my father quit the movies," Amy continued, "he'd been his own boss. Now he has to compromise with David and me—and now my mother. We battled over having certain things in, and he'd insist on having other things in, and he'd fuss and fume, but he said, 'Maybe, maybe.' "

"That must have been a great thing for your relationship," I commented.

"Oh, yeah," she said. "He said that he had to go through a big struggle when he wrote the first book with my brother—they both did. He had to stop being a father and be a collaborator. And he had to go through the same process with me."

"To learn to see his children as adults and people, instead of just his children?" I proposed.

"And as creative sparks of their own, with input that could be valuable to him. It really has been exciting. But it's not all harmonious, either. The hardest part is when our traditional roles as father/daughter creep up on us, and we get stubborn in ways that sound to me like a teenager arguing. If we can just drop that and talk as work partners, we can compromise and work it out.

"We had a harder time on the first book. Instead of my father saying, 'I don't like it,' or, 'I don't think this is how it should be,' he'd say, 'That isn't how you do it. This is how you do it.' He doesn't do that as much now, and I'm sure I have my own obnoxious habits. A joke is good. That's one of our greatest tools for compatibility. David is an irrepressible punster. He has a very dry sense of humor and cruel to the extreme when it comes to puns. So we pun a lot, and that keeps things tolerable.

"It was interesting because they had both worked before and, being intellectual men, tended to sulk when they were mad, whereas I tended to fly off the handle. So that added a whole new ingredient.

"I've not suffered too many illusions about being famous," Amy said a little later, "because I've always been close to my mother. She's had a difficult time until recently, when she started writing on her own. I've certainly heard the other side of it, of having to live with someone else getting all the attention.

"There are always going to be people saying, 'Oh, you got your books published because you're Irving Wallace's daughter,' or, 'Oh, that didn't hurt, huh?' no matter what I do. If I wrote a three-volume novel, if I wrote the next Anna Karenina, if I wrote forty books, there will always be some hostile person saying that. You have to come to terms with it in yourself, you know? You can't wait for other people to see it's really you."

"I know that as soon as I started achieving something in my own right," I said, "I could stop getting embarrassed when people made a big thing about my father."

"Oh, yeah," she agreed. "That's one way to get to that place where it's okay. Where you know who you are. I think one of the hardest things must be kids of famous people who haven't been able to get some kind of career—it doesn't even need to be a career, but some kind of satisfaction. If they aren't sure who they are, it can just put salt in the wound.

"My father is always asked, 'You've got a real writing factory here; what did you do?' Call it nepotism, or call it what you want, but no one criticizes when a lawyer's son becomes a lawyer."

Probably half the people I had interviewed had mentioned that same analogy—if it's okay to follow your parent's career in other fields, why isn't it okay in the arts?

"There's a mystique about the arts," Amy postulated. "Similar to the mystique about the psychic, that it's a strange godly gift you received when you were in the cradle, that you were the blessed one. The idea of being in an environment that supports it, or learning it from your parents, destroys that myth. People seem disappointed that whatever ability you have is something to be learned or developed, that it's not going to just drop on them someday."

17.

Mothers:
The Hidden Strength

I think it must somewhere be written that the
virtues of the mothers shall be visited on their
children as well as the sins of the fathers.
—CHARLES DICKENS

"I'm very grateful for having a mom who is sometimes a
gigantic pain in the—neck," Susan Newman said with unusual
gentility. "She may not always give me what I want, but she is
very consistent in what she gives. And very blunt. You don't bullshit with her, because she'll see through you, and whenever I get
too cocky, my mother can bring me down to earth. But when she
gives me compliments, well, euphoria!

"I really love my father a lot, but if I didn't have my mother
. . . I'd be a very different kind of person—probably a lot more
fucked up—because she has a certain stability about her. And
reality.

"A major problem in my family is that there's no consistency.
Major rules are made, and then they're broken. And, you know,
you can't do that. Particularly since the overall *life* is so unreal
anyway," she said.

"Two years ago, [Dad and Joanne] gave me a fur coat for
Christmas. Now, I had been working, I could have bought my
own fur coat, but the message was, 'Oh, you're really coming up

in the world.' It just blew my mind that they gave it to me. It was very extravagant for them.

"Anyway, I didn't tell my mother about it for months, because I knew that she had thought out so carefully what Christmas presents to give me that year, things that would really help me in my work. She gets some really imaginative ideas, like a wonderful thing for me to carry my scripts around in that no one else would have. She really puts in time and effort. She can*not* compete on that level financially, and I know she probably feels, 'No matter what I do, Paul can always one-up me.' Even though I don't really care, and I don't ever play them against each other that way, I know that it creates a lot of problems for my mother.

"When I finally did tell her about the coat, everything that I thought would happen did. We had one of those great conversations where we both wound up in tears. I said, 'Don't put me in the middle of this; I don't want to deal with this; I can't help it if he's rich. I wish I was never born in this family, anyway.' All that sort of *wonderful* stuff comes out. I imagine it's been damn hard for her.

"But thank God for my mother. She's a realist, and I think it's primarily because of her that I have my feet at all planted on the ground."

Although not all of us have had the tangible evidence of inequality, like Susan's fur coat, I suspect that the competition between parents, especially divorced ones, is amplified when one of the parents is famous. If the children of famous men have identity problems, imagine what the wives must go through as they are pushed aside and overlooked.

But they are our mothers. To us, they are on a par with our famous fathers. Yet I am always asked, "How is your *father*, Kathy?" "Say hello to your *father*." (Except by people who know *both* my parents.) It was Samantha Drake, daughter of producer Alfred Drake, who said, "People always make me feel as though I am the product of just one parent."

After I had interviewed Susan, I went home and told my

mother this anecdote, commenting how sad I thought it was that Susan's mother felt she couldn't compete like that.

"She's right," Mom said bluntly. "She can't."

I was stunned into silence. Awkwardly, we changed the subject. What I wanted to say to her was, "No, Mom. I mean, isn't it sad that she feels she *has to* compete on that level?" The point of the story to me was not that Paul had in some way "won," but that each parent, each gift, was valued for itself in its own way.

It was frightening to realize that I had never suspected how strongly Mom felt about this. I was shaken for several days and thought about how difficult it must have been for Mom. Always in the background, always the primary disciplinarian, and feeling, as she often said, like the heavy.

It must be especially difficult now and in the last few years when much of my life, both publicly and privately, has revolved around my relationship with my father. Dad and I have been slowly working toward détente in our personal relationship, and at the same time, because of my profession, a lot of attention has been paid to the "daughter of a famous man" aspect of my life. Which leaves my mother out. Most of my energies for the last three years have been going into the writing of this book about, bottom line, Dad and me, even to the exclusion of time that Mom and I might otherwise have spent together.

When I was a young girl, even a young lady, many of my needs were filled by her; and it was to her that I turned for advice, although I suppose she may have felt that even then my financial needs were being taken care of by Dad. But as I grow, advice and response to my professional needs are more likely to come from Dad.

Yet I love and admire her so much and owe so much to her. It was my mother who helped me with my homework, not just by criticizing, but by making suggestions like, "How could you say this better?" or, "Are you sure this is the right word? Let's look it up." She quoted Shakespeare in context in everyday conversations and always lovingly made us conscious of our speech, correct or not. Although she disparages her own abilities, it was she who molded our appreciation of music with wonderful informal gatherings around the piano, playing and singing together.

I was surprised when I first started to attend the opera as an adult to hear familiar tunes that I had heard whistled over the scrambled eggs as a child.

She is educated, brilliant, witty, and loving but has so little faith in herself or belief in the impact she has on others. People who don't know my mother ask the usual questions about my father, but people who have met both my parents ask first about her.

"I've sat next to your mother at parties," Christopher Buckley told me, "and I think there are some similarities between her and my mother."

"It must be awfully hard for them," I commented. "I've never met your mother, but what I've read and heard about her does remind me of my own mother. They both seem to be so bright and so witty and so overshadowed."

"Well," he replied, "you are *Mrs.* Walter Cronkite and *Mrs.* William Buckley. And if they happen to be professional house-wives, they tend to be even more slotted into being 'the wife of.' I'm not sure it's any harder on me than it is on my mom.

"She's a very strong person. She was raised British colonial and has never changed her citizenship. She lives for me and my dad. She's never gone out and done anything professionally, but the way she runs a house is sheer art, and that's not so easy. It gets dumped on a lot, but it's just not easy. She's also very active in charities and stuff.

"But my temperament is equal parts of my mom and my dad. I can tell exactly which parts. It's true, occasionally people remind you that you have a famous father, but it doesn't mean that you forget who your mother is. Even if she's not famous."

I would not presume to speculate on how much the shadow of my father's fame has affected my mother; I imagine that her character was pretty well formed before he ever stepped into the limelight. I only heard her complain about it once, and with good cause.

We had sailed into a small harbor where some friends of my parents lived. The man greeted Dad as we pulled in to the dock, and almost before we'd stepped ashore, he brought over another friend of his to be introduced to Dad, totally unaware, it seemed, of my mother's presence. The man neither acknowledged nor introduced her.

My mother is far too much of a lady to have made any comment at the time, but later in the evening as she was fixing dinner, she mentioned it almost casually, standing at the sink. Although her words were calm, her hands betrayed her anger; as she talked, she had been peeling potatoes for dinner, almost mangling them in a vicious rhythm.

She is a strong woman, stoic and enigmatic. In the late sixties and early seventies, when encounter groups were in and we all tried to tell everybody all our feelings all the time, my mother's sense of privacy about her feelings was annoying to me. I misspent several years hammering at her to try to find out what she thought about everything, how she felt every minute.

Somewhere along the line, I realized that she would never change; she is who she is and I am who I am, and what's important to me is not necessarily going to be important to her. One step beyond that, I realized that I admired her for those attitudes of keeping her problems to herself, that same strength and stoicism for which I had condemned her. It wouldn't work for me, but I admire her beliefs and her strengths.

"My mother had a tough way to come up," Nora Davis told me. "She's had to work for every *inch* of whatever she's had, and she instilled in us respect for what a *woman* is. She never made us think, 'Well, all you're going to have to be is a wife, dear, so you just go over and play with your dollies.' She demanded things of us and demanded things of our *minds*, as well as making us stand up straight.

"I think she caused my father to come to some greater understandings as far as women are concerned, so he was able to say, 'Okay, since you're tired of washing diapers, I'll stay home and you go to acting classes.' She used to come home and teach him what she'd learned in class while he was at the sink with his apron on. They *worked it out*. But it was never easy.

"I never felt that my mother wished she didn't have us, and

I've seen a lot of people, not even *in* show business, tell their children, 'Listen, if I didn't have you . . .'

"It's a very interesting thing, though; there's a part of my personality that's very family-oriented. I believe in families and especially in terms of the survival of *my* people, but still . . . sometimes my mother would talk about careers and 'Do something with yourself,' and I would say, '*Mom*! Please! Okay, I'm going to *do* something with myself, all right?' Now I'm getting older . . . I'm beginning to realize what she meant and realize that I grew up with a woman to whom anything you want to do is possible. It was almost like a threat: 'Oh, God, my mother can do that; that means I have to be able to say *I* can do it.'

"But as I grew older, I realized that she was trying to prepare me. I do feel lucky because we can talk as women and as friends about those kinds of things, and she can give me insights into how to mix both [career and family].

"I think it comes from her being basically a loner, and having a burning desire to create in terms of art, and never thinking of herself as just a woman. I picked that up, and so did my sister. Even though my sister's chosen to start her family earlier, she has a very independent spirit. She's very much like my mother. I'm more like my father in many ways."

"The first thing I had to do was discover how wonderful my dad is," Debby Erhard said. "I spent a while neglecting my mother in my thoughts. Then a couple of summers ago I realized how wonderful my mother is, and I had to stand back for a second, because I'd never realized it before. I had always taken her for granted; you know, 'She's my mom, had her for years.'

"I don't know why Dad's the most powerful relationship in my life. I think anyone that relates to him comes out of their relationship with him. If my mom didn't give that thing up, of him being the powerful source in our life, I think there would be lots of problems. But my mom's experience with him is the same."

"I think probably my mother's attitudes influenced me more than my father's," Christie Hefner said, "because she's the parent that I lived with—although she happens to reflect many of the same ideas and ideals that he does. I think if I turned out well, she deserves the credit.

"The fact that both my parents are very easy to talk to, and that I didn't have a lot of the generation gap experiences that my peers had, made it much easier. My parents' attitudes were much more in sync with my generation than they were with theirs. It became possible to go with my mother to get the pill, rather than hiding the fact that I was living with someone and wasn't married."

My appreciation of my parents continues to grow and especially my appreciation of the longevity of their relationship. Exactly half of the people I interviewed had divorced parents. Linda McMahon said, "The biggest obstacle in my relationship with my parents was when they split up. That was a real bad time. I knew it was best that they live apart, but, at the same time, I wanted them together. I was pretty young, seventeen or eighteen.

"A lot of things happened during that time. I was very concerned about my mother, naturally; we all were, the four kids. It took a long time, but eventually Mom realized that it was important for the four of us to have a relationship with Dad, too. It's just time, really. The old saying—time heals all. Almost all If it's taught me anything, it's taught me that I'll never be that dependent on a man. Never.

"It must be really hard for a woman in that position," Linda reflected. "Mom was married very young, married for twenty-seven years, and she really lives for her children. A true mother. When my father comes back to town for graduations and holidays and such, he's the celebrity, so he's always the center of attention. I've always felt that it wasn't fair for my mother to be in the background in those situations.

"I guess what I'm trying to say," she concluded, "is that my mother is a great woman. She's really kept our family together. It's nice to have a chance to say that."

All my life I have been asked, "Is it difficult to live up to your father's image?" But it was not until I was twenty-nine years old that it occurred to me that I was also struggling to live up to my *mother's* image. Though it may not be as public as my father's, it has had just as powerful an effect on me. It is *her* superior intelligence, as well as his, that has intimidated and inspired me; her selfless devotion to her family that has made me despair of ever living up to that image of ideal motherhood; her strengths that have made me intolerant of my own weaknesses.

Our mothers are usually the ones from whom we draw our day-to-day strength, the ones who provide us with a sense of stability in the especially chaotic world of celebrity. But they are also the ones with whom we are likely to have day-to-day conflicts. This may be one of the reasons that our relationships with our fathers are easier to resolve—we don't have a history of emotional text to relearn. Perhaps we don't have as three-dimensional a notion of who they are to reevaluate; we're more likely to be exploring new territory.

Because of the public nature of our relationship, my father and I have been forced, to a certain extent, to reassess it, to clean it up. Somehow we've learned to accept each other for who and what we are. My mother and I are still suffering growing pains.

Our mothers are unlikely ever to achieve public recognition for their love and strength and all the things that make them special. Yet as wife of the President and mother of the presidential family, Betty Ford reached a level of celebrity unknown to most wives and mothers. After she became First Lady, she also made a name for herself through charity work and the book she wrote, but basically she is just a mom like mine. The fame and respect Betty Ford received were primarily because of the kind of person she is, the way she dealt with her own and her family's problems, because of the woman and the mother and the wife that she is, not because of her career, or her husband's.

"When you become First Lady," Jack Ford said, "your outlets are increased tenfold. There are lots of things that she got a great deal of recognition for when she became First Lady that she had been involved in for years. Everything from charity work to her saying, 'I brought my kids up to tell the truth, and I'm not afraid for them to say maybe they tried smoking pot or that Susan might have an affair.'

"That's the way she was all her life. Nobody said, 'God, that is unbelievably honest,' until she said it as First Lady. A lot of that greatness was already there; it was just never appreciated in a public sense.

"Of course, you know that nobody is as great as the image that the public has of them. So I tend to see, as I'm sure you do, the more human sides of my mother and my father that make them more lovable but make them more imperfect than maybe most people would see them."

"Are the things you admire about your mother the same things that the public admires?" I asked.

"I would say it's the private things. My admiration is more of a human admiration. She has her feelings and frailties just like the rest of us," he said.

Some of her frailties were made public when Mrs. Ford admitted herself to a drug and alcohol abuse program after an emotional confrontation with her family.

"It was a difficult decision that we all made as a group," Jack said. "I don't want to go into great length about it, because it's really for her to speak about."

"You can speak about your feelings about it," I said.

"I was scared to death. It was terrifying. Here you love this person, and you're having to say such terrible things right to their face. You know, you are telling them the truth. It's not easy to say, 'Look, you have a problem with drinking.'"

"How did that recognition of her problem affect your relationship with her?" I asked.

"Well, the fact that she responded so positively was tremendous in terms of feeling closer to her. We were saying, 'We're telling you this because we love you,' and she's having the normal reactions of—well, it's hard to say, 'Yes, I have problems.' But as quickly as she did respond, she understood that we were doing it because we loved her, and she loved us, and we got over that most difficult hurdle very quickly.

"It was a reinforcement of the strength of the family in general and ours specifically, and about love for your mother and a mother's love for you. To be honest, I felt closer to her at that point than I had at any time in my life."

"What about publicity?" I asked. "Did you think that her choice to go through it all publicly was right?"

"Absolutely. It wasn't easy. I wouldn't call it embarrassing, but it certainly wasn't easy. First of all, in that instance, you have all kinds of people who want to say very nice things—'I think it's wonderful that your mother did that'—but after about the hundred thousandth time, you get a little bit testy about it. You get to the point where she's put it behind her, and you've put it behind you, and that's the way you would like it to be. We all have our pride and self-images, and an admission of that type is obviously not the kind of thing you look forward to discussing. At some point, you want to let sleeping dogs lie."

"I've been thinking a lot lately," I told him, "about how frustrating it must be to be the wife of a famous man—the feelings of inadequacy, the inability to compete—"

"Oh, I'm sure my mother has felt that kind of frustration," he said. "Certainly, I think Mother felt all kinds of frustrations. The first ten years, when my father's career was progressing very rapidly and very successfully, were exciting for her because she was progressing right along. But, ultimately, you say to yourself, 'I want more. I want to have my own sense of self-esteem, and I can't operate entirely out of my husband's successes.' I didn't understand at the time, but I can remember when my mother went through that sort of self-examination and self-criticism. It was competition for internal self-respect and self-esteem.

"The more I think about it, the more difficult it would be for me to conceive of a way to overcome that problem as a woman. But then again, you've got to think that your closest friends are the most important ones, and that's where it's least important that your father be who he is or Susan Newman's father who he is. Because they're either friends or they're not friends.

"My father does not feel the need to be the compelling dominant figure amongst their close group of friends. In a private-home setting, I don't think my mother ever felt those kinds of inadequacies. My father was, consciously or unconsciously, always so good about building her up; he was always respectful and careful [to create] a joint relationship on an equal-treatment basis. More so than any other man I have ever met. I even have friends who consciously try really hard to have a fifty-fifty relationship, and it just doesn't work. It seems so effortless for both my parents to have that kind of give-and-take relationship. They're my ideal of life and marriage and family. [When I was younger] I was more impressed with the outside forces and their deference to my father than I was to [the beauty] of their internal relationship.

"So seldom did they really argue. Maybe they did and I never saw or heard it, but I don't really think that's the case. I think they just have an exceptional marriage. As I grow older and closer to that possibility myself, I find myself more frustrated at my failure to be able to achieve the harmony that they enjoy in their relationship.

"That's an interesting question," he reflected, referring back to the competition—and frustration—of some wives. "My first instinct is no, that my mother didn't go through that. But when I think about it, I think maybe she did and I was insensitive to it, or circumstances suddenly gave her new outlets, and those problems didn't really exist anymore. Because as the kids grew up and went their own ways, I think she *did* have a certain sense of frustration and lack of purpose. But very soon thereafter, she became the wife of the Vice-President, and very soon after that, she became the wife of the President. That was, maybe, the ultimate ointment to soothe those wounds.

"Of course, I guess the bottom line is that there is no way for a woman to compete with a man of Walter Cronkite's stature and station. Maybe the one saving grace for the wife of a politician is that if he becomes President, she becomes First Lady. That's the only way she can compete, and then it's not so hard. But there *is* no First Anchor Lady position."

18.

Francesca Hilton:
All That Glitters

I'm tired of all this nonsense about beauty being
only skin-deep. That's deep enough. What do you
want—an adorable pancreas?
—JEAN KERR, *The Snake Has All the Lines*

Every time I called Francesca to ask if I could interview her,
she said not today, not right now, not this week. She never said
no; she never exactly said yes.

Then one day in March, I came home to find a phone message
hinting that she might be ready to do the interview. I was damned
if I was going to be strung along anymore, but I decided to
give her the benefit of the doubt and at least return her call.

A pleasant, confident voice answered the phone saying, "Ca-
marillo State Hospital, information desk."

I paused for just a second before saying, "Hello, Francesca."
I couldn't believe that anyone could sound so different, and I
was curious to try to find out what had changed.

She asked if I was still interested in the interview. I explained
my time limitations and decided to lay things on the line. I told
her up front that I was only interested if she was willing to be
honest with me, to stop saying that she might want to write her
own book or that she was afraid of repercussions from what she
might reveal to me. Not only did she agree, but we actually set
a firm date.

239

The Gabor and Hilton names conjure up an image of elegance and glitter, of opulent crystal-chandeliered hotels and restaurants with white-coated attendants, of legendary minks and diamonds and glamorous gowns; Francesca's Beverly Hills address had seemed appropriate. However, not all of Beverly Hills is made up of pink-tinted mansions, and, more often than not, it seems, the children of the famous reject their parents' life-styles.

Francesca answered the door of her modest one-bedroom flat in a dark-blue jogging suit and ushered me in, introducing me to the dogs as they ran by. She put on a tape of Middle Eastern music, retrieved falafel dip and wine left over from a party the night before, and sprawled on the couch, saying, "Ask me anything you want, and if I can, I'll answer."

Francesca had hinted, in one of her earlier refusals to be interviewed, at "repercussions" and said that she didn't know if what she had to say should be said at all. However, when I asked her about those fears, she backed away and said, "I don't like to give [interviews]. I've been used by a lot of people who have interviewed me. A lot.

"Once I gave an interview to someone, and it ended up in the *National Enquirer*. I tried to sue, but they're very clever the way they write it. I had a one-hundred-and-one fever, but I did this guy a favor because he's an old friend, and it ended up as a whole page in the *National Enquirer*. I can imagine my family must have loved that.

"I've been very afraid since then to talk too much to anybody. I'd rather write [the articles]." I mentioned my negative feeling towards the *Enquirer*, and she responded, "I don't hate them. You know why? Because they don't pretend to be anything they're not.

"I've been very *honest* with interviewers," she went on. "And it's been to my disadvantage. Because they print everything you say. There are very few journalists who don't. I've gotten—they've written—well, my mother knows how to be a very good interview. She knows just what to say and what not to say."

"Tell me about some of the heavy changes that you mentioned on the phone," I asked. "You said you'd gone through a lot since your father died."

Scott Newman at Mammoth Mountain, California, 1978

Debby Erhard, age five

Jack Erhard, age five

Debby, Werner, and Jack Erhard in San Francisco, 1980

Michael Keeshan at his Dartmouth graduation, 1975, with his father, Bob Keeshan (who received an honorary degree at the same time)

Michael Keeshan, with Bob Keeshan, on the day of his first communion, 1959

Linda McMahon with her father, Ed McMahon, and a friend, 1978

Francesca Hilton, age seven, with
her mother, Zsa Zsa Gabor, 1954

Francesca Hilton and Zsa Zsa
Gabor, in London, 1973

Nancy Sherman (*right*) with her mother, Dee Sherman (Golden), and her father, Allan Sherman, in Beverly Hills, California, 1966

Nancy Sherman, 1980

Polly Styron (*center*) with, left to right, William, Susannah, Tommy, and Rose, 1980

Amy Wallace (*center*) at a café in Stockholm in 1960 with her brother, David, and her father, Irving Wallace

Amy Wallace at the typewriter, in Paris, with her father, Irving Wallace, 1967

Amy and Irving Wallace, 1977

John Blyth Barrymore sharing a drink with his father, John Barrymore, Jr., 1953. Photo by Frank Worth, godfather of John Blyth Barrymore

John Blyth Barrymore,
1980

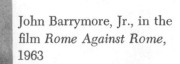

John Barrymore, Jr., in the
film *Rome Against Rome*,
1963

Christopher Buckley with his father, William F. Buckley, Jr., 1980

Christopher Buckley, 1980

Susan Newman (*far right*) with Scott and Paul Newman, her stepmother, Joanne Woodward, and her half sisters, Lissy, Stephanie, Nell, and Clea, 1970

Dad and me at Martha's Vineyard, 1980

"Oh, yeah, growing up," she laughed. "I grew up. I think everyone must go through [not wanting] to grow up, and all of a sudden they realize they have to. I guess it must have happened because my father died, but I don't think it was because he was famous. I don't know . . . maybe he is . . ." she trailed off.

"The week after my father died, before the contents of the will were published, I had at least ten offers from people to go into business with them. Once the will [became public], they found out I got a hundred thousand instead of a hundred million, then I didn't get any more calls. It was very strange, very interesting. Maybe I misread it, too. Maybe I'm overly sensitive. But I don't know.

"I was in a restaurant Saturday night, and I ran into someone I've known for a long time, [although] not as a close friend. She said, 'You look so fit and beautiful now. It must be all the money you inherited.' Everybody assumes that I'm rich now; that's fine, let them think that. I have more money now than I used to have, but I never thought that money made you so happy. I don't know why people always assume that money is the answer.

"Of course, in this town, it does talk, but what about all the rich people who are so unhappy? *Especially* in this town, people's vision is based on materialism. I mean, the more money you have, the bigger you are, right? All of a sudden, you lose all your money and nobody speaks to you anymore, right? I just don't think it's really important what I have."

We got sidetracked by the dip and the dogs, and chatted until the conversation returned to her photography and her acting careers.

"Here I am in a situation where I have very little money right now," she said. "I'm working hard, and I'm doing my second assignment for *Look* right now, and I'm really pushing myself in photography. I'm not an aggressive person," she asserted, a statement that many people who know her would dispute, "and it's very hard for me to push myself. As it was in acting. But in acting, instead of pushing your photography, you're pushing your *flesh*," she said with disgust.

"When I started out acting, I never thought of it as competing with my mother; I really never did. Of course, they would compare me to her a little bit. But once you're in the door, you still have to prove yourself," she said, reiterating a common theme. "And you know that as well as I do.

"I'd rather produce the film and put myself in it—you have much more control. You can end up on the cutting room floor in one minute, but if you're the producer, you're controlling the film.

"It takes longer, though, if you're the kid of a star. I *know* it takes longer, because unless you become an instant star, which is rare, they want to make it very hard for you. They want to make sure you really want to—because they figure you've had everything you need, there's no reason for you being an actress. Haven't you noticed that?

"If we're successful, they'd much rather put us down than if we're nobody. [They think] it's so easy for kids-of. It's *not* easy. It's just as hard; in fact, harder. But everyone thinks you just walk into a casting office, and they'll just give us the part. Well, that's not the way it will ever work.

"They'd much rather give [the part] to an unknown, [because] an unknown doesn't know enough about show business, and they can sock 'em into contracts real easy.

"I think another reason is that they don't believe kids of stars are really serious. They all think we're loaded. I don't know. I suspect, if someone is right for the part, it shouldn't matter who it is. That's the way it's supposed to be. But that's not the way it is. It's all politics.

"But on the other hand, you can have a lot of contacts, too, to help. I'm sure you have a lot of contacts at CBS that help a lot. No?"

"Not as much as one would think," I told her. "Not as much as I would like."

Although Francesca's parentage did not necessarily help her to get acting roles, it was a help in more material ways.

"Usually you can at least get things wholesale. I used to do that with my mom. When I wanted something, I'd call and say, 'This is Zsa Zsa Gabor's secretary . . . ' and I used to say that she likes something very much, or that her daughter wants it."

She seemed amazed when I told her I couldn't do that, that my father hadn't set that example.

"Well, does he make so much money that he can afford to do that?" she asked, trying to find her own explanation. "Or does he just not believe in it?"

I tried to make clear the importance of my father remaining unencumbered by any taint of partiality; accepting favors might compromise his editorial judgment. "For example, if he were to accept an auto from General Motors, and then GM had a safety problem, would he report it? If he chose not to, for editorial reasons, would anyone be sure it wasn't because of his personal relationship with the company?"

"Well, now I understand," Francesca said. "I understand that. In his job, he really can't do that. But he could say his *daughter*—"

"But he won't," I said, and gave up.

"Now I want to ask you something that's rather delicate."

"I don't care," Francesca answered. "Ask me anything."

"Well, to be honest, I've never seen your mother's work, but many people seem to feel that she's not really an actress at all, that she's made it purely on being a glamour girl, a manufactured celebrity."

"Let's face it," Francesca replied, "they always say bad things about famous people, right? They always like to pick on famous people. I guess if my mother wasn't talented, she wouldn't still be around—don't you think? I don't know; she's lasted pretty long. Sure, she's glamorous and made it on her looks, too, but how many people bother anymore about their looks? She's one of the [few] people who cares enough about it to still look good.

"I asked Elizabeth Taylor one day—she was married to one of my brothers once. I said, 'Elizabeth, you can't even go to the bathroom without being in the papers.'

"She said, 'I don't read any of that crap.'

"My mother once told me that if she believed half the things she read about herself, she'd hate herself. There's an old saying: 'When they don't talk about you at all is when you're in trouble.' It's true. The more famous you are, the more they have the tendency to put you down. I'm sure your father gets it, too.

"My father—my father was a bit different. He was a business-man. My mother is still doing what she's doing, still making a lot of money, still working. She's a very bright person. She's not *dumb*.

"You know, when Jack Paar gave up the *Tonight* show, she was offered it. She turned it down. That was before Johnny Carson. Listen, how many actresses and actors go on those shows and can't open their mouths? She can talk, and she's entertaining. People love her. She's *bright*! I don't care what people think about her. I know what I think about her. And that's all that really matters to me."

"What image do you think people have of you because of your parents?"

"When I was doing a show in Las Vegas," Francesca began, "called 'The Name's the Same,' which was with all kids of stars, they had me billed as Francesca Gabor-Hilton. I think they expected us—at least, me—to be a carbon copy of my mother. I would imagine that's what they expect of most kids of stars, you know?

"I can remember hearing people in the audience saying, 'She doesn't look like her mother. . . .' I don't know, I think it depends on what the people are looking for. I *know* they expect a lot of my parents.

"My mother always goes out of the house looking good," she went on. "I don't think the stars of today do it as much, but she really is one of the few glamour ladies left. Which is *great*."

Francesca was starting to become restless and asked if perhaps I could come back another day to finish the interview. Knowing how much difficulty I had had obtaining even this much time with her, I thought I had better not count on a continuation at a later date and instead asked for just a few minutes more.

"One thing I wanted to ask is whether you feel people take advantage of you because of your mother and father?"

"I don't know," she said. "I don't think I've ever had a casting-couch kind of thing, but I've had guys take me out for that reason."

"How do you know?"

"Usually too late," she answered. "You end up falling in love with them and then find out. You can tell if people are phony. They always bust themselves one way or another. Can't you tell?"

"Either I'm terribly naive, or I've never had that happen to me," I said.

"You didn't grow up around here, did you? It's different."

I asked her how old she was when her parents were divorced.

"I wasn't born yet," she said. "I was still in the stomach. Six months when they were divorced. I don't know if you really want to use that . . ."

"Were you close to your dad when you were growing up?"

"Yeah. He was sixty years old when I was born— Maybe we should do the rest of this when you come back," she said suddenly. "Do you mind?"

But we never did get to do a follow-up, and I was left wondering at her seeming avoidance of discussing her father.

Although Francesca's inheritance was substantial, according to *The New York Times* she felt she had been dealt with unfairly and contested her father's will, maintaining that she had been renounced as a result of her father's guilt over marrying her mother outside the Church. I tried to understand the effect that her share would have had on her. After growing up with the onus of a world-renowned name like Hilton and struggling to reach some acceptable attitude about money with the knowledge that someday you would inherit a portion of an enormous corporation, it may indeed have come hard to be rejected with what was by comparison a token sum.

Yet one comes away with the certainty that she will parlay whatever assets are hers to her own advantage. For above all else, Francesca is a survivor.

19.

The Family Name

Oh! while along the stream of time thy name
Expanded flies, and gathers all its fame,
Say, shall my little bark attendant sail,
Pursue the triumph, and partake the gale?
—ALEXANDER POPE, *Essay on Man*

Once the honor of the family name was an important factor in one's code of behavior, but now nobody seems to care much. It is considered old-fashioned, and nowhere except perhaps in movies like *The Godfather* do you ever hear anyone talk of dishonoring the family name.

But for us kids of celebrities, the name has a definite, unavoidable significance. We may not all share a strong sense of pride in the family name, but those of us who have an immediately recognizable one, like Cronkite or Barrymore, are frequently and most definitely made aware that we are not the only ones, or the most important ones, to carry those names.

It is difficult having two lives, two identities. I can't be just Kathy, who goes on dates and gets married and flunks history, because I'm Kathy, Walter Cronkite's daughter, who goes on dates and gets married (with attendant press) and—what? Flunks history? Granted, it makes an amusing anecdote, it may even make a not-so-amusing psychological point about rebellion, but couldn't it also be just that I'm not very good at history? Where does Walter's daughter stop and Kathy begin?

Sometimes people can be unintentionally cruel in their disregard of children apart from their parents. Nancy Sherman related that she went to summer camp when she was ten or eleven, "and all the kids would follow me around, saying, 'Sing your father's song, sing your father's song!' It was just so embarrassing. I had no life of my own. I was just insecure enough that I was only my father's daughter, and nothing else. Other people gave me that identity. I'm probably overemphasizing the way I felt, but I hardly saw my father. He'd be on the road for months at a time once he became famous, and my mother was gone a lot. I was heavy and unattractive, and nobody really seemed to care about Nancy; everybody seemed to care about Nancy, Allan's daughter. I was probably a good student because it was my only sense of identity."

Christie Hefner grew up using her stepfather's surname. "A lot of people didn't really know who my father was until I had my sweet sixteen party at the Playboy mansion," she told me.

"I changed my name back to Hefner when I was in college. I'd been elected Phi Beta Kappa, and I wanted the name Hefner on my certificate. I don't know what it would have been like growing up if everyone had immediately asked if my father was Hugh Hefner. But I believe it was easier growing up with anonymity. By the time people found out that Hugh Hefner is my father, it became an interesting fact about me, rather than the most important consideration.

"Although one summer when I went to the National Music Camp to study voice and drama, I had a crush on a boy who was a couple of years older. At the end of camp, he said he wanted to introduce me to his parents. I was really flattered, because I liked him very much. He brought me over to them, and he didn't even say my name, just, 'Mom and Dad, I want you to meet Hugh Hefner's daughter.' It was very painful for me. But I think I remember it so vividly because it was exceptional; that really did not happen very often.

"Now, being introduced as an executive of *Playboy* makes the rest unnecessary. The people here have been terrifically supportive about letting me have my own identity and my own space.

More and more, people introduce me based on who I am and treat me independently of my father."

"I'm proud of my father," Jenny Buchwald said. "At one point, I wasn't so proud of him, but I'm so damn proud of him now that it's easy to say my name. Because I know there's me, and then there's him, too. I think it was hardest when I didn't believe in myself. There was a time when people would come up and say, 'Yeah, your father's Art Buchwald—let me borrow a thousand dollars.' So then I got in the habit of never telling people what my last name was. They would introduce themselves with both their names, and I would just say, 'That's nice; my name's Jennifer.'

"I couldn't accept it, because people wouldn't see me as me. I hated that. I was trying to find me, and they were relating me to my father. It was too much for me."

Most people admitted to using aliases at least occasionally to avoid entirely the "Are you any relation to . . . ?" problems. Many seemed relieved to learn that they were not alone in their desire sometimes to hide behind another name.

"I've done that," Susan Newman said. "I changed my name and had no communication with *that* side of my family at all, but everyone still knew who I was. I suppose if I went to some remote place and was surrounded by people that had no 'in' to show biz in any capacity, then maybe . . . But I'm always surprised when you're just introduced as Susan Newman, and they say, 'Any relation to Paul?' I don't know how they make these connections."

Monte Schulz concurred: "I do not understand at all how people make the connection with the author Charles Schulz and *Peanuts*. When they see Charles Schulz on checks—I have to sign my name Charles Schulz, Jr.—or if I use his credit card, people say 'Oh, is that *the* Shulz?' It varies, depending on how involved each individual is with The Strip.

"See, no one even mentioned Charlie Brown to me till I was in the sixth grade. Some kid says, 'Are you the son of Charles

Schulz?' I couldn't believe that he'd know that. I went to school with William Wyler's son and nine or ten kids that were more well known. God, nobody ever mentioned Schulz!

"I still don't understand. *Who knows Charles Schulz?* Because I would think, who cares, really? Who cares who writes it? If you like it, you like it. Fame is such a transitory thing, but The Strip, it just exists. It's just being added to, day by day. It's always going to be there. I think The Strip is the only thing that matters."

I was nineteen when I was first married, and I kept that name for some years after my divorce because I liked the anonymity it offered. It was very handy to have a legitimate alias, not to have to answer The Question all the time. I also used to use it when I was broke, for example, and going to the free clinic. I figured they'd just laugh if someone named Cronkite came in and said they were broke and needed help.

I must admit that the power of the Cronkite name was probably a significant factor in reaching people for interviews, but I find it hard to believe that there are people naive enough to think that I "have it made" in my acting career because of my father.

When I first came out to California, I was still using my ex-husband's name. I battled with myself, not to mention with various advisers, about which name I was going to use professionally. I knew whatever name I used at the beginning of my career I would have forever, and I wanted it to be my *own* name, not my ex-husband's.

I think that one way in which the name has helped in my acting career is that because of its familiarity, a director or casting person might be more likely to remember me than if I were Kathy Smith. And that certainly helps.

Besides, in an odd way I felt that I owed my father that, the pleasure of pride in me if I did make it. I hoped to bring further honor and fame to an already famous name.

I assumed that, having grown up in the theater, Mary Crosby probably never had to make that decision. "Well," she said, "that came with who I am. I don't really like my name. Crosby is fine, but Mary . . . it can't go any lower. I wanted to change my name to Karen, or something. Anything but Mary. And Mary Frances, which I used until recently, sounds either Southern or pretentious to me. 'Mary Frances!'" she demonstrated in a disciplining, convent-school tone of voice.

"Because of my name, I was able to get things that I never would have gotten otherwise," she continued. "I'm very proud of who I am, and when people know me, they know *what* I am. And until they know me, they couldn't know, anyway. I'm proud of what the family members have done. I think Daddy gave our name a lot of respect, and I respect it. I'm not into rebelling."

In the film business especially, it is impossible to know the real reasons why one has lost a job to someone else, but how sad to lose a job because of one's parents. I was once told by a casting director that if he had the choice between two equally qualified actors, "one wealthy and one struggling," he would choose the one who was "struggling." The assumption that we are not struggling, or do not need the job because of our parentage, is a cruel and galling one. It doesn't matter how well off your parents are— or even you yourself—there are more important reasons for needing work.

I have been challenged by people in the industry saying bluntly, "You can have anything you want; why would you want to be an actor? You can't really be serious about it; you don't have to starve." And, "Why should I give you a job? What about those poor kids who come here from Iowa with stars in their eyes?"

In fact, those of us who have grown up on the fringes of the industry may actually be better equipped to deal with the realities of the business. We know that it *is* a business; we have seen first-hand how hard one must work and what a heavy toll it takes on one's life. We have seen behind the façade and know that being a celebrity is not all limousines and champagne. If we do choose to pursue that career ourselves, we do it with our eyes open, able to commit ourselves simply to doing our job, less distracted by the glitter. No one can feel satisfied without meaningful work to do, and to be denied that because of the success of our parents is ironic indeed.

❊   ❊   ❊

"My parents were very supportive," Mary Crosby said. "They never said, 'Look, I know this producer. . . .' I'm sure my father could have done that, but he never wanted to, and I wouldn't have wanted that. Having doors slammed in your face is a good experience, and I'm glad I've had it."

"The whole industry is built on nepotism," Chris Lemmon stated, "whether it comes from a father or a friend or an agent: what gets you in the door on an interview is the fact that you know somebody who knows the person who's interviewing you. Now, once you get in the door, it doesn't make any difference if you're the president of Universal's son or Carter's son or the trash collector's son. It all depends on how good you are. My father named me Christopher Boyd Lemmon, so that if I ever did go into the industry I could be Christopher Boyd. But I don't want to be Christopher Boyd. My name is Christopher Lemmon. I don't care. I'm proud to be his son. I've been noticed more as his son than as myself, but it doesn't bother me."

Lorenzo Lamas had never considered changing his name either, but Allen Carr, the producer of *Grease*, suggested he change it to something less ethnic, "because Tom Chisolm [the character Lorenzo played] is supposed to be this all-American guy," Lorenzo said. "So I said, 'To what? Can you think of a name that would stand out more? Do you know of any better name than Lorenzo Lamas?'" he said with a movie-marquee flair. "Allen said, 'How about Larry?'"

Werner Erhard's children have had the opportunity to try out several different surnames; they prefer Erhard. "For one thing," Debby said, "I'm in the world of *est* a lot, and it takes a lot of time to explain, 'Yes, I'm his daughter, but I have a different last name.' People have their stuff about me being Werner's daughter, anyway, and I might as well be right up front and have my last name be Erhard."

Jack and Debby's famous name is not universally recognized, but when it is, "People are interested, and they want to talk,"

Debby said. "And if they have bad feelings about est, they want to tell me that, too."

Jack jumped in to assure me that, "Usually, though, they're pretty turned on. They're more interested in the training than in us."

"When did you decide to take Erhard as your surname?"

"We were actually asked a year and a half ago," he said. "You know, I love being Werner Erhard's son. It's a privilege, and I like people finding out who I am."

John Barrymore felt differently. "In a way, it's really an albatross, you know? I resented being John as a kid. I figured, after having used the name twice, did they *have* to use it again? I felt like I really got stiffed by not getting an original name. I hated being John Barrymore the Third. Especially John, the most common name in the English language. "

One way in which having the same name can be confusing is illustrated by an incident that happened at the restaurant where John works. "I heard somebody say my name, and I walked over and said, 'Yes?'

"They said, 'What do you want?'

"I said, 'Didn't you just call me?'

"They said, 'No, we were talking about John Barrymore.'

"And I said, 'Oh. Excuse me.'

"Unless I'm being introduced to someone specifically about work," he told me, "I always just introduce myself as John. Sometimes, just for a joke, I'll introduce myself under an assumed name. Very often, in fact. I'll say, 'Bill.'

" 'Bill who?'

" 'Bill me later.'

"They think I'm kidding when I introduce myself anyway. I went on an open call, an audition, in New York. You put your name on a list when you get there, and then you have to wait for hours. Finally, the guy gets to my name and says, 'Hey, some joker put John Barrymore.' He skipped it. Never called my name.

"It does put a burden on. It's impossible for me to get an objective review. They're gonna go hard on me, no doubt about it. Sometimes there's an attitude of, 'Oh, fuck, here's another Barrymore to look at,' and sometimes it's, 'Here's another Barry-more—well, he'd better be good.' Thank goodness I've never played Hamlet!"

Francesca Hilton, with two famous parents, feels ambivalent about her family names. "I think it's hard to have two parents [who are famous] but my father was never a movie star or any-thing, so it's a little bit different. I don't think, because my name's Hilton—it's probably a little bit easier than if it was *Gabor*-Hilton.

"When I tried acting, one agent wanted me to change my name to Gabor-Hilton. I said, no way. The first thing a casting director would ask me was, how is my family and my mother. Then I found out that my agent was selling me on my family's name, you know? I'd been an actress in England for three years and studied hard and was a really good actress, and they were selling me on my family's *name*. I got furious. Finally, eventually, I just gave it up."

The children of famous people often consider whether or not to adopt a more common name. Occasionally, other people will decide to adopt a famous name. I was horrified to hear that the Cronkite name was being used as an alias by a football fan. My father was surprised to receive a call one day from the manager of a West Coast football team, asking if he would please explain to my brother that union rules simply forbade him to sit on the bench with the football players.

"Mr. Cronkite," the man said, "we're glad to give your boy the fifty-yard-line passes every year, but he just can't be allowed to sit on the bench."

"I don't know what you're talking about," was my father's reply.

"Well, your son, Jim—"

"For one thing," my father said, "I don't have a son named Jim, and for another, the son I do have is in boarding school in New England, not in California watching football games." He tactfully did not mention that my brother was not even much of a football fan.

Apparently, somebody had gotten in touch with the manager of the team through the local CBS station by saying that he was Jim Cronkite, Walter Cronkite's son. Not only had he finagled tickets to the games, but to the local opera and theater as well, and who knows what else.

They never did catch the fellow but, by making it known that they were onto him, stopped his activities. I wonder if that kind of thing is going on all over the country? I find it bizarre and a little creepy to think that someone might be impersonating me, especially to get privileges that I would not take advantage of myself, or that, to sound a little old-fashioned, someone might dishonor the name.

I know there are those who are quick to accuse me of "using" my father's name professionally, whatever that means. I find that sort of thinking not only absurd but also infuriating. It is yet one more denial of who I am, as separate from who my father is.

Cronkite just happens to be my name. It is my name as well as that other famous Cronkite's name. Is it to be his exclusively by rights of prior use? Must every generation pick a new surname to insure a separate identity?

I have not been raised to use the name; my father has not set that example. He does not go on junkets, accept favors from foreign or domestic governments, or live on freebies from generous companies. He is appalled by the attitude of some famous folk of "anything you can't get for free isn't worth having," and he would not risk people questioning his impartiality, no matter what the advantages.

I remember one rather sweet example of his attitude when we went into a crowded restaurant with no reservations. He hung back and said, "Let's see how we're treated without using The Name." It didn't occur to him, I guess, that his face would be recognized, anyway, and we would be whisked immediately to a good table.

But as familiar as his face is, it is not always recognized. Once, in Maine, we were walking down a back road to town when it began to rain. A nice old man stopped to offer us a lift, and, after talking to Dad in the front seat for a mile or so, he said, "What's your name, buddy? If you don't mind saying . . . ?"

"Uh, it's Walter Cronkite," Dad said, a little surprised.

Luckily, the road was clear as the man recklessly peered around into Dad's face. After a long moment he said, unconvinced, "Naaaah," and turned back to his driving.

20.
John Blyth Barrymore:
Life in the Theater

I am thy father's spirit,
Doom'd for a certain term to walk the night,
And for the day confin'd to fast in fires,
Till the foul crimes done in my days of nature
Are burnt and purg'd away. But that I am forbid
To tell the secrets of my prison-house,
I could a tale unfold whose lightest word
Would harrow up thy soul, freeze thy young blood,
Make thy two eyes, like stars, start from their spheres,
Thy knotted and combined locks to part
And each particular hair to stand on end,
Like quills upon the fretful porpentine:
But this eternal blazon must not be
To ears of flesh and blood. List, list, O list,
If thou didst ever thy dear father love—
         —WILLIAM SHAKESPEARE, *Hamlet*

Although John Blyth Barrymore may at times be discomfited by his name, he is proud of his heritage. John is a handsome, craggy-faced young man of twenty-six, with an identifiably Barrymore profile and demeanor, and a thick red mane of hair. He swears frequently, laughs loudly and cheerily, and tells stories with an eloquent flourish. He lived in Los Angeles most of his life, moving back to New York City from time to time to pursue his career on the stage. At the time of this interview, he had a paying job waiting tables, which he hates, while appearing in nonpaying showcase productions so far off Broadway that they're almost in New Jersey.

John was on his way to an uptown movie theater, so we met for the interview at my parents' house. He bypassed the arm-

273

chairs, choosing instead to sit alone on the sofa where he could more easily stretch out his lanky frame. He turned down a drink, but, as we talked, occasionally bummed cigarettes, saying with a grin, "I'm trying to quit, but my doctor says I'm not getting enough nicotine."

I asked him where he fit into the complex Barrymore family tree.

"I am John Barrymore the Third," he began. "I am John Barrymore, Jr.'s, son, John Barrymore's son's son. Ethel and Lionel were my grandfather's brother and sister."

"So you're the third generation?"

"Well, you could look at it that way. I'm really the fourth generation of actors. My great grandfather, Herbert Blyth, was a famous stage actor in his time. It was just because there were no movies that he wasn't world-famous.

"I've always wanted to change my name back to Blyth and someday will. My full name is John Blyth Barrymore," he said, letting it roll off his tongue with pride, "but I think of myself as John Blyth, because Blyth is the real family name. In Herbert's day, you were a pimp or a whore if you were an actor, so he changed his name to Maurice Barrymore to save his family from disgrace. He married a famous actress of that time, too, Georgianna Drew.

"Now, my cousin Tony Fairbanks—he's no relation to Douglas, he's my grandfather's daughter's son, right? John and Delores Costello had two children, my father and my aunt. And he's my aunt's son. But he's changed his name to Barrymore now, because he's an actor and because there's a lot of confusion. They always think he's Douglas Fairbanks' son," he laughed.

"Ethel built the theater," John said, continuing the family saga. He assumed I knew he referred to the Ethel Barrymore Theater on Broadway. "I don't know what happened when she died, but somehow it belongs to the Schuberts now. Ethel's grandson lives in New York—John Drew Miglietta. He's a stage actor."

I asked him about the current crop of Barrymores.

"Well," he replied, "I have five half sisters, none of them from the same pair of people. My father has three daughters, and my mother has two. All except one are much younger than I am. I'm the last chance, as they say. The last of the Mohicans. The last of the Barrymores. It's up to me. Unless my father has another son. But I don't think that's likely.

"Except that now my cousin's changed his name, and he's about to get married, too, so that'll start a whole new branch over there. Meanwhile, I'll probably change my name back to Blyth and start another branch down this way.

"As an actor, watching actors, I relate most to and I understand more about acting through my own family's work than through anybody else's. There's an incredible connection. I see so much of myself in it, and so much of my father in my grandfather's work, that it's really personally affecting more than any other actor that I see. I can see what he's doing to himself to evoke the performance.

"My grandfather did the same thing that I'm doing, although he was an artist in Manhattan before he was an actor. It's always the same for an actor—you do plays, you build your way up. Except my father was different because he was so close to my grandfather's generation that when he decided he wanted to be an actor, they threw twenty movie scripts at him immediately. I didn't have that advantage. On the other hand, I'm not an alcoholic. That's a good start. Although I am enough of a womanizer that I probably will get some horrible disease someday," he laughed. "Fortunately, penicillin has been invented.

"I'm a lot like my grandfather and my father, I guess. I'm into having a good time. Not to the level where it interrupts my life, but as long as it's a nice diversion. That's the thing. My grandfather was a brilliant actor. So were Lionel and Ethel, but they were essentially doing it for the money. And because their parents were actors. They were all into their own lives, their own pleasures, having a good time. I'm the same way. I really enjoy life itself, and when I'm not acting, and I'm not breaking my balls in a restaurant, that's how I spend my time. So I guess you could say I'm following the tradition all around.

"My grandfather died in the forties of drinking; my great-grandfather died of syphilis. He went nuts. It was a heavy thing for my grandfather, according to a book I read about the family, 'cause they all—John, Lionel, and Ethel—all watched their father go nuts for five years before he finally died.

"I'm certain, though, that I won't die the same way—unless the damage has already been done—and that my father will.

"My grandfather, [Errol] Flynn, W. C. Fields, [John] Carradine, John Decker—they were like a group of Hollywood madmen. And the same thing with my father and the group he was in with. He has at one time or another rubbed elbows with all of the underground of Hollywood—Dennis Hopper, Peter Fonda, [Jack] Nicholson—all of those characters. He's about the same age as Dennis Hopper—he's only forty-six, my father. His hair went completely white almost overnight when he was thirty-two. It's hereditary. My father started going gray when he was seventeen. It was helped along, I'm sure, by the dope thing. Over the years he's been a doper, a yogi, a raw-food vegetarian, then back to something else. Don't get the image that he's been drinking since he was sixteen years old, because he hasn't. Whatever he does, he does very intensely, whether it's being healthy or being destructive.

"It's common knowledge that he's experimented with drugs. He's gotten into it heavy, and then he's gotten out of it. He's an absolute extremist. He can be so intelligent, beautiful-speaking, warm—he can be a saint. Or he can be Colonel Dorf. And there are very few in-betweens. He's everything from heaven to hell.

"One thing about him—he's never boring.

"You ever hear of a series called *T.H.E. Cat*? They put money on the table, the highest bread they'd ever offered, for him to do that series. After he'd walked out on ten pictures. And they wrote the thing for him. He would have been brilliant. My father is an incredible athlete. He was perfect for that show. All he had to do was sign his name, and he said, 'I don't think I can do this shit.'

"My father's been busted over and over. He's the king of the victimless crime. After a while they just did it as a joke. Last time I went down there [to the police station], I said, 'I'm here for John Barrymore.'

"They said, 'Take him. Please.' They sort of like him, the L.A. cops. They've just made sure he hasn't gotten too drunk before getting behind the wheel. I mean, he's sort of like a cult hero to them.

"Do you know about my Aunt Diana? She was John's first daughter, and she died. Of overindulgence. Just because the—you know—the Barrymore thing killed her." The movie *Too Much Too Soon* was based on Diana's tragic life and death. "It's the same thing that's happened to my father. His being a 'Junior' destroyed his career. My father survived, but it killed her.

"I'm going tonight to see my grandfather in *Jekyll and Hyde*, which I've already seen, but I love. God, you know, it's been thirty-five years since the guy died, and they're still talking about him. People talk about his *Hamlet* like they've seen it, you know?

"One of those pop-art poster companies called me and said, 'We want to use your grandfather's profile and a marquee that says "The Great Profile" on a Cadillac commercial. Is that okay?'

"I said, 'Sure, it's okay. How much?'

"They said, 'What do you mean?'

" 'How much are you willing to pay us?'

" 'What do you mean, pay you?'

"I said, 'You'll be hearing from us.'

"Got together with my father and our lawyer. We got about fifteen grand out of it We split it three ways, because my father owed him a lot of money. But that was the only time we actu ally received any recompense from all this exploitation. If I had the bread, I would pursue these things. It just pisses me off that all these people are cashing in. You know, when a fuckin' bar with my name on it won't even give me a free drink, there's something wrong."

21.
Family Friends

Be . . . rather sweet than familiar; familiar than intimate; and intimate with very few, and upon very good grounds.

—JAMES PUCKLE, *The Club*

One of the questions I'm asked most often is, "Did you know a lot of famous people when you were growing up?"

Well, I never thought of family friends as famous people; they were simply Aunt this or Uncle that. Most of my parents' closest friends weren't famous people at all. They were chums from long ago, from college, from starving young reporter days, ordinary people like Mom and Dad.

Most people who don't know my parents may not think of them as "ordinary people," but they are. They grew up as old-fashioned, small-town kids (although that may offend my mother; she still thinks of Kansas City as the center of the universe), and even now they are very much that way. We are more likely to have pot roast than filet mignon, and "use it up, wear it out, make it do, or do without" is Mom's ingrained credo. I never have been able to understand why people are surprised when they meet my parents for the first time. "But they're so warm and friendly and down-to-earth," they say.

That in itself may be a reason why we didn't have a lot of

279

famous friends. My parents aren't caught up at all in the trappings of fame, the movie-star mentality and games, and they don't have a lot of patience with those who are.

I must admit that I still become star-struck and speechless when introduced to people I admire. My most embarrassing moment was probably when my parents treated me to a Broadway show, *Two By Two*, and a trip backstage to meet the star, an old friend of Dad's and a longtime favorite of mine, Danny Kaye.

When we entered the dressing room, he greeted my father enthusiastically, kissed my mother, and then turned to be introduced to me.

I had sat through *The Five Pennies* over and over, weeping at the same scenes every time; I had spent hours when young chanting the tongue-twisting "The vessel with the pestle is the brew that is true" rhymes from *The Court Jester*, and every week at the end of his television series, I had wished that I could skip around that circle with him. Face to face with this most warm and loving man whom we had just seen in yet another magical performance, I lost control and fell into his arms, sobbing inexplicably with emotions that had no other expression.

He laughed kindly and gave me a hug, but I was mortified by my behavior and retreated as soon as I could, without having said a word to him.

Although our home life was pretty quiet, we often met interesting people when we traveled with Dad on assignment. We always kept our shots and passports up-to-date, so that we could leave at a moment's notice if the opportunity arose. But because Mom worried about our being in his way when he was working, and Dad would never allow us to miss school, we didn't travel with him when we were younger as much as we would have liked. With all the traveling he does in the course of his work, when he has a vacation, he would rather be on the boat.

One place we did go was Cape Canaveral in the early days of the space program. Luckily for us, the missile launchings often took place right around spring vacation, so we could accompany Dad. Sitting on the night-chilled sand, reporters, astronauts, scientists, and families, we watched across the bay to where the first unmanned rockets rose into the dark, their brilliant fire dominating the clear star-shining sky.

I vividly recall watching those first rockets, but I can't remember the excitement of my first plane trip because I was so young. I don't ever remember *not* traveling, and there's nothing I'd rather do. To Mom, too, who was raised in plain old K.C., Mo., traveling is one of the greatest rewards of being married to a reporter.

She summed it all up by saying, "I used to think that it would be heaven to spend a vacation seeing all the great monuments of the world. But now that I've seen all of those monuments, I can go to Spain and just stand in front of one Goya."

Chip has traveled with the folks even more than I have. When I was young, there were three of us kids, rather an unruly group to manage. By the time Chip was old enough to take along, Nancy and I had pretty much flown the coop—gone off to boarding school or gotten married. It seems to be a family tradition that married children have to pay their own way, and the nature of setting up housekeeping being what it is, it often worked out that married children stayed home.

Eventually there was only Chip, the last of the litter, left, and he went everywhere with them. Therefore, he had more opportunity to meet various celebrities. He remembers meeting Arthur C. Clarke in Mexico when Clarke was working on his book, *Rendezvous with Rama*. He sat with Chip, drawing on a cocktail napkin the complicated satellite world he had invented for the book and saying, "Let's see what Kubrick can do with this!"

Nora Davis told me that her parents had worked with Sidney Poitier and Harry Belafonte in a basement theater group in Harlem. "They all came up through the ranks together and then went their various ways. There's a fellowship among actors, anyway, but it's especially keen among black actors, as far as I can see.

"When I was in the fifth grade or so, my father and Sidney

and some other actors came to my school and did *Little Red Riding Hood*," she said, laughing at the memory. "I can't remember whether Daddy was the wolf, or Sidney."

"We first moved to Hollywood when I was eight and a half years old," Nancy Sherman related. "One morning, really early, my parents heard this harp music and thought, 'What, are we dead? Are we in heaven?' This was like seven in the morning.

"They went next door to inquire about the music, and this sweet little old man opened the door and introduced himself as Arthur [Harpo] Marx.

"This is how my father got discovered. He was still working on game shows at that point, and Harpo gave this party and invited my parents. George Burns and Gracie Allen were driving up just as my parents were walking over, and George Burns looked at my father and said, 'Boy, please park the car,' and my father said, sure. He was so excited to meet George Burns. So my mother just stood there while he went and parked the car.

"He overheard George Burns saying to Jack Benny at the party, 'Isn't that nice how Harpo invites the car-parking boys into the party? He's so great like that.'"

I was particularly curious about the relationship between Ed McMahon and Johnny Carson. Linda McMahon clarified it for me.

"They consider each other one of the best friends they both have," she said. "They've known each other for a long time, and after my parents' divorce, when my father was single and Mr. Carson was single, they used to pal around a lot. But it's different now, and Mr. Carson is not a social man. I guess there's a line you have to draw. I think people sort of forget that he's my father's boss, but they're very good friends."

Christie Hefner, whose parents were divorced when she was young, told me, "I didn't really grow up meeting famous people, so I can remember very well the first trips to L.A. and the first time I looked around the room and realized there were actually famous people there, people who, when they walk down the street, cause other people to turn and look at them. I don't remember ever thinking, 'How exciting!' I remember thinking, 'Great, I really want to talk to that person.' It would never occur to me to ask for someone's autograph. It just seems silly to me. But mostly when I was with my father, it was just family," Christie went on. "Sometimes we caught somebody coming or going, and there were a couple of people like Shel Silverstein who had been a longtime buddy. He's wonderful. He's sort of the uncle that everybody wants to have.

"I've never been awestruck by people. I don't think it's because I've met well-known people. I just think some people are awestruck, and some people are not. It's not in my nature.

"But I love the fact that I have the opportunity to meet people like Masters and Johnson, Bella Abzug, and Warren Beatty, people who are so creative and have achieved so much. It's like a dream to be able to sit and talk with those people."

"In a lot of ways, I've led a life that other kids from upper- or middle-class families would not," John Blyth Barrymore said. "I've associated with thieves, dealers, murderers, counterfeiters, bank robbers, famous crazies. I've met people that the average kid from Beverly Hills would never meet. Not only met them but worked for them or spent time with them.

"As a result of my father being who he is, the circle that he hangs out with, I've gotten closer to the seamier side of life. I spent a few days with Tim Leary before I left L.A. Tim is a strange guy. I don't know him that well, but I kept seeing him around L.A., and one day I ran into him at a party.

"He said, 'Who are you?' I told him. 'Oh, I knew your dad in Switzerland,' he said. 'You seem like a really intelligent guy. I'm looking for intelligent agents.'

"I said, 'What does that mean?'

"He said, 'Well, you know.' Later, he invited me over to his house, and we rapped about politics and all the stuff he's into. The average kid wouldn't end up in Tim Leary's apartment talking about all that. It's just because of who I am."

* * *

For several years, there has been a small informal travel group consisting of my parents; James and Mari Michener; the late Bob Considine and his wife, Millie; Willis and Doris Player; Art and Ann Buchwald; Neil and Judith Morgan; and Dick Barkle—plus assorted children—who explore such places as Tahiti, Java, and Mexico. Most of them turned their experiences into articles. My family just went for the adventures.

Chip has been on several of these trips, accompanied always by one of his Frisbees. He was even mentioned in Michener's book, *Sports In America*.

"I turned him onto it," Chip said, "like at airports waiting for the plane. Michener would call out after many a throw, 'Did you see that flight?' enthralled by the aerodynamics of it, as well as the fun."

It was Chip who pointed out to me that Dad doesn't travel like the average tourist. It's all planned out, his secretary has typed up an itinerary in quintuplicate, he is expected everywhere he goes, greeted by the manager, never left waiting, and never bumped from flights or left without a room in an overbooked hotel. He gets right in and is taken care of right away.

However, this does not apply to tennis courts. One year, Mom, Dad, and Chip visited Australia and New Zealand. As always, the men traveled with their tennis racquets and played whenever they got the chance. That wasn't often in New Zealand, where their hotel seemed to be filled with tennis-playing travelers who had booked the courts night and day.

One morning, just at dawn, they were awakened by a violent earthquake. Mom was thrown clear out of bed, and by the time she had gathered her wits together enough to realize what had happened, Dad and Chip had already jumped into their tennis clothes, grabbed their racquets, and run out the door, calling back, "At least there'll be no one on the courts!"

I have also had the opportunity to meet interesting non-famous people I probably would not have met if I had come from a less renowned family. Not Timothy Leary. Not even politicians and movie stars, just people living what they may feel are ordinary lives, but lives that are endlessly fascinating to me, lives as foreign to most of us as the supposedly glamorous world of the movie star.

For instance, how many people have a chance to glimpse the life of a Down East lobsterman, a man who gets up every day before dawn and spends all day motoring around in the fog, setting and retrieving lobster pots, because that's what his father did, and that's what his brothers and cousins do.

One summer, I spent some time on the family boat, *Wyntje*, cruising the Maine coast. One evening, as we sat at anchor in a tiny harbor under gathering rain clouds, a lobster boat pulled up alongside.

"Mr. Cronkite? I thought you might like to have these lobsters. I'm sorry there aren't more, but it's the off season, and these are all I got today." A young man held out a box full of small, sweet lobsters.

"Oh, no, I . . ." my father started to protest.

"Now, you gave me your autograph on the dock, and I want to give you these. Like I said, there would have been more, but . . ."

Dad interrupted his apologies and invited him to stay and help us eat them. The man seemed embarrassed and refused, but when Mom intimated that her inexperience in cooking lobster might not do them justice, he agreed to stay for a drink and help out.

I think, in fact, we got a little drunk, but what a dinner! What an evening! Good food—the sweetest, most tender lobster we've ever eaten, lemon butter, freshly dug Maine potatoes, beer—good company, and good conversation.

"Now imagine," our guest said, poring over a chart of the bay, "that my hand is the lobsters. They come right up the channel, here, so this is where you want to put your traps . . . right . . . here."

He told us that most of his colleagues don't know how to swim, even though they live and work on the water. "A fellow just drowned here a couple of weeks ago. If he knew how to swim, I guess he would have been saved. Actually," he added, *sotto voce*, "he was a cousin of mine." We started to offer our sympathies, and he stopped us, saying, "Oh, no, that happens. When this is your life, you know that that's a chance you take . . . and it happens. That's all there is to it."

We waited and waited the next morning for him to show up in his funny little lobster boat and take us out with him to see how it's done, but he never showed. Finally, we had to cast off, or we wouldn't have made the next night's port before dark.

We heard the end of the story weeks later from a friend of my parents who lived on the bay. Our lobsterman had indeed been a little tipsy when the party broke up. So much so that he had run his boat up on the rocks and had spent all night on board, drinking and carousing with his buddies. They teased him mercilessly about being such a fancy yachtsman now, after spending the evening on Walter Cronkite's yawl, that he couldn't even keep his own boat off the rocks. They didn't get it afloat until near dawn.

If my father had not been a recognizable figure, we would have seen the lobstermen, we might have taken pictures of them as they passed, but one in particular would not have come over to the boat. And we would not have spent the evening talking to this fascinating man about his life, his life-style.

As Chip and I discussed the various people we had met, he spoke of "the Zen of being Walter Cronkite's son," whatever that means. When I asked him to clarify for his less philosophical sister, he mentioned one of his several trips to the LBJ ranch with Dad. He was sitting on the front porch of the ranch house with Dad, LBJ, and Lady Bird when a bee landed on him.

"Lady Bird said something, and I didn't say anything. That," he said, "is the Zen of being Walter Cronkite's son."

I still don't know what he means.

22.

Susan Newman:
Points

Yet in my lineaments they trace
Some features of my father's face.
—Byron, *Parisina*

I met Susan for the first time in December 1978, when we appeared together on a talk show. She seemed at first defensive, almost hostile, but as we became better acquainted in the following months, she began to be more open. Susan describes herself as "suspicious" and "protective." Several of her acquaintances and childhood friends have said, "I don't think anyone's ever really known Susan."

We met at her parents' luxurious antique-filled East Side apartment. It was a rainy evening, and, after the doorman admitted me and I took myself upstairs in a cranky old elevator with a hand-operated grate, I was welcomed with the warm and comforting aroma of freshly baked brownies. I perched on the edge of the velvet couch and looked around, trying to decide which was more intimidating, the owners of the apartment or the furnishings: gilded wood statues of Jesus, old dark portraits of somber faces, and spindly-legged chairs. Susan offset the tone of the room by sitting cross-legged on the floor. She was wearing an eclectic outfit composed of a long velveteen skirt, a Université de Paris sweatshirt, and, over that, a very pretty silky cocoa-colored blouse.

Susan fascinated me, and I was pleased that she gave me the opportunity to get to know her even a little, to enjoy her intelligence, her unique perspectives, her humor. Also, she was one of the few people I interviewed who was willing to talk about the anger and about some of the problems of being a celebrity's child.

I asked her whether she had grown up mostly with her mother or with her father.

"With my mother," she replied. "Really, my relationship with Dad probably started when I became a little older. I think he relates to his children better when they're older; I'm sure he'd agree with me on this. He just can't get into babies. I can understand it, but it makes for a very peculiar time growing up. In the beginning, Dad and I mainly had those glorious, divorced weekends, fairy-tale weekends, really. We'd have lunch at the Plaza and then maybe go to F.A.O. Schwartz and pick out one toy, of which mine were mostly dolls; then we'd take a carriage ride around Central Park or go to the zoo, or something like that. They were very magical. And had nothing to do with reality.

"And then if we went someplace for dinner, people would make more of a to-do than if you walked in with your mother, and you don't quite understand what's going on.

"There are people interrupting, and you're never quite clear what they want. Even though you know what an autograph means, you don't know why they want it from your father.

"I think that constant interruption is probably the most bothersome thing about the fame. Maybe that's where some of the anger comes from: you haven't seen your old man in four months, and you're trying to tell him how you flunked out of school and your boyfriend is a junkie—or whatever the major catastrophe is—and people are coming up and . . ." She finished the sentence with a frustrated gesture. "Time elements are very disproportionate," she went on, "and I think that affects the relationship."

"Do you have ways of compensating for the lack of time together?" I asked.

"Not really. Sometimes if I feel too neglected—whether it's my fault, his fault, or nobody's fault—then I just withdraw. I'm not real good at unpleasant encounters and particularly when they're family-oriented. So if it gets too out of hand, I put my tail between my legs and make a quick retreat. There are certain things I just won't deal with.

"I think, in some ways, it's very alienating, this life. It depends on your personality makeup, like my being suspicious of new people, but I think it alienates the entire family on different levels."

"Alienates from the outside world, you mean?"

"From the *real* world," she answered. "Because I don't think that these people are living in a particularly real world. Doesn't make it bad, but it's just not real.

"I think my father's as confused by his fame as we are. He was just a nice blue-eyed kid from Shaker Heights. Who was to know that old Skinnylegs Newman was going to become such a big thing? Obviously, it's changed and affected him, but I do think he's pretty down-to-earth.

"My fear for him is that he's so isolated. There are certain things about life that he doesn't even remember how to do anymore, basic, basic things that most people have to deal with. He doesn't know how expensive something is, and you'll get really pissed off and say, 'Dad! Don't you realize . . . ?' Or he'll ask you to go into a store on Rodeo Drive and see if they have this shirt he wants, and you're dressed *comme ça*," she said, gesturing at her rumpled clothes, "and you walk in and cannot get anyone to look cross-eyed at you. Five minutes later, when he comes walking in, fifteen employees come running over. That's when I'll say, 'Gee, Dad, I was in here ten minutes, and I couldn't get anyone to wait on me by screaming "Fire!"' And he'll look apologetic. I don't think he even realizes how much people do for him."

She returned to the subject of her father's economic ignorance. "Right around the time that the hippie business was going on for me, I had gone to Sears and bought two summer shifts—for a dollar ninety-eight apiece. I thought I had really discovered the bargain of the century, but when I went to spend the weekend in Connecticut with my father, I remember being really hurt that he did not applaud my very down-to-earth, pragmatic approach to finance. It's something that has stuck with me ever since as an example of how he's in a different league. Because he is insulated from certain avenues of life, it just doesn't mean anything to him anymore, although I suppose if he bought a racing car on sale, that would mean something to him.

"And again, there was my father's naiveté when I did the movie for Steven Spielberg [*I Wanna Hold Your Hand*], and Dad said, 'How many points did you get?' *

"I said, 'Dad, I hate to tell you this, dear, but I was glad to get the *salary* I got—what do you mean, *points*?' He doesn't know —he thinks anyone who makes a movie walks away with five million dollars."

"Yet he's one of the few big stars that you never hear about pulling star trips and throwing his weight around," I commented.

"No, but . . ." she replied hesitantly and then launched into her story. "This was one incident that really pissed me off and made me think, 'How unfair.' All men are created equal and all that, right? Well, we were driving back from New York to Connecticut in one of Dad's souped-up VW's—this was quite a few years ago. He was driving like a banshee, and I was holding on to my seat, and the cop's red light goes off behind us. Dad pulls over to the side. Obviously the policeman did not realize"—she hesitated just a moment—"who Dad was.

"The policeman got out of the car with a chip on his shoulder and yelled, 'Do you realize how fast you were going? Your back taillight is out, and you're getting a ticket for that, and your front tire . . .'

"He was almost going to search the damn car!

"Dad was just sitting there, and I'm beginning to wonder: is he going to say, 'Officer, excuse me, I don't think you know who I am'? He didn't do that, but he knew that in two minutes his license was coming out, and if the guy didn't put it together then, he's a moron.

"So: 'Let me have your license.' Really gruff. Out came the

---

* Percentage points of the film's profit, over and above one's ordinary salary.

license. It was a classic scene: the cop looks at the license, and it's still not clear who this person is, and then he looks at Dad with a sheepish half-turn, focuses back on the license, a little double take back at Dad, and says very heartily, 'Oh, well! Mr. Newman! Why didn't you tell me—gee, I'm so sorry. Listen'"—Susan leaned in and lowered her voice confidentially—"'you were going a little fast; get the taillight fixed at your convenience. I won't even write you a citation.'

"I remember saying to myself, Dad's a qualified race driver, but that doesn't excuse his driving that fast on public highways. It's not the same, and I don't care who he is. I think for the children involved, it creates a highly distorted framework for your life. You never know.

"It's not *your* power. If you're centered at all as a person, you're always asking yourself if you're overstepping your bounds. But I know for a great deal of my adult life, I have been overly cautious, 'Oh, no, I can't do that!' Well, anyone else would be doing it, so why can't I do it? Whether it's traveling or—it's very hard to keep things realistic. On every level—the way my parents eat, the way they travel, the way they live—although they don't live that extravagantly, but not everyone coughs up x amount of thousands of dollars to rent a little beach house for the summer."

"But," I commented, "a lot of people *do* have expensive houses and dine in fine restaurants who are not Paul Newman and Joanne Woodward. You know it's a double standard: if our parents do it, it's extravagant; if a Wall Street broker does it, it's okay."

"Yeah," she agreed. "I don't know how you get around that, either.

"Let's face it, artists are notoriously self-indulgent people. I didn't know until I was fifteen years old that it's illegal to drink alcohol in a car, because I saw so many people doing it.

"Or, how am I supposed to judge what real relationships are? Because what I see around me are storybook couples, devoted people, and then the husband is at the party with a fourteen-year-old girl, and when they see you, they slink around and make a quick getaway. I think my parents are monogamous, but I have no way of knowing that, and I don't want to know. Any time someone comes up ready to divulge some family skeleton, I say, 'I'd rather not know that.'

"I think it's highly confusing sometimes—what are *real* people doing? If people use their authority—you know, if there's a 'No Trespassing' sign, and I'm with some people that have a certain amount of power, they say, 'That's okay, that's not applicable to me.' So next time, when I'm eight, or twenty, or thirty, I see a 'No Trespassing' sign, and I say, 'Well, that's okay, that's not applicable to me.' Because of my adult role models."

"It's not just your family, then?" I asked. "It's the whole—"

"The whole circle," Susan said. "Everyone. So what is your frame of reference for being a responsible person in life?

"They didn't grow up with these same advantages. Joanne was quite poor, and Dad was not poor—he was in a middle-class family, but it wasn't like *this*. I think they are really relatively down-to-earth. Still, I can see that, through the years, they've had ambivalent feelings about how that should be dispersed to the children. Consequently, there's inconsistency. One minute, it's okay for you to fly to Europe after graduation because everyone else you know is doing that, and then six months later, when you get back to the States, and you haven't seen the family, and you want to go to Connecticut for Easter— they say, 'No, no, it's too extravagant.' I think they're confused about priorities, and they're not sure how to make you the best person without making you power-crazy or money-nuts."

"What about your kids?" I asked, starting to frame a question about how she would mold her own future success with the possibility of having children. But she cut me off.

"No kids."

"No kids?" I repeated, taken aback at her vehemence.

"Very antichildren. Why? Probably because I'm one of six. And I was the baby-sitter for everybody. I would be sterilized if I knew that it wouldn't create other bad things. I mean, I believe that there are female energies in that zone of your body, and if you cut those tubes, it has some 'cosmic' effect on you. Some way. Something. It disrupts the normal bodily functions.

"I'm a pretty independent person. When I cannot stand dependency, I cannot stand it. There is no gray. I'm very much an extremist, on almost every level of my life. I'm working very hard to find all those in betweens. You know, it was fine when I was unemployed, and I was in a blue-jean skirt, and my two cats were lounging all over my body like a chair. But during more successful years, when I was always dressed very jazzy, I just didn't want the cat hair on the black silk anymore. So I gave them away. I just wasn't being a good mother to them.

"All my girl friends have babies now, and it's very weird, because I'm 'Aunt Susan.' Babies are dirty; they slobber all over you; it's disgusting. I have no desire at all. I don't think I could handle children."

"What do you see for the future, Susan?"

"Well, because of a certain lack of domestic stability growing up, I crave it now. I want a country house where I can go and be left alone, and I want an apartment somewhere in the city that is mine. I may only spend three weeks a year there, but I want to know that that nest is there somewhere. Relationship-wise, it's difficult, because I have yet to find the guy that puts up with me going away for three months on location. They're usually not sitting around when you get back. Or if they are, things have changed, and the relationship is on its way out.

"So I may not have the temperamental makeup to be an actress. I'd almost rather know I was going to make two hundred dollars a week, but that that check was really going to come in every week, than to make ten thousand dollars but not know when the hell even another penny was coming in."

We chatted for a while about the future, about politics and religion and philosophy, and Susan mentioned the idea that one chooses, prenatally, the world into which one is born.

"Okay," she said, "if I chose this lot in life that has at times caused me a great deal of discomfort . . ." She stopped to think for a moment. "It has also been"—she paused again, betraying her ambivalence—"nice, in terms of, for example, the knowledge somewhere in the back of my mind that I will never absolutely starve to death. If I'm laying face-down in the gutter and my father hears about it, he may not come in person, but he might send someone to get me." She laughed and continued, "Or if I had to have a major operation and my SAG insurance had out, I could have that operation. And that's comforting, but I think that there aren't that many constructive things about being a famous child."

"If you accept the metaphysical premise that you choose this life in order to learn something you didn't learn in all your previous lives, what would you say you needed to learn in this life? By going through what you're going through, by being Paul Newman's daughter?"

She took a moment to think and said slowly, "Well, I would imagine some of my friends think I need to learn a little humility. It's not that I'm outrageously cocky, but when I say I'm going to form a company, someone says, 'Well, where do you get off thinking that you can bypass all the little preliminary steps to get you to that level?' Where I get off thinking that may be an overinflated ego. I know I have my cocky moments, but I don't think that's the major portion of my being.

"I'm trying to get out of this denial trip, of saying, 'This is the way it is, and unless I move to Timbuktu, change my name, dye my hair, and never go anywhere socially where any of my old man's movies are playing . . .' Instead, if I can use him, in the best sense of the word, or if we can trade off on each other's abilities . . .

"There comes a time when you have to be able to say, 'He can help me now,' or, 'He can be a positive force.' Which is what I'm trying to get into now. Maybe I can use all the talents he's built up, and by incorporating what I have to offer, make his product even better.

"A year ago, if I were to start that production company, I never would have thought of asking him to be any part of it."

"I would love to be able to collaborate with my dad on something like that," I said. "But on what? I can't think of any way I could contribute to anything he would do. Our areas don't overlap enough, and that's really sad, because I would love to do that. What a wonderful experience that would be; what a wonderful extension of our relationship."

"I hope that sometime I could work as an actor with my ther," Susan said. "Or have him direct me. He's a really good ctor, and he works particularly well directing women. It could go one of two ways: either he would tap things in me that no other directors could know existed, or it could be a nightmare." She laughed at her imaginings of how bad it could be. "But he's worked well with Nell and with Joanne; I think he can transcend that initial nightmare syndrome and tap the juicy stuff.

"Sometimes I think my job in my father's life is that I bring him a lot of comfort. I'm very responsible; some of the other kids in the family are not so responsible. I take less from him, financially and emotionally, than a lot of the other kids do. So when he sees me, he says, 'It's such a joy to see you, Susan.' You know? Maybe that's what my function is for him.

"His function for me? I'm not really sure. If I could go through life with the same knowledge I have from this lifetime into the next lifetime, I imagine what I'd want to seek out would be—could I get as far on my own steam?"

Surprisingly, Susan had come full circle back to the question I had asked earlier.

"It's the syndrome everyone seems to be locked up in," she continued. "I believe that you should applaud yourself for your own victories, and I believe you should kick yourself in the ass for your failures. So why do I have to work twice as hard when probably just starting out I've been better educated than a lot of people? Do I hate him because he educated me better? So I'm bright; why should I start out at the bottom if I can start out at the middle? Yet I'm always wondering: maybe I *am* out of line; maybe I should start out at the bottom like everybody else.

"But I don't even get to see the bottom that often. You know? In my hippie days, I went around and fought for all the causes, and I went into the ghettos and painted the houses, but those people hated my guts. Those people thought, 'Great. Paul Newman's daughter. She comes down, kills a few roaches, paints the wall, and then goes home to her mansion in Beverly Hills. Well, fuck *her!*'

"People imagined that I was politically active because Dad was politically active. Well, Dad was politically active years before I even knew what politics were. It really annoyed me. Can't I do anything and just do it for myself?

"In a lot of ways, he was frequently more liberal than I was in my views. In fact, I had a certain amount of anger about that at times. 'You're the father—have some limit here on your imagination of the way life should be, because I need that.'

"Actually, you don't get to see what he's really thinking many times. I'm sure part of that is due to [being who he is]. As freaked out as *we* are, and as protective as *we* feel, think about being Paul Newman and sitting down and confessing some deep dark secret to someone, and you weren't sure if they had a tape recorder in their purse. Do you know what I mean?"

Although Susan and her father seem to have that in common, she said later, "We're as different as night and day. Our priorities in life are very different. I have no compulsion to be like him, to mythologize him. He's a very nice man; he's very supportive to me *most* of the time, and I don't think I can really ask for more. Now.

"It hasn't always been that way, but [it is] for now. He's not going to change. If I should make a lot of judgments on him, all it's going to do is alienate us. The world he lives in is part of what's created him. I'm just coming to a point now where I'm trying to create a space between us as two adults that are dealing with each other, but without losing the affection.

"There were times when I didn't get along with my father that well. I guess I felt that he was making judgments on me. He expected me to be a certain way, and I didn't want to be that way, so 'To hell with you!' Better to withdraw.

"Another misconception about life-styles: I don't live the way my father lives. I don't go to the restaurants he frequents, I don't keep that circle of friends. Most of my friends aren't even actors. I think it's extremely important to keep as many civilian friends as you possibly can.

"My father always said to me, 'The people you have as friends *before* success are going to be your only true friends.' A lot of people, when they start to achieve that success, find that there's no one to turn to. That's when they start overdosing on pills and this and that. You're probably not going to run right out and trust the girl you met a year ago when you were making two million dollars a year, and you're not quite sure what her motives for friendship are. My best friend is a girl I met when I was twelve. She went home one day and said, 'Oh, I just saw the girl next door, Susan Newman, and, gee, we're going to be best friends. Oh, boy, oh, boy.'

"Her mother said, 'Susan Newman, oh, my God, that's Paul Newman's daughter!'

"And my friend said, 'Who's Paul Newman?' It's been the basis of our friendship ever since.

"This famous kid routine's a highly alienating situation. I'm not really sure yet the toll that it's taken on my life. I know the relationships it's interfered with and the paranoia it's created for me. It changes, it seems to be changing all the time.

"It has a tremendous effect on boyfriends," she said, referring to fame in general. "I was never aware of that until a couple of years ago. I don't think it's anything that I have done, and the men that I've been involved with have agreed with that. Even though I don't have a clear-cut picture of what this Paul mythology is, I can imagine that as a twenty-eight- or a thirty-five-year-old male, having to live up to that myth—whatever it is in their own minds—is sort of an instant divorce from me. Which is a real shame."

"How do you deal with that?"

"Lately, I've taken to putting the family off limits to conversation. It's not a conscious thing, but it seems to have worked in a mutual consent lately. I've found that when I talk it all out, I just dig my grave deeper; it seems to blow all out of proportion.

"What I find kind of disheartening is that everybody puts up a front," Susan said. "I don't know why anyone would assume that all the typical family problems—and the new ones that money and power and fame create—are not also present in our family. Of course, they are. We have some of the very primal life problems taken out of our frame of reference, but a whole new set of them are created."

"Like?"

"Like identity problems. Like having any semblance of a normal family structure and the support that I imagine that would lend you. Just having normal dinner times with everyone there and . . . you know, there are times I don't even know where my father is in the world."

"Oh, I know what you mean," I said. "It makes me feel so out of touch with him to hear secondhand what Dad's up to."

"Oh, I get lots of information secondhand," she said. "I never knew about Dad and Joanne and my mother and what sort of a scene that was until I read it in a movie magazine when I was twelve years old. Then I asked somebody if it was really like that, and they said yes. Well, that had been quite a scandal while it was happening, and no one had ever mentioned it. I'm very ignorant about my family history."

"It would be very hard for me to imagine not knowing my family history," I commented. "It would be almost like being adopted."

That set Susan off on another tangent. "I always tell them, 'I *know* I'm adopted,'" she said. "'I know you're a speed freak, you drive these racing cars, you're a lunatic; and I'm the most cautious person in the world.'

"I sometimes feel like I have no connection to my family, in a way. The way they approach their lives is a little bit too foreign to me. I'm not making any judgments on the way they lead their lives, because I think they do quite well. But the things they are cut off from are things that I think people should not be cut off from. They would be the first to deny it. My girl friend was sitting here the other day and said, 'You know, I've been thinking about your father, and, yes, he's really down-to-earth, but damn it, if you've been treated like a king for thirty years, eventually you're going to pick up the crown and stick it on your own head.'

"See, I've only gotten in touch with the anger recently, with my brother dying, you know? And, uh, I don't know exactly where the anger stems from.

"I am awfully sick of having to justify myself. Damn it, I was the assistant treasurer of two box offices, the youngest person in the union, you know? I have my own things that I do well, that my father's particularly bad at. Actually, most of the things that he's very gifted in, I'm not, and vice versa. So it's just a matter of your independence, somehow, and not having always to apologize. I'm really sick of that, now.

"It's hard to cut off from outside judgments, but if you know that's out of their own jealousies, that's *their* problem. I just did a scene in acting class, and it went abominably. I was really upset about it, and a friend of mine from class said, 'Didn't you realize that the girl you were working with couldn't get past the point that you were Paul Newman's daughter, and consequently the scene was *never* going to work?'

"It really took me aback. I really had figured I was at least past that level. But I never will be to some people. That's maddening.

"What more can you do? You work, you don't wallow in your parents' name, you create your own respectability as a human being—and even then it's not good enough. What more should you have to do?

"It's something that will haunt all of us until we die. Because you never *do* know. My one plea to people is, don't make judgments on us, because everybody really does react differently. You know, all of our backgrounds have one common denominator, but all the other elements are completely different. If both your parents were into some heavy power trip, but you had a nanny that kept your feet on the ground; or if your father was famous and a drug addict, and that created a whole different problem in your family—it's going to affect you in a completely different way. Not that there aren't little things where we come together, things we all share—certainly, we all know what it's like to fight for our own identity; we certainly know what it's like to have a distorted viewpoint of money. Luckily, my parents always said to me, 'If you want to be a garbage collector, Susan, be a garbage collector. Just be a decent garbage collector.' And it gave me a lot of leeway."

But whatever leeway may have been given, both Susan and her brother, Scott, chose their parents' field.

"Really, it all gets down to the identity," Susan said, "and why some people make it and why some people don't. Joanne asked that, you know? 'What happened with your brother? And why are you the way you are?' Well, I don't know. Maybe part of it is male; maybe part of it is that one of us had a more addictive nature than the other. Maybe it was some lack of connection, of differentiation between someone else's power and your own power."

Certainly, the pressures on Scott as the only son and the oldest must have been different from those on Susan: the expectations would be higher, the disappointments greater. Certainly, his life centered more around the pursuit of escape through chemicals. But I think more telling than either of those is the "differentiation of power." Susan seems able somehow to hold herself a little apart from her family; she knows who and what her father is, and who and what she is in comparison; she analyzes, examines, questions. And when, as she said over and over, there were no rules set down, no boundaries defined for her by her family, she developed her own. Somehow, Scott was never able to do that.

After talking to Susan, I wished more than ever that I had had the chance to interview Scott. In Susan I could see the same odd sense of humor, the same intensity, the same defensiveness, the same arrogance that I had known in Scott. But where in Susan was Scott's love of beauty, his artistic sensitivity? Was it just better hidden and yet to be discovered? Or had that very sensitivity been Scott's downfall? And why had Scott lacked the survival instinct that Susan had in abundance?

There is a resilience about Susan; Susan is making it—at least she has the chance to work through her problems. One of the tragedies of Scott's premature death is that he will never have that chance. All the people in this book are dealing with their parents' fame one way or another—some embrace it, some reject it, some are still learning. Scott is dead.

23.
Endings and Beginnings

We have come a long way in a gold canoe, over many waters both bright and surly, sometimes sending a bitter spray asplash in our faces. But you were ever listening for the beat of the wings of the angel of fear, so you got out to walk safe on the crowded road.
—SEAN O'CASEY, *Red Roses For Me*

On Monday morning, November 10, 1978, as on any other day, the clock radio turned on at nine A.M. On any other day, I would have gradually drifted up out of my dreams. But on that day, I snapped abruptly into full consciousness as I lay listening to an anonymous professional voice announcing that Scott Newman had died from a combination of drugs and alcohol.

There was no funeral for Scott, but I heard that some people were gathering in an informal commemoration. I didn't know what I was looking for, but I went.

The newspaper headlines announcing his death were so sensationalized, and the accompanying articles sketchy, unsatisfying, and, I discovered, largely inaccurate. "Paul Newman's Son Dies at 28, Apparent Overdose: Drugs, Alcohol," said the New York *Daily News.* But I needed to understand how and why he died, and why his death left me with so many questions. What was the obligation I felt to find answers? Was it because Scott had been unable to find his own solutions when he was alive, and now his search was precluded? Was that why I wanted so badly

301

to find answers for him now? Was it guilt that I had not given him enough help along his way? Or was it because of my own unresolved feelings about my life?

"In Scott, the panic was always right there, and he was always trying to find a solution. It was so powerful he didn't know how to help himself. They have all the money, and they try to do so much for you, but . . ."

At the memorial gathering, one person stood up and spoke about Scott's reaching out to his father. That was when the sobs came, and the fear. If Scott's troubles were at all related to his father's fame, then it could have been any of us. It could have been me, identified only as "Walter Cronkite's Daughter Found Dead." My God, we can't even have our own identity when we die. Even if we escape through death the pressures of reflected fame, it is regarded as just another Hollywood casualty.

I needed to know if that was the ultimate answer to Scott's death.

"I don't think Scott was afraid of death at all."

Scott lived fast; he took chances; he was unafraid of many things. He was a stuntman, a skydiver, a motorcyclist, and he was proud of his accomplishments in those fields. He took drugs, he drank, he was in some ways reckless, even self-destructive. But still, he was young and full of life, and one never expects one's friends to die. For weeks after he died, I kept dreaming that he called and sent messages saying, "Everything's fine; I'm very happy. And don't worry—it was an accident." But I wasn't sure—and I needed to know.

I uncovered less than I had hoped of the facts of his death and of the reasons, if there are any. But in talking to those who were closer to him than I had been in the last few years, I learned to know, and to miss, sides of him that I had never seen.

"He had a way of coming into people's lives that they noticed it."

"When he was thirteen, he used to ride to school on a unicycle."

"I don't think I ever saw him jump into a pool; he always did triple flips."

Everyone who talked of him mentioned his smile, and I suppose that is the first thing everyone loved about Scott: a smile that lit up the room, a Cheshire cat smile that lingered, a gentle good humor that you couldn't help but be charmed by. He had his darker side, to be sure, but whatever the trials, his smile, at least, would always win you back. He would eat the middle out of the apple pie that you were saving for company, and you wouldn't be able to get too angry about it. He had that childlike sweetness and sincerity that turns anger aside. And he had that smile.

He would sometimes call in the middle of the night, rousing me from sleep with a hearty, "Hey, Cronkite!"—the first person to call me by my surname since my sixth-grade gym teacher. Sometimes it was to ask for a loan—to buy a motorcycle or to pay his rent. I never gave it to him; he didn't strike me as a good risk. But he'd still call.

I hadn't really spent time with Scott for two or three years. We had gotten to know each other in acting class, which he attended sporadically. After a while, everyone in the class had refused to work with him, and I was asked if I would give it a go.

"I remember when Scott first came to acting class. He seemed so self-assured—and that smile! But what I always remember is the nervous laugh behind the smile."

"He was always competing with his father's image—lover, actor, race-car driver."

"Scott was the talented one. He just was."

He was difficult, I will admit. I assume that he had some ambivalence about the class, or about the work he was doing there, or perhaps about acting altogether. I only know that he had a well-deserved reputation for sabotaging rehearsals. Not only would he fail to show up for scheduled sessions, but he would even absent himself from the class period in which we were to perform. And take his phone off the hook. And disappear from his apartment for days at a time.

It was a battle for the poetry, the humor, the talent to be able to thrive. But I remember the melody of the brogue he worked so hard on for the Sean O'Casey play we were doing. He liked poetry and classical music and computers. When he was well, he ran religiously, worked out at a gym, and dieted on a horrible-looking green fluid recommended by his nutritionist. The rest of the time, he immured himself in his apartment and lived on alcohol and junk food.

I fed him, cajoled him, bullied and babied him. I tracked him down, followed him around, and when he wouldn't answer his phone, I knocked at his door until he let me in.

Then in the middle of a rehearsal, when I'd say, "Jesus, let's take a break," he'd tease me into working longer. When I'd slack up and just walk through the scene, he'd put my heart back into it. I'd never worked so hard in my life.

We did the best damn scene either of us had ever done. And when it was over and had been performed in class, we asked to work together again.

> *" 'Do you know the answer?' Scott asked me once. When I didn't answer, he said, 'You do know the answer, don't you? I think I know it—I just can't seem to get there.' "*

I had spoken to Scott several times when I was interviewing people for this book. I'd hoped he would be able to talk to me about his needs, his fears, his perspectives on his life. He never gave me any real indication that he might, but still I called every few months to see if he had changed his mind. I know he had something to say, and I hoped he would say it. But as far as I knew, he would not.

What I did not know was that, even up to a few weeks before his death, he was seeking advice from his closest friends about whether or not he should do the interview.

One of them told me that when she was sorting through the few belongings he had left at her house, she found on top of his things his address book, open to a page with two names on it: "Dad," and underneath, "Kathy Cronkite."

She told me that he had always felt a special bond with me

because the stature of his father was probably equaled only by that of my father, so I would be one of the few people who could really understand. Yet, Scott and I never talked about our fathers. Not that I can remember.

"Scott didn't die because he was a celebrity's kid; he died because he had a terrible disease called alcoholism. And alcoholism doesn't care who your father is."

"His father drinks two cases of beer a day; how can he tell his son he has a drinking problem?"

There are still those who assume that Scott died because he was Paul Newman's son, but the one thing I *did* learn is that there are no easy answers. Yet, I would like to think that this exploration of the children of the famous might help even one person, one child-of or one parent, to a greater understanding of some of the pressures. Or at least to open a dialogue. One of the saddest similarities I found in all the people I interviewed is that not one of them ever sat down and talked about it with his or her parents.

But the real message is this: The son or daughter of a teacher, a farmer, a shopkeeper may become famous or may not, may be healthy or confused, may be happy or may live in darkness. We can no more be categorized or stereotyped than the members of any other group. We each carry our own dreams and struggles and fears and ambitions.

This book started out as a survey, an exploration of who we are, and how we are alike and how we are not. But as I talked to these varied people, as I explored my own feelings about being a famous person's child, I realized more fully why I wanted to write this book.

I found similarities of experience and outlook, but I found much more. I found twenty-eight individuals.

The parent-child relationship is at best difficult, but how complicated it becomes when the parent is famous. Our parents are simply living their lives, doing the best they can in their chosen fields, and if they are successful, they should be praised, not condemned. But when their children's lives are as tumultuous as they are because of the results of that success, it is too easy to blame them for the turmoil.

Over and over we have said, "The children of plumbers be-come plumbers; why can't I be whatever I want? Why can't my work be evaluated on its own merit, not in comparison to my parents'?" Over and over we have said, "My parents say, 'Be whatever you want to be,'" but even that reassurance cannot lift the pressure; it is not only from our parents and their fame that the pressure arises. It is not always our parents who judge us, who badger us, who expect us to live up to their fame or to live it down, who require us to protect their image or accuse us of arrogance if we are rightfully proud of their achievements—it is also the public. But since we cannot lash out at the public, we lash out at our families—and at ourselves.

One of my friends said, after reading the manuscript of this book, "They all have an overreaction against money; none of them seems to be able to deal with being rich kids."

"But the point is," I responded, "that they're *not* all rich kids, no matter what everyone thinks."

But when I thought back over the individuals I had met, I realized that, rich or poor, they all had an atittude of privilege, an assumption about their place in the world and the importance of their lives, a certain aura if not of wealth, at least of power. It is something that, no matter how long we might choose to lie in the gutter, we cannot shake. But can we learn to take ad-vantage of it?

To be happy one needs more than the things money can buy and the advantages power can bring. One needs a goal, a reason to get up in the morning. "Love, work and knowledge are the wellsprings of life and they should also govern it," Wilhelm Reich said.

Over and over while writing this book or while talking to people about it, I realized that most of what we are saying ap-plies to everyone, not just the children of celebrities—the fear of failure, the competition, living up to an image, learning to accept ourselves and our parents for who we are—it is all part of the process of growing up for all of us, no matter who our parents are. And I've grown up a lot in the two years it has taken me to write this book.

I always thought that growing up was something that happened to you; I didn't know it was something you have to work at, conscious decisions you have to make, sometimes with pain, sometimes with a great rending as you leave precious parts of your childhood behind.

Because of my father's values I think that I was a lot less influenced by peer pressure than many young people. By his example, he taught me honesty, integrity, and professionalism; to stand up for what you know is right for you.

I haven't necessarily gotten any answers from this work, but just through the process, I have changed and grown. My self-image is vastly different. I do things differently: I am a writer and a success. A friend said, "When I met you two years ago, you were Walter Cronkite's daughter. Now you're a writer."

I was just finishing this book when I met my new husband, Bill Ikard, the son of a former congressman. Late at night, on our first date, we sat huddled against the cold at the end of the pier, on Martha's Vineyard, bathed in moonlight reflected off the water, and talked about our fathers, about the never-ending desire for their approval and love, and about meeting them halfway. It was Bill who suggested that perhaps as much as we need their approval, they need ours. As deeply as I longed to hear from my parents, "I'm proud of you; you did a good job," when was the last time I had said that to them? Or had I ever? As much as I needed to find out who I am in relation to them, I needed to help them learn that, too.

We talked also about the long years spent trying to live up to the example our parents set. Compared to the achievements of such an illustrious man as my father, any effort of mine seemed to fall short, and there appeared to be only two levels of accomplishment: perfection and failure.

I had great difficulty finishing this book, saying, "Done!" I had to reconcile myself to the fact that it would never be perfect, or even complete. As long as I live, I will be growing, and my feelings toward my life and my family will be changing. As I talk to more people, I learn more about myself and my familial relationships; and the more I learn about other people, the more I grow to appreciate the exceptional relationship my parents and I have.

In my family, we have often said to each other those precious words, "I love you," and I take for granted not only the words but their truth. When people ask me what I value about my relationship with my parents, I name our communication, our respect, our playfulness, but too often I neglect to mention the one most valuable ingredient—our love.

These are the strengths that set me apart; these are the reasons, I am convinced, that I made it. Ultimately, the major influence on our lives is not our parents' *fame*, but our *parents*. I've always known that my parents love and support me totally, and that no matter what tragedy or disgrace might befall me, I can always go home. I forget sometimes that not everyone has that assurance; I forget sometimes to stop and thank my parents for that.

In a sense, this book is a thank you, a love letter, to my parents. It never will be finished, for love—like growth, like change—has no end.

Photo Credits

Page 92: Chris Lemmon and Jack Lemmon—Tony Costa.

Page 93: The Ford family—David Hume Kennerly.

Page 94: The Woody Guthrie family—from Marjorie Guthrie.

Page 95: The Arlo Guthrie family—Peter Simon.

Page 96: Tex Ritter with sons John and Tommy—courtesy, Dorothy Fay Ritter.

John Ritter—Jim Britt.

Page 241: Photo of Scott Newman by Kathy Connell.

Page 242: Debby Erhard—courtesy of the Erhard family.

Jack Erhard—courtesy of the Erhard family.

Page 243: Debby Erhard, Werner Erhard, and Jack Erhard—Kenneth Yamamoto.

Page 244: Michael Keeshan and Bob Keeshan, 1975—courtesy of the Keeshan family.

Michael Keeshan and Bob Keeshan, 1959—courtesy of the Keeshan family.

Page 245: Linda McMahon and Ed McMahon—Photo by Victoria McMahon.

Page 246: Francesca Hilton and Zsa Zsa Gabor, 1954—reprinted by permission of Photoworld/Freelance Photographers Guild, Inc.

Page 247: Francesca Hilton and Zsa Zsa Gabor, 1973—Wide World Photos, Inc.

Page 248: Nancy Sherman with Dee Sherman (Golden) and Allan Sherman—courtesy of Nancy Sherman.

Nancy Sherman—Jay Sandrich.

Page 249: The Styron family—Peter Simon.

Page 250: Amy Wallace with Irving Wallace and brother David—courtesy of Sylvia Wallace.

Page 251: Amy Wallace and Irving Wallace, 1967—courtesy of Sylvia Wallace.

Amy Wallace and Irving Wallace, 1977—Photo by Gerry Shenson.

Page 252: John Blyth Barrymore and John Barrymore, Jr.—Frank Worth, godfather to John Blyth Barrymore.

Page 253: John Blyth Barrymore—Photo by Sealy.

John Barrymore, Jr.—Preben Sirensen.

Page 254: Christopher Buckley and William F. Buckley—Pat Buckley.

Christopher Buckley—Pat Buckley.

Page 255: The Newman family—courtesy of the Newman family.

Page 256: Kathy Cronkite and Walter Cronkite—Peter Simon.

Index

Abzug, Bella, 283
Allen, Gracie, 282
Allen, Rex, 173
Allen, Steve, 164
Altman, Robert, 28
Armstrong, Neil, 25, 162
Armstrong, Rick, 25, 54, 162
Arnaz, Desi, 160
Arnaz, Desi, Jr., 160
Arnaz, Lucie, 160
Autry, Gene, 173
Axton, Hoyt, 33

Ball, Lucille, 160
Barkle, Dick, 284
Barrymore, Diana, 277
Barrymore, Ethel, 274, 275, 276

Barrymore, John, 26, 76, 274, 275–276, 277
Barrymore, John, Jr., 26, 76, 274–275, 276–277
Barrymore, John Blyth (John Barrymore III), 25–27, 76–77, 269–270, 272–277, 283
Barrymore, Lionel, 274, 275, 276
Barrymore, Maurice, 274, 275–276
Beatty, Warren, 283
Belafonte, Harry, 281
Benny, Jack, 282
Blyth, Herbert, 274
Boone, Debbie, 75
Boone, Pat, 80
Buchwald, Ann, 27, 284
Buchwald, Art, 27, 201, 265, 284